Economic Development Law
for North Carolina Local Governments

Economic Development Law
for North Carolina Local Governments

David M. Lawrence

2000

INSTITUTE *of* GOVERNMENT
The University of North Carolina at Chapel Hill

Established in 1931, the Institute of Government provides training, advisory, and research services to public officials and others interested in the operation of state and local government in North Carolina. A part of The University of North Carolina at Chapel Hill, the Institute also administers the university's Master of Public Administration Program.

Each year approximately 14,000 city, county, and state officials attend one or more of the 230 classes, seminars, and conferences offered by the Institute. Faculty members annually publish up to fifty books, bulletins, and other reference works related to state and local government. Each day that the General Assembly is in session, the Institute's *Daily Bulletin*, available in print and electronically, reports on the day's activities for members of the legislature and others who need to follow the course of legislation. An extensive Web site (http://ncinfo.iog.unc.edu/) provides access to publications and faculty research, course listings, and program and service information and links to other useful sites related to government.

Support for the Institute's operations comes from various sources, including state appropriations, local government membership dues, private contributions, publication sales, and service contracts. For more information about the Institute, visit the Web site or call (919) 966-5381.

Michael R. Smith, DIRECTOR
Thomas H. Thornburg, ASSOCIATE DIRECTOR FOR PROGRAMS
Patricia A. Langelier, ASSOCIATE DIRECTOR FOR PLANNING AND OPERATIONS
Ann C. Simpson, ASSOCIATE DIRECTOR FOR DEVELOPMENT

FACULTY

Gregory S. Allison	James C. Drennan	Janet Mason
Stephen Allred	Richard D. Ducker	Laurie L. Mesibov
David N. Ammons	Robert L. Farb	Jill D. Moore
A. Fleming Bell, II	Joseph S. Ferrell	David W. Owens
Maureen M. Berner	Susan Leigh Flinspach	William C. Rivenbark
Frayda S. Bluestein	L. Lynnette Fuller	John Rubin
Mark F. Botts	Milton S. Heath, Jr.	John L. Saxon
Phillip Boyle	Cheryl Daniels Howell	Jessica Smith
Joan G. Brannon	Joseph E. Hunt	John B. Stephens
Anita R. Brown-Graham	Kurt J. Jenne	A. John Vogt
William A. Campbell	Robert P. Joyce	Richard Whisnant
Margaret S. Carlson	David M. Lawrence	Gordon P. Whitaker
Stevens H. Clarke	Charles D. Liner	Michael L. Williamson
Anne S. Davidson	Ben F. Loeb, Jr.	(on leave)
Anne M. Dellinger		

Contents

• • •

ACKNOWLEDGMENTS

• • •

As is always the case, I have benefited from the help of many others in writing this book. My colleagues Frayda Bluestein, Joe Ferrell, and Don Liner each read one or more chapters and provided many helpful comments and suggestions. Alex Hess, the Institute's librarian, helped with inquiries about the various incentive programs offered by the State of North Carolina. Tom Lee, a bond attorney with Poyner & Spruill in Raleigh, saved me from a good many errors in explaining industrial revenue bonds and the tax code's treatment of private activity bonds. Mike Smith, the Institute's director, released me from other responsibilities for five months in 1999, which enabled me to complete this book months, or even years, earlier than I would have otherwise, and I am grateful to him for doing so. Finally, over the years I have had conversations with and answered inquiries from economic development officials at the state and local government levels, and from them I have learned much about the practical issues they face. I hope the book is as helpful to them as they have been to me.

DAVID M. LAWRENCE
PROFESSOR OF PUBLIC LAW AND GOVERNMENT

Chapel Hill
Spring 2000

INTRODUCTION

• • •

COUNTY COMMISSIONERS and city council members regularly list economic development among those local government activities to which they give highest priority. Elected officials typically seek a number of common objectives through economic development. First, they hope that economic development will help their residents achieve a better life through the provision of jobs for those who are unemployed and better jobs for those who are. Second, they hope that economic development will reduce the financial strains on government itself (and on its taxpayers) by building a stronger tax base. Third, they hope that economic development will create buffers against economic instability by diversifying their local economies, building a mix of businesses to help the community ride out economic cycles.

Governments attempt to accomplish these economic development objectives through a wide range of programs. Good jobs don't help unless people have the skills to do the work, so the public schools and the community college system are a foundational part of economic development. Companies cannot locate or expand in a community that does not have the infrastructure to support their businesses, so traditional governmental efforts in road building and water and sewer system construction also are foundational parts of economic development. Then there are the more direct activities of economic development agencies, such as assisting in local business creation and development, counseling business owners, providing worker training, and seeking to attract business growth through relocation and expansion of companies.

This is a book about the law that frames and guides economic development programs undertaken by North Carolina local governments. Because it is about economic development law and not economic development in general, the book centers on those topics that have attracted legislative and judicial attention. Law develops from policy conflicts; resolution leads to statutory authorizations and limitations, litigation, even constitutional amendments. Much of the public debate about economic development concerns how government should go about attracting business growth through company relocation and expansion; more particularly, much of the debate centers on the use of economic development incentives. As a result, most of the law of economic development is about incentives, and so too most of this book is about incentives.

Over the past decade, the value of incentives given to companies by state and local governments across the country has greatly increased, and those increases have fueled the continuing national debate about incentives. We sometimes forget, however, that state and local governments, including those in North Carolina, have been offering economic development incentives to companies for a very long time. North Carolina's earliest efforts, beginning in the late 1830s, sought to assist the private sector in building the industrial infrastructure that the state so clearly lacked. The major incentives before the Civil War aided the state's fledgling railroads: The state guaranteed railroad bonds, issued its own bonds in return for bonds of the railroad companies, and, most often, issued its own bonds to railroad companies in return for railroad stock. By the time the war began, most of the state's bonded indebtedness had been issued in order to assist railroads. But railroads were not the only recipients of state incentives.

> While the railroads began stretching across North Carolina, the state made other political decisions that affected its economic future. A commercial society needed banks to provide credit and a flexible paper money supply. The state accordingly invested large sums in bank stock, not only because the investments were very profitable but also to ensure that business interests would not suffer. . . . Businessmen pointed out that cotton culture would be more profitable if the fiber were turned into yarn before it left the state. The government agreed and supplied the infant mills with loans from the Literary Fund when private banks refused to accept the risk. In the 1850s, the state supplemented its subsidies of railroads and navigation companies with generous subscriptions to plank road companies.[1]

It was not just the state. Local governments along the routes of proposed railroads also issued bonds in order to subscribe to railroad stock, a practice they continued throughout the remainder of the nineteenth century. Indeed, communities continued to subsidize railroads into the 1920s at least, buying land to donate for rights-of-way and constructing stations for railroads.[2] In the early twentieth century, local governments began offering assistance to industrial companies by constructing special infrastructure and making other promises. In 1907, for example, the Cabarrus County Board of Commissioners agreed to construct a new macadam road stretching seven miles from the Concord town limits to "a place on the main road from here to Salisbury which has been christened Kannapolis," accepting J. W. Cannon's offer to loan the county the money to do so.[3] In 1928 Asheville and Buncombe County agreed to construct a water line to carry at least five million gallons of water a day to a new rayon-producing plant located some distance from Asheville, to improve roads leading to the plant, and to construct a sewage treatment facility for the plant if it could not simply discharge its wastes into a nearby stream. The city of Asheville's resolution in support of the plant concluded "that owing to the distance of the proposed plant location from the City Limits of the City of Asheville, and the vast amount of vacant land lying between said location and said City Limits, that the incorporation of said plant and land adjoining the same into the City of Asheville is impractical, and said City of Asheville would oppose such a proposition."[4] The quoted language was cited against the city (unsuccessfully) some sixty years later when the city at last did attempt to annex the tract including the rayon plant.[5]

Not only are incentives not a new idea; early efforts to provide incentives also introduced the legal issues that continue today. The pre–Civil War railroad assistance led to inclusion of a loan of credit provision in the state constitution, and local government assistance to railroads later in the nineteenth century led to the state supreme court's recognition of a public purpose limitation on government expenditures. The town of Sylva's unsuccessful effort to assist a railroad and the city of Asheville's annexation promises to the rayon plant illustrate the need for statutory authority to offer incentives (and the reality that sometimes governments don't worry overmuch about their need for authority). But these earlier efforts also show that incentives sometimes work: by the later nineteenth century, North Carolina had a widespread network of railroads; J. W. Cannon's predictions for his new community proved modest; and American Enka built its rayon plant in Buncombe County.[6]

This book takes no side in the ongoing debate about whether governments should use incentives and whether and to what extent incentives actually influence company decisions. Rather, it recognizes that incentives are part of economic development. North Carolina local governments (and the State of North Carolina) offer incentives, and this book seeks to help them work through the statutory authorizations and procedures that regulate their doing so. It does so with five chapters:

Chapter 1 discusses the constitutional issues that continue to affect economic development programs. It is the most densely legal chapter of the book and probably will be of more use to county and city attorneys than to their clients.

Chapter 2 discusses the statutory authority for substantive economic development programs in North Carolina and considers various legal issues that arise under the current statutory framework. It also discusses incentive policies and offers suggestions for incentive contracts with companies that receive incentives. The chapter should be of use not only to attorneys but also to economic development officials, county and city managers, and county and city governing board members.

Chapter 3 discusses the statutory procedures that governments must follow in carrying out economic development. These procedures by and large are activated whenever a local government wishes to offer incentives to a particular company. The chapter also includes example forms that local governments may use in conjunction with the described procedures. This chapter should be useful to attorneys, economic development officials, managers, and board members.

Chapter 4 covers two topics. First, it addresses financing economic development, especially the state and federal rules that govern borrowing for economic development projects. Second, it describes three possible organizational forms for economic development within local government (line departments, economic development commissions, and private nonprofit corporations) and compares legal characteristics of the three forms. This chapter should be useful to attorneys, economic development officials, managers, and board members.

Finally, Chapter 5 describes the principal incentives offered by the State of North Carolina to companies locating or expanding within the state. Largely informational, this chapter should be of interest to attorneys, economic development officials, managers, and board members.

Notes

1. Harry L. Watson, *"Old Rip" and a New Era, in* THE NORTH CAROLINA EXPERIENCE 217, 220 (Lindley S. Butler & Alan D. Watson eds., 1984).

2. *See Brown v. Walker*, 188 N.C. 52, 123 S.E. 633 (1924), which details how the town of Sylva acquired right-of-way for donation to a railroad, and *Hudson v. City of Greensboro*, 185 N.C. 502, 117 S.E. 629 (1923), which involved Greensboro's participation in construction of a private train station. The state supreme court held that Sylva acted without legislative authority, but it upheld Greensboro's actions.

3. Cannon's letter to the board of commissioners and the board's positive response are set out in the meeting minutes for June 3, 1907, and I am grateful to the Cabarrus county attorney, Fletcher L. Hartsell, Jr., for providing a copy of the minutes' pages. Cannon's letter continued: "We expect to have these [two large mills] completed and in operation early in the coming year, and we expect to have a population of two to three thousand people. This plant will bring quite a large taxable property into Cabarrus County. . . . I estimate that before the end of the five years term [of the loan] expires, that the taxes collected from this new enterprise and the enhancing of property adjacent will pay for this amount of indebtedness." *Plus ça change, plus c'est la même chose.*

4. The resolutions of commitment from the city and county are found in the record on appeal of *Thrash v. City of Asheville*, 95 N.C. App. 457, 383 S.E.2d 657 (1989), 327 N.C. 251, 393 S.E.2d 842 (1990), at pages 334–37 and 346–49.

5. In *Thrash, supra* note 4, the court of appeals held that a city could not enter into a binding contract promising not to annex specified property.

6. These early incentives also sometimes did not work. In the early 1880s the town of Fayetteville had become so heavily burdened by railroad-related debt that it asked the General Assembly to abolish the town, hoping thereby to escape paying the debt. The town remained legally nonexistent for twelve years, until the General Assembly incorporated the city of Fayetteville with the same territory as the abolished town. The state supreme court ultimately held that the stratagem did not work; the new municipal corporation was required to repay the indebtedness of the abolished one. All of this is detailed in *Broadfoot v. City of Fayetteville*, 124 N.C. 478, 32 S.E. 804 (1899).

Economic Development Law
for North Carolina Local Governments

I

CONSTITUTIONAL CONSIDERATIONS

• • •

I

CONSTITUTIONAL CONSIDERATIONS

• • •

ECONOMIC DEVELOPMENT efforts have always raised state constitutional issues and sometimes precipitated constitutional change. This chapter looks at three constitutional doctrines and the effect of each on economic development programs. The three doctrines are the public purpose limitation, the limitations on the ability of local governments to grant exemptions from or abatements of property taxes, and the limitation on loans or gifts of credit. Although in 1996 the North Carolina Supreme Court settled the fundamental question of whether economic development incentives serve a public purpose, several constitutional issues affecting economic development activities remain unresolved.

The Public Purpose Limitation

Public Purpose in General

The state constitution recognizes the public purpose doctrine in Article V, Section 2(1), which declares that "the power of taxation shall be exercised . . . for public purposes only." The constitutional language, however, understates the breadth of the doctrine as developed by the state supreme court. The public purpose doctrine is not a limit on *taxation* but actually a limitation on governmental *expenditure*: If an expenditure does not serve a public purpose, it may not be made, regardless of the source of its supporting revenues.[1] Thus the doctrine limits what government may do, what activities government may undertake.

Although the constitutional provision recognizing the public purpose doctrine entered the state constitution only in 1936, it followed fifty years of public purpose case law in which the state supreme court had found a public purpose limitation inherent in the constitution's Law of the Land Clause.[2] Fittingly for this context, the court's first public purpose case dealt with an economic development issue: In 1887 the court held that a city's donation of funds to a railroad company served a public purpose.[3] Many of the court's subsequent important public purpose cases have involved economic development programs, and the history of those cases reflects a judicial ambivalence about economic development activities. Nevertheless, the court's most recent decision, *Maready v. City of Winston-Salem*,[4] places economic development and economic development incentives firmly among those governmental programs that serve a public purpose. To help explain the court's decision in *Maready*, this section begins with a brief review of the public purpose doctrine and of economic development legislation and litigation after 1960.

Background to the *Maready* Decision

In discussing the public purpose limitation, the North Carolina Supreme Court frequently distinguishes between public and nonpublic purposes with language much like the following:

> It is clear, however, that for a use to be public its benefits must be in common and not for particular persons, interests, or estates; the ultimate net gain or advantage must be the public's as contradistinguished from that of an individual or private entity.[5]

Although this language doesn't help much in deciding particular cases, it does identify a fundamental public purpose principle: There must be *public* benefits from public expenditures, not just benefits to private individuals or entities. Economic development activities embrace a wide variety of programs, and many unquestionably provide a public benefit. For example, programs that advertise a community, provide technical assistance to small businesses, or maintain a written inventory of sites suitable for industrial or commercial development clearly serve a public purpose.[6] Their benefits are widely available with no significant special benefit to one or a few persons or companies. Other economic development programs, however, most significantly incentives to a single company to induce it to locate or expand within a community, target significant benefits to a single, private entity. These kinds of programs raise much more difficult constitutional issues and, predictably, have been the focus of a number of public purpose decisions of the state supreme court.

In the two most important decisions before its decision in *Maready*, the court held that industrial revenue bonds *did not* serve a public purpose under the state constitution.[7] In its simplest form, an industrial revenue bond is issued by a state or local government agency to finance an industrial facility for a private company; the company's lease or loan payments are the sole security for the bonds.[8] Because the interest on industrial revenue bonds is exempt from federal income taxation, their use allows the company to finance an industrial facility at a cheaper cost than would be possible with a direct bank loan to the company. In its two decisions, the court held that the companies' benefits from industrial revenue bond financing outweighed the public benefits of new jobs or an increased tax base. Although the state's voters later overruled the decisions by approving a constitutional amendment that permits counties to establish county authorities that may issue industrial revenue bonds,[9] the amendment was narrowly drafted and did not overturn the basic judicial philosophy underlying the decisions. The two decisions continued to raise questions about other kinds of economic development incentives offered to specific companies.

The *Maready* Decision

These questions, as noted above, were finally resolved in 1996 in *Maready v. City of Winston-Salem*.[10] Between 1990 and 1995 Winston-Salem and Forsyth County had agreed to twenty-four separate industrial or commercial incentive packages.[11] The total public cost for the twenty-four projects was $9.1 million for the city and $4.2 million for the county. From this public investment, the two units calculated that they had attracted almost $240 million of private business investment and more than 5,500 new jobs. In 1995 a local attorney brought suit against the city and county, claiming that these various incentive transactions violated the constitution's public purpose limitation. In March 1996 the supreme court held that the entire set of incentives served a public purpose.

Although the *Maready* court offered several arguments to distinguish the two earlier industrial revenue bond cases, the most fundamental difference is that the justices in the majority had a view of the effect of and need for economic development incentives that was different from that of the justices who had decided the two earlier cases. The earlier court had assessed the predominant benefit from incentive programs as private, that is, as flowing to the company whose facilities were being financed. The current court reached a different judgment—that the predominant benefit from incentive programs is public, increasing residents' employment opportunities and strengthening the government's revenue base. There is no fundamental difference in the activities at issue in *Maready* and in the earlier cases; rather, the passage of a quarter century changed the perception of those doing the judging. As the court said in *Maready*, "the passage of time and accompanying societal changes now suggest a positive response" to the question of constitutionality.[12]

After *Maready*, the decision as to the constitutionality of particular incentive packages rests with the governments and agencies offering the incentives rather than with the courts. Although the *Maready* opinion indicates that if a particular incentive is more for the private benefit of the company involved than for the general public, the rule of the industrial revenue bond cases would cause the incentive to be unconstitutional, the court's recognition of that possible consequence is not an invitation to citizens to sue and challenge specific incentive packages. The court noted that Section 158-7.1 (the basic authorization for incentives) of the North Carolina General Statutes (hereinafter G.S.) requires a public hearing before expenditures are made pursuant to the statute and stated that these "strict procedural requirements . . . provide safeguards that should suffice to prevent abuse."[13] That is, if a local government has held a public hearing and given the public a chance to comment on a proposed incentive package, and if the government thereafter has decided to go forward, the incentive carries a presumption of public, rather than private, benefit.

Some Specific Constitutional Provisions

During the quarter century that the two industrial revenue bond cases were North Carolina's ruling case law on economic development under the public purpose limitation, the state's voters approved several specific amendments to the state constitution, each validating a financial incentive program that otherwise was questionable under the two cases. The first of these specifically permitted the issuing of industrial revenue bonds themselves, under narrow circumstances.[14] Subsequent amendments permitted cities and joint agencies of cities to own and operate electrical generation and transmission facilities jointly with private investor–owned utilities and to finance such facilities,[15] permitted public financial assistance to private agricultural facilities,[16] and permitted public-private ownership of and public financial assistance to airport and seaport facilities.[17]

Each of these amendments establishes only a narrow exception to the principles underlying the two industrial revenue bond cases. For example, each permits only the use of *revenue* bond financing for the projects authorized by that amendment; the amendments do not give any independent constitutional support for *general obligation* financing for the projects. Because the amendments were necessitated by the industrial revenue bond decisions, and because *Maready* has effectively superceded those decisions, the amendments have probably become unnecessary surplusage. If so, their failure to permit other forms of financing besides revenue bonds ought not to bar the General Assembly from authorizing the state or its local governments to use other forms of financing for a project otherwise covered by one of the amendments. Some residual uncertainty about that consequence probably remains, however, and therefore some bond counsel might resist approval of a financing package that is beyond the strict confines of the amendments.

Cash Grants, Loans, and Equity Investments

That a local government may grant a broad range of incentives to private companies, in consideration of the new jobs provided by the company and the tax proceeds and other revenues that will be received by the government as a result of the company's operations, has been settled by *Maready*. The incentives involved in *Maready*, however, paid for *specific* costs that were otherwise the responsibility of the benefited company, such as land purchase, site preparation, or employee training. Three forms of incentives were not at issue in the case, however, and therefore were not clearly sanctioned by the decision. The first of these is grants of cash to a company, with the company entitled to put the cash to any use it wishes. The second is loans to a company for working capital, capital acquisitions, or other company uses. The third is providing capital to a company by becoming an investor (an owner) in the company. Is there any reason to think that the rule of *Maready*—that incentives serve a public purpose—does not apply to these forms of assistance?

Cash Grants

There is no apparent reason to doubt that the *Maready* decision supports a local government's authority to make cash grants or to loan money to a company in order to encourage economic development through the company. The incentives at issue in *Maready* included the following: making site improvements on company-owned land, paying the cost of relocating utilities on a company-owned site, paying the company's rent on a headquarters building, paying the cost of moving one private tenant out of a private office building so that a new private tenant could occupy the space, donating land to a company, and renovating a privately owned industrial facility. Each incentive used public money to pay directly for costs that otherwise were the responsibility of a private company; as a result, each benefiting company could use its own funds, which it otherwise would have spent for these costs, for other company operations, perhaps in North Carolina, perhaps not. Each incentive was constitutional because it caused the benefiting company to locate or expand its operations in Winston-Salem or Forsyth County, thereby increasing the employment opportunities and tax base in that community. If it is constitutional to pay $250,000 for a company's land or for training a company's employees or for paying the company's rent, in each case freeing $250,000 of company funds to be spent elsewhere, why is it not equally constitutional to give the company $250,000 in cash to be used as the company decides? The outlay of the local government is the same, the practical benefit to the company is the same, and the public benefit of attracting jobs and tax base is the same. The *Maready* decision clearly supports cash grants to companies in consideration of the companies locating or expanding in a community.[18]

Loans

If it is permissible to *give* money or other items of value to a company, then it is difficult to see why it is also not permissible to *loan* money to a company. Indeed, the public treasury is less harmed by a loan than by a gift. There is an extensive history of government-sponsored loan programs in North Carolina, some of which have been specifically upheld by the North Carolina Supreme Court. For example, in the general area of economic development, G.S. 160A-456 and 153A-376 specifically permit cities and counties, respectively, to make loans for building rehabilitation as part of a community development program; and G.S. 143B-437.01 establishes the Industrial Development Fund, under which the state makes grants to local governments, which in turn may loan the proceeds to qualifying industries.[19] More importantly, in *State Education Assistance Authority v. Bank of Statesville*,[20] the state supreme court held that it served a public purpose for a state agency to make loans to college students to finance their educations; and in *Martin v. North Carolina Housing Corporation*,[21] the court held that it served a public purpose for another state agency to make loans to persons of low and moderate income to help finance their homes. Clearly loan programs are a permissible method of furthering a public purpose, and there is no reason to think the rule is any different for economic development.[22]

Equity Investments

The constitutionality of equity investments is less clear. Assisting a manufacturing company differs from owning one, a difference perhaps reflected in the state supreme court's statement that "it is not the function of government to engage in a private business."[23] The statement appears in one of the industrial revenue bond cases and thus might no longer reflect the court's views, but there can be no automatic assumption that local governments may make equity investments to further the public purpose of economic development. It is more likely than not, however, that the courts would uphold equity investments as an economic development tool, perhaps in reliance of the following points.

First, unlike that of many other states, North Carolina's constitution does not specifically prohibit the state or its local governments from becoming a shareholder in a private company.[24] Because the fundamental notion of state constitutional law is that the state may do, or authorize, anything unless it is barred from doing so by the state constitution, the absence of a specific bar to becoming a shareholder suggests that it is constitutionally permissible.

Second, the state has for many years been the majority shareholder of the North Carolina Railroad, a private corporation; and during the nineteenth century both the state and its local governments acquired stock in many other railroads and other kinds of private companies.[25] Perhaps significantly, government made these investments to further economic development.[26] These earlier practices, however, may offer less support than they appear to at first. That the state or local governments may own shares in a railroad corporation, a type of enterprise already quasi-public in character, does not necessarily mean it may own shares in a corporation that manufactures railroad engines.

Third, economic development programs frequently seek to provide financial assistance to small businesses, which are recognized as vital generators of new jobs.[27] One way of doing so is to make loans to such businesses or to subsidize private loans made to them.[28] But small businesses are often in fragile financial condition and may have difficulty in repaying loans; many don't meet loan underwriting standards. If a government's goal is to help such businesses financially, providing equity rather than loans may be the most feasible way of doing so.

Finally, in *Maready* the state supreme court seemed to want North Carolina and its local governments to be on a level playing field with other states in the economic development realm. Seemingly the court's policy is that in the absence of a specific constitutional bar, if other state or local governments are using an important economic development tool, North Carolina and its local governments should not be prohibited from using the same tool.[29] Other states operate economic development programs that support companies by acquiring equity interests;[30] to be able to compete, North Carolina governments should have the same capability.

Eminent Domain for Economic Development

The *public purpose* doctrine limits governmental expenditures. The closely related *public use* doctrine limits government's power of eminent domain. Just as government may not expend moneys on activities that do not serve a public purpose, so too it may not condemn property for projects that do not serve a public use. The *Maready* litigation determined that it was a public purpose for a local government to expend public moneys on economic development incentives. The case did not directly address whether it would serve a public use if a local government were to use its power of eminent domain to condemn a site for an industrial location or expansion, but the litigation may have indirectly answered that question in the affirmative as well. Although there is no current statewide authority for local governments to use eminent domain for economic development projects, the General Assembly has enacted at least one local act permitting this use of eminent domain, and therefore the issue of constitutionality may well arise.[31]

Arguments in Favor of Constitutionality

In recent years the North Carolina Supreme Court has treated the terms *public purpose* and *public use* as essentially synonymous. For at least fifty years, the court has regularly used *public purpose* in discussing whether a government could condemn for a particular project, blurring any distinction between the two doctrines.[32] More recently, in a 1960 eminent domain case, the court not only used the terms interchangeably, it also cited a public purpose case (involving the constitutionality of an expenditure) in support of its conclusion that condemnation for an urban renewal project did serve a public use and was therefore constitutional.[33] Finally, in 1968 the court used the congruence of the two terms to support its first decision invalidating industrial revenue bonds. In *Mitchell v. N.C. Industrial Development Financing Authority*,[34] the court wrote:

> In passing upon the validity of an act, this Court must consider the consequences of its decision. Were we to hold that Authority serves a public purpose when it acquires a site, constructs a manufacturing plant, and leases it to a private enterprise, we would thereby authorize the legislature to give [the] Authority the power to condemn private property as a site for any project which it undertook.[35]

The court now has held that it is a public purpose to subsidize industries in order to further economic development. If future decisions follow the logic of the *Mitchell* opinion, it also now would be a public use to use condemnation to acquire sites for industries, again in order to further economic development.

Upholding eminent domain for economic development would accord with the case law in about half the states that have considered the issue. Four cases illustrate the decisions that uphold condemnation for economic development projects. In *Prince George's County v. Collington Crossroads, Inc.*,[36] the Maryland Supreme Court upheld the use of eminent domain to acquire the site for a 323.5-acre county industrial park. In *Poletown Neighborhood Council v. City of Detroit*,[37] the Michigan Supreme Court upheld the use of eminent domain to acquire several thousand acres to be conveyed to General Motors for a new Cadillac automobile assembly plant.[38] In *City of Duluth v. State*,[39] the Minnesota Supreme Court upheld condemnation of an existing (but currently unused) industrial facility in order to provide a site for a privately owned paper mill, noting the congruence of public use and public purpose.[40] And in *City of Jamestown v. Leevers Supermarkets, Inc.*,[41] the North Dakota Supreme Court upheld the use of eminent domain to acquire downtown parking lots to be conveyed to the developers of a new grocery store.[42]

Arguments against Constitutionality

Despite the existing pattern of equating public purpose and public use, and despite the national case law that supports eminent domain for economic development projects, the North Carolina courts still might refuse to extend *Maready*'s public purpose holding to eminent domain. After all, there is something unsettling about a government condemning property owned by private owner A simply because the government believes that future private owner B could use the property more productively.[43] The court's equation of public purpose and public use in *Mitchell* was to some extent rhetorical: making the equation strengthened the court's argument against the constitutionality of industrial development bond financing. In discussing eminent domain in *Mitchell*, moreover, the court went on to argue: "That the power of eminent domain should or could ever be used in behalf of a private interest is a concept foreign to North Carolina, and it transcends our Constitution."[44] That attitude toward the use of eminent domain might well outlast the court's change of heart about the constitutionality of expenditures for economic development.

A comparable constitutional attitude lies behind those cases from other states that have rejected use of eminent domain for economic development. For example, in *City of Little Rock v. Raines*,[45] the city proposed to condemn property in order to develop an industrial park; the Arkansas Supreme Court held that the condemnation did not serve a public use. Similarly, in *Karesh v. City Council of City of Charleston*,[46] the city proposed to condemn a half block of downtown property and then lease the property for up to sixty years to the private developer of the remaining half of the block, who would construct and operate a parking deck and convention center on the site. The South Carolina Supreme Court viewed the long-term lease as equivalent to conveying the fee and held that it was not a public use to condemn the site for the benefit of the private developer. The developer planned to include street-level shops in the parking structure, and the court remarked that "[w]e cannot constitutionally condone the eviction of the present property owners by virtue of the power of eminent domain in favor of other private shopkeepers."[47]

Each state that has rejected eminent domain for economic development has upheld expenditures for the same purpose. That is, the courts in those states have used a different standard for public purpose than for public use. Some of those courts have explicitly uncoupled public purpose and public use in order to distinguish between expenditures for economic development and eminent domain for that purpose. A set of cases from Maine are illustrative. In *Opinion of the Justices*,[48] the Maine Supreme Judicial Court held that the city of Bangor's proposal to condemn land within an industrial district for reconveyance to manufacturing companies would serve neither a public purpose nor a public use. The court supported its holding with the common argument that government should not condemn one private use for the sole purpose of helping another:

> An existing shoe factory or paper mill, let us say, within the proposed industrial area or park could not, for reasons clear to all, be authorized under our Constitution to acquire additional facilities by eminent domain. That such a course could well be of great value to the particular enterprise and so to the city or community would not affect the application of the law.[49]

Twenty-five years later, however, the Maine court was willing to uphold *expenditures* for economic development projects, even when those expenditures directly benefited a private company. In *Common Cause v. State*,[50] the court allowed both the state and the city of Portland to spend large amounts of money in order to bring a ship-building facility to Portland's harbor. In explaining its conclusion, however, the court emphasized that it no longer equated public purpose with public use; its holding allowing expenditure of public moneys did not thereby offer support for eminent domain for comparable projects.[51] Although current North Carolina case law supports holding that condemnation for an economic development project serves a public use, it remains possible that North Carolina courts could, like those of Maine, uncouple public purpose and public use when and if a case reaches the appellate level.[52]

Property Tax Exemptions and Abatements

The Constitutional Provisions

State and local governments throughout the country use property tax exemptions and abatements as an economic development incentive. Exemptions, which remove a class of property from the property tax base, are normally established by statewide legislation; abatements, which reduce or forgive property taxes for several years, often are granted by local government and apply only to specific parcels of property or to the property of a single owner. Abatements often are given through a contract under which a private company makes an investment on the property in return for a specific abatement. In South Carolina, for example, a manufacturing company that constructs a new plant or expands an existing plant with an investment of at least $50,000 is eligible for an abatement from county and municipal property taxes for up to five years. In addition, South Carolina law permits abatements for significant investments in distribution facilities, research and development facilities, and corporate headquarters and office facilities.

The North Carolina General Assembly has enacted a number of statewide property tax exemptions that are intended to promote economic development. The most prominent of these exclude the following classes of property from the statewide property tax base:

- manufacturers' inventories;[53]
- retailers' and wholesalers' inventories;[54]
- poultry and livestock and feed used in the production of poultry and livestock;[55]
- various forms of intangible property, such as bank deposits, stocks and bonds, and business accounts receivable;[56]
- certain kinds of computer software;[57] and
- cargo containers and container chassis used by ocean-going ships.[58]

Abatements, however, are another story. Two North Carolina constitutional provisions combine to effectively bar legislation that would allow local governments to negotiate and offer specific property tax abatements to specific industrial or commercial property owners.[59] These two provisions read as follows:

Article V, Section 2(2). Classification. Only the General Assembly shall have the power to classify property for taxation, which power shall be exercised only on a State-wide basis and shall not be delegated. . . .

Article V, Section 2(3). Exemptions. . . . Every exemption shall be on a State-wide basis. . . . No taxing authority other than the General Assembly may grant exemptions, and the General Assembly shall not delegate the powers accorded to it by this subsection.

The two provisions place North Carolina policy making on exemptions exclusively at the state level. Only the General Assembly may grant exemptions and establish classifications,* and it may not delegate this power to any other agency or level of government. Thus the constitution prohibits legislation that allows local governments to grant exemptions. In addition, the constitutional provisions require that any exemptions be granted on a statewide basis; it is not constitutionally possible to fashion exemptions or abatements that explicitly apply only to a single property or a single property owner or that only apply in a single city or county. Together these provisions bar any legislative attempt to authorize local governments to negotiate and grant explicit tax abatements to particular properties and particular property owners.[60]

---

* The constitution provides for both exemptions and classifications, but there is no important practical difference between property that has been exempted from the tax base and property that has been classified and the class excluded from the tax base. In this discussion, the term *exemption* refers to both.

Cash Grants Based on Property Taxes Paid

Against this constitutional backdrop, a number of North Carolina counties and cities—apparently starting in 1996—have adopted and implemented incentive policies that approach tax abatements in effect. It is unknown whether a court would consider the payments made under these policies to be so much like abatements that it would declare them unconstitutional.

The policies follow a common pattern, and therefore the description below is generalized and not intended to depict any particular local government's policy. In brief, these policies offer to make annual cash grants over a number of years, for example five years, to industrial companies that invest certain minimum amounts in the county or city. (The investment might be either a new facility or the expansion of an existing facility.) The policy ties the amount of the cash grant specifically to the amount of property taxes paid by the company. For example, if a company invested at least $5 million, the county might agree to pay it an annual cash grant in an amount up to 75 percent of the property taxes the company paid on the resulting facility; larger investments would make the company eligible for a grant that represented a larger percentage of the property taxes paid.

These policies do not entitle companies to these grants. Rather they set out the minimum criteria for receiving grants, making it clear that each grant will be negotiated, with factors other than investment playing a role in whether a grant is made and how large it is. These other factors include the number of jobs created by the investment, the types of jobs created, the potential for further investment by the company, the demands the company will place on public infrastructure, and so on. Once the local government has determined the size of the cash grant it is willing to make, and the government and the company have agreed on the grant and the commitments the company will make to support the grant, the agreement is reduced to a contract between the parties.

As noted above, it is impossible to know whether a court would hold that implementation of the sort of policy described above would be an unconstitutional attempt to grant a tax abatement.[61] All that is possible is to suggest the arguments that might be made on each side of the issue.[62]

The principal argument against these policies and contracts focuses on effects. When the policy is implemented, it results in a contract between the local government and the company under which the company receives an annual cash grant from the government that is measured by the amount of property taxes paid by the company. The contract differs from an explicit tax abatement contract only in that the company does in fact pay the property taxes due on its facilities. Once the company receives the cash grant, its financial position is nearly identical to what it would have been had the company received an abatement and never paid the taxes.

The opposing argument begins by emphasizing the one difference just noted: the company does in fact pay its property taxes. Therefore, it has not received a property tax abatement; rather, it has received a cash incentive.[63] The earlier discussion of public purpose argued that incentives structured as cash grants are constitutional after *Maready*. That being the case, the method of measuring the amount of the cash grant should be irrelevant. Why should cash grants in general be permissible but not this single form of cash grant? Why should *measuring* the grant by the amount of property taxes paid be unconstitutional when property taxes have been paid?

Given the uncertainty associated with these policies, local governments might consider alternative ways of structuring cash incentive policies. There is obvious attraction to tying the amount of any incentive package offered to a company to the amount the company has invested in the local community; measuring incentives by the amount of property taxes paid is one way of doing that. Another way to the same end, however, is to base the incentive on the actual investment made by the company rather than the taxes paid on the investment; that is, a local government might offer incentives measured as a percentage of investment or of taxable property rather than as a percentage of property taxes. Ending the direct reference to property taxes paid reduces the cash grant's resemblance to an explicit tax abatement program and thereby offers greater constitutional protection to the policy.[64] In any event, a local government should not characterize the cash grant as a "reimbursement" of property taxes. Doing so gives evidence that the grant is a tax refund, which the statutes clearly forbid.[65]

Cash Grants Based on Sales Taxes Paid

The cash grant policies discussed above attempt to encourage *industrial* development. A grant policy based on property taxes paid, however, is not as attractive to new or expanded *commercial* development; property taxes are a considerably smaller relative cost for most commercial enterprises than for industrial ones. Recognizing that, at least one county has adopted a commercial development policy that awards cash grants on the basis of sales taxes paid rather than property taxes paid. Such a policy is on a stronger constitutional footing than are the industrial incentive grants just discussed. The explicit constitutional provisions on exemptions and classifications apply only to property taxes, not to sales taxes or other forms of taxation. Therefore the strong constitutional policies of exclusive state-level decision making expressed in those provisions are irrelevant to a cash grant policy based on amounts of sales tax paid. Furthermore, although the statutes that levy the sales tax characterize it as a "privilege tax . . . imposed on a retailer,"[66] they also make it very clear that the retailer is in fact a conduit: the tax is to "be borne and passed on to the customer, instead of being borne by the retailer."[67] It is the customer who in fact pays the sales tax, but it is not the customer who receives the cash grant; the grant goes instead to the state's agent in collecting the tax. Therefore, because the grant does not go to the taxpayer, it obviously is difficult to characterize the grant as a tax abatement. It is more clearly just a cash grant, one that happens to be measured by the amount of sales tax generated by the business receiving the grant.

Loans and Gifts of Credit

Constitutional Background

The final constitutional provision with significant implications for local government economic development is found at Article V, Section 4(3), which reads as follows:

> No county, city or town, special district, or other unit of local government shall give or lend its credit in aid of any person, association, or corporation, except for public purposes as authorized by general law, and unless approved by a majority of the qualified voters of the unit who vote thereon.[68]

Throughout the remainder of this discussion, Article V, Section 4(3) is referred to as the *credit provision*. As its quoted language makes clear, North Carolina's constitutional credit provision (unlike comparable provisions in many other states) does not prohibit loans or gifts of credit in all circumstances. Rather it restricts them, imposing three requirements before a local government may make a loan or gift of its credit: (1) the loan or gift of credit must be for a public purpose; (2) the loan or gift of credit must be authorized by a general law (that is, not authorized by local act of the legislature); and (3) the loan or gift of credit must be approved by the unit's voters.

This constitutional linkage of public purpose and voter approval emphasizes the significant point that the credit provision is not a substitute for the public purpose doctrine; it actually bears little connection to it. A North Carolina local government may not loan or give its credit, even with voter approval, unless the transaction serves a public purpose (just as it may not expend money unless the expenditure serves a public purpose); but also, even when the transaction serves a public purpose, the other two constitutional conditions—voter approval and general law authorization—must be met.[69] The credit provison is instead part of the constitution's system of limitations on a local government's use of its credit, both for itself and for others. By and large, the constitution permits a local government to use its credit for its own purposes, by direct borrowing, or for the benefit of others, by loans or gifts of credit, only if the unit's voters have approved that use in a referendum.

The present constitutional language regulating loans and gifts of credit dates from 1973, when a complete rewrite of Article V became effective; since then no appellate cases have interpreted its meaning. Although the constitution has had both a state and a local credit provision since 1868, and though a number of appellate decisions interpreted those earlier provisions, the relevance of the earlier cases is uncertain. The 1973 revision of Article V was proposed to the 1969 General Assembly by the Local Government Study Commission, and the legislature enacted the credit provision's language exactly as proposed.

The study commission's report does not indicate any intention to change the developed understanding of what constituted a loan or gift of credit; indeed the thrust of the report is that no change was intended.[70] The commission's proposal did for the first time, however, include an explicit constitutional definition of a loan of credit (as will be discussed below), and that definition fails to include every type of transaction that the supreme court had held to be a loan or gift of credit under the 1868 provisions. If the definitions are exclusive, the consequence is that the 1973 revisions narrowed the field of transactions that constitutes a loan or gift of credit. At least two reasons might be raised, however, that could cause a court to hold that the definitions are not exclusive. First, as stated above, the study commission's report includes no indication that it intended any change in the then-current understanding of what constituted a loan or gift of credit. Second, the constitutional definition covers only a *loan* of credit; it does not define a *gift* of credit. A court could use that fact to continue the former credit provision case law (and perhaps expand the coverage of the provision beyond both that case law and the express definition) by characterizing transactions not included in the constitutional definition as gifts (rather than loans) of credit.

The new constitutional language, however, has created uncertainty about the current boundaries of the credit provision and about its application to economic development. For that reason, what follows is a set of suggestions and speculations about the meaning of the provision based upon the current constitutional language; the appellate cases decided under the former provision; and, because some form of credit provision is almost universal among state constitutions, appellate cases from other states.

The Meaning of Credit

If the credit provision is to apply, a transaction must involve a local government's *credit*. What does that term mean? As the earlier discussion indicated, the credit provision is in the section of the state constitution that regulates local government borrowing. The section does not specifically define credit, but it comes quite close by specifically defining a *pledge of faith and credit* as a "pledge of the taxing power."[71] Therefore, a government's faith and credit is equivalent to its taxing power. Although the term faith could add something to the meaning of the phrase, it is more likely that the single word credit also is equivalent to the government's taxing power. If so, a local government's credit is loaned or given only if its general resources are at risk, only if it might be made to use its taxing power. Such a meaning of credit accords with the case law interpreting the pre-1973 constitutional provisions, in which the state supreme court had held that those credit provisions did not apply in instances when a local government pledged only project revenues and not its general taxing power.[72]

The credit provision probably also does not apply when a government makes other pledges that, like project revenues, fall short of its taxing power. Most importantly, if a local government enters into an installment financing agreement pursuant to G.S. 160A-20, in which the only security pledged is the financed asset, and does so for the benefit of a private entity or person, probably no gift or loan of the government's credit has occurred—the government has not pledged its general credit. When the state supreme court upheld the constitutionality of installment financing agreements, it held that the agreements did not pledge the faith and credit of the local government.[73] In reaching its conclusion, the court emphasized the nature of the security (the financed asset), the government's ability to refuse to appropriate moneys due under the agreement (the contract's nonappropriation clause), and the inability of creditors to draw upon the general credit of the borrowing government in case of default.[74] A court should apply the same reasoning to the applicability of the credit provision to installment financings.

As a practical matter, then, this understanding of credit significantly limits the application of the credit provision when a local government borrows money. The provision does not apply when the security for the borrowing is either project revenues (as with revenue bonds) or the project itself (as with installment financing agreements), nor does it apply when the borrowing is subject to a right of nonappropriation. Rather it applies only when the security is the government's taxing power; that is, it applies only to general obligation borrowing.

Futhermore, the credit provision does not establish an additional constitutional hurdle for most general obligation borrowing, even if that borrowing otherwise constitutes a loan or gift of credit. Ordinarily, when a local government borrows money with a general obligation pledge, the borrowing itself satisfies the three requirements imposed by the constitution on gifts or loans of credit. It is for a public purpose; it is authorized by general law; and it has been approved by the voters. The state supreme court has made clear that a local government may not issue general obligation bonds except for a public purpose;[75] the constitution requires that all laws authorizing the borrowing of money be enacted by general law,[76] and the constitution requires that almost all general obligation borrowing be approved by the voters.[77] Therefore the credit provision restricts loans or gifts of credit that involve a government's general obligation debt only if one of the three constitutional requirements is not met. The only requirement that is not always and automatically met is voter approval. As applied to governmental borrowing, then, the credit provision restricts only government use of *nonvoted* general obligation bonds issued under the constitutional authority to issue nonvoted debt under the so-called two-thirds provision of the constitution.[78]

What Constitutes a Loan or Gift of Credit

Five different kinds of transactions either constitute or might constitute a loan or gift of credit under the North Carolina Constitution. They are: (1) borrowing through nonvoted general obligation debt and lending the proceeds to a private person or private entity, (2) borrowing through nonvoted general obligation debt and acquiring stock in a private company, (3) guaranteeing private obligations, (4) borrowing through nonvoted general obligation debt and using the proceeds primarily to benefit a private person or private entity, and (5) engaging in a joint venture with one or more private persons or private entities. The remainder of this chapter discusses the five types.

Lending Borrowed Moneys to Private Person or Entity

The first express constitutional definition of a loan of credit states that one occurs when a local government "exchanges its obligations with . . . an individual, association, or private corporation."[79] Specifically, if a local government issues its own nonvoted general obligation debt through bonds or other debt obligations and then exchanges the bonds or other obligations for the bonds or other debt obligations of a private individual or entity, the local government has loaned its credit. An exchange of obligations returns to the mid-nineteenth-century roots of the credit provision, when the state and local governments exchanged obligations with railroad companies as a way of assisting in railroad construction and thereby encouraging economic growth.[80] An actual exchange of obligations, however, would be rare today. A local government is more likely to issue bonds on the public debt markets and then lend the bond proceeds to private individuals or entities.

Lending bond proceeds is functionally equivalent to exchanging obligations. When a government exchanges obligations with a private person or entity, the other party sells the government's bonds on the secondary market, thereby obtaining the cash necessary for that party's purposes. In return, the government holds the obligations of the private party. Similarly, when a government sells its bonds itself and lends the proceeds, the transaction places both the private borrower and the government in the same position that each would have held after an exchange of obligations and sale of the government's bonds by the private borrower: The private borrower has cash and the government holds the borrower's debt obligations. Therefore, even without an actual exchange of obligations, a local government lends its credit when it uses that credit to borrow and then loans the proceeds to private persons or entities. This understanding of loans of credit accords with the interpretation of both the pre-1973 constitutional provisions[81] and the credit provisions contained in other state constitutions.[82]

Making Loans from Current Revenues

A local government loans its credit when it borrows money and loans the proceeds. If instead the government uses current revenues to fund loans to private individuals or entities, a loan or gift of credit does not result. Without a borrowing, the government's credit is not involved. Both current North Carolina practice and cases from other states support this understanding of the credit provision. The state and its local governments currently operate a number of programs under which they make loans to private persons or entities using current appropriations to fund the loans, and it is assumed that no loan or gift of credit has been made.[83] Furthermore, a number of other state courts have interpreted their constitutional credit provisions to exempt from constitutional regulation loan programs that do not involve moneys borrowed by the government.[84]

Borrowing and Purchasing Equities

The earliest North Carolina case interpreting a credit provision, *Galloway v. Jenkins*, was decided in 1869, just one year after the original constitutional provision took effect.[85] While the court held that the railroad assistance at issue was a loan of the state's credit, the case did not involve an exchange of obligations with the railroad. Rather the state proposed to exchange its bonds for stock in the railroad, which at the time was the more common method of assisting in railroad construction.[86] Given the current express constitutional definition of a loan of credit, it is unclear whether this case remains good law. Borrowing and using the proceeds to purchase equities does not fit within the definition. Nevertheless a current case offering a similar set of facts ought to be decided the same way as the 1869 case was.

The loan of credit provision does not apply to all investments of bond proceeds in the equities of a private company. For example, if a local government were to issue bonds to fund pension liabilities, it should be allowed to invest the bond proceeds in stock without concern for the credit provision. The key to understanding *Galloway* lies in remembering that the railroad in question was a new company, its stock having only nominal value; the state was purchasing the stock not as an investment of public funds but rather to provide capital to a new business enterprise. If a government today were to use bond proceeds for a comparable investment—aiding a company by providing capital—the government's own credit would in fact be used for the company's benefit, and the constitutional provision should control.[87]

Guaranteeing Private Obligations

The constitution also expressly defines a loan of credit as occurring whenever a local government "in any way guarantees the debts of an individual, association, or private corporation."[88] A local government cannot act as guarantor of loans made to private individuals or entities, act as surety on such loans, or in any other way guarantee payment of such loans.[89] Several comments need to be made about this definition and some of its effects.

Limited to guarantees of private debts. The definition of a loan of credit limits its coverage to guarantees of debts of *private* individuals and entities. This limit conforms to the credit provision itself, which applies to loans or gifts of credit to "any person, association, or corporation." That is, the constitution does not appear to regulate the ability of one government to guarantee debts of another government, although no current statute authorizes such a guarantee.[90]

Probably extends to guarantees of obligations other than loans. Clearly the credit provision regulates guarantees of loans made to private individuals or entities. Unclear, however, is whether it also regulates guarantees of other sorts of liabilities and obligations of private parties, such as liabilities arising from nondebt contracts or from torts committed by a private party. The same constitutional provision that defines a loan of credit to include guarantees of private debts defines *debt* as the borrowing of money. If the word debt is given the same meaning in both definitions, the credit provision does not extend to guarantees of private liabilities and obligations that were incurred other than through borrowing money. A court might not interpret the word in that way, however. The constitutional definition of debt is concerned only with governmental debts[91] and so might be held to apply only to governments, allowing a broader meaning for the word when applied to private individuals and entities. Certainly the policy behind the credit provision is as engaged when a local government guarantees other sorts of private obligations as when it guarantees a loan to a private party, and for that reason a court might accept a broader reading of debt.[92]

Probably covers indemnification agreements. Many local government attorneys believe that the ban on guaranteeing private debts restricts a local government's ability to agree to indemnify, or hold harmless, a private individual or entity. If a local government enters into an indemnification agreement, it is in effect agreeing to assume responsibility for specific obligations of another party; in a sense it is guaranteeing payment of those obligations.* (The obligations in question usually will not be obligations arising from loans made to the other party, so the applicability of the credit provision to such agreements depends first on the resolution of the issue discussed in the preceding paragraph.) An indemnification agreement differs from a standard guaranty in that it is made directly to the obligor rather than to the third-party obligee, but that structural point ought not control.[93] A government entering into an indemnification agreement is subjecting itself to the same kinds of potential future liabilities faced by a government that agrees to guarantee or insure payment of private loans. Although there is virtually no case law addressing the effect of credit provisions on indemnification agreements, both a Massachusetts court and a Texas court have suggested that such agreements are restricted by loan of credit limitations,[94] and at least two state attorneys general have reached the same conclusion.[95]

Status of guarantees funded by current appropriations unclear. A guarantee that is limited in scope to moneys already appropriated might not be a loan or gift of credit. The earlier discussion of the meaning of credit indicated that a loan or gift of credit under the constitution probably has to involve some possibility of recourse to the government's taxing power, some possibility that the government might be forced to levy a tax in order to meet its commitment. But if a guarantee is limited to moneys that the local government has already appropriated for that purpose at the time the guarantee is made, there can be no additional or future demand upon government resources, no recourse to the government's taxing power. For example, a local government might set aside $50,000 and agree to use those funds to guarantee loans made by banks to small businesses. If the $50,000 became exhausted, the government would have no further obligation. With such a guarantee it may be that the credit of the local government is not involved and therefore that the credit provision does not apply. Policy and textual arguments, as well as case law from other jurisdictions, both support and oppose this suggestion.

The credit provision, as previously noted, is concerned with limiting demands on the government's credit, that is, on its taxing power. It does not apply to borrowing that is secured by resources other than the taxing power, so why should it apply to guarantees that also cannot call upon the taxing power? A majority of the courts that have considered this issue have held that guarantees limited to current appropriations do not give or lend the government's

---

* Some hold-harmless provisions only guarantee that the promisor will hold the other party harmless from having to pay the obligations of the promisor. These promises do not guarantee obligations of another party and therefore are not affected by constitutional credit provisions.

credit.[96] Furthermore, one North Carolina decision interpreting the pre-1973 credit provision offers support to this argument. In *Fuller v. Lockhart*,[97] the Wake County School Board wished to purchase insurance from a mutual insurance company. The issue was whether the school board's potential liability, as a member of the company, for the company's liabilities constituted a loan of credit. The court held that it did not, emphasizing that the county's liability for additional assessments was limited to the amount of its premium. Other courts also have allowed the purchase of mutual insurance in cases where the assessment liability was comparably limited.[98]

On the other hand, the constitution itself defines a loan of credit as occurring when a government *in any way* guarantees a private debt, not just when the guarantee is open-ended. Although "in any way" may refer only to the nature of the promise (that is, including not just guarantees but also surety and insurance contracts), a court might easily read it also to make irrelevant the source of moneys that supports the guarantee. At least one state court has extended a credit provision to limited guarantees of the kind in question.[99] Until the North Carolina courts have had an opportunity to interpret this state's credit provision, the issue will remain unresolved.

In summary, as applied in the context of economic development, the credit provision restricts a local government from guaranteeing repayment of loans made to private entities, whether private businesses or private economic development agencies. It probably restricts a local government from guaranteeing payment of other sorts of private obligations as well. It also probably restricts a local government from entering into an indemnification agreement with a private business or a private economic development agency, under which the government agreed to pay the other party's obligations. Finally, it may apply whether the guarantee is open-ended or restricted to moneys already appropriated.

Using Borrowed Moneys to Assist Private Person or Entity

If a local government borrows money and pledges its taxing power, it is using its credit. If it uses the proceeds of that borrowing for expenditures that primarily benefit a private entity, it is using its credit for the benefit of that entity; and in many states such a transaction constitutes a loan or gift of credit. This sort of transaction is not included within the definitions in the North Carolina constitution, however, and therefore, as has been noted, the North Carolina provision might not cover them. Given that governmental credit is being used for private benefit, however, and given the precedents from other states, it is certainly possible that a court would extend this state's credit provision to these sorts of transactions.

What kind of transactions are meant here? The case law from other states suggests three primary categories, a discussion of which follows.

One, a local government borrows money and uses the proceeds to purchase or construct an asset that will be conveyed to, leased to, or used by a private person or entity.[100] For example, a local government might buy land for conveyance to a manufacturing company. If the conveyance or lease is for fair market value, many courts find no loan of credit.[101] Some courts find a loan of credit even in those circumstances, however,[102] arguing that the government may have better access to the credit markets than the private person or entity and that the government's credit is being loaned in that fashion.

Two, a local government borrows money and uses the proceeds to improve an asset owned by a private individual or entity.[103] It might, for example, purchase and install new machinery in an existing manufacturing plant. Again, if the government receives adequate consideration, some courts might find there is no loan of credit.[104]

Three, a local government borrows money and gives the proceeds to a private individual or entity.[105] Again, if adequate consideration is received, a court might find no loan of credit.[106]

Entering into Joint Venture with Private Person or Entity

In a couple of states, the courts routinely hold that those states' constitutional credit provisions forbid any kind of joint venture between public entities and private partners. In a string of cases, the Ohio courts have concluded that if a transaction is characterized as a joint venture between public and private entities it is enough to invalidate the transaction under that state's credit provision.[107] In reliance on the Ohio cases, the Mississippi Supreme Court has held that a joint venture is per se a loan of credit.[108] Unfortunately the opinions in these cases are not helpful in explaining why it is that joint ventures automatically, or even ever, constitute a loan or gift of credit. We can get some notion of the potential problem with joint ventures, though, by looking at cases from a few other states, both those in which courts found loans of credit and those in which they did not, and by looking at the law of joint ventures.

In *Johnson v. Young*,[109] an Idaho county held a number of judgments against several judgment debtors. It proposed to join with other judgment creditors and appoint a common trustee to bid on properties of the judgment debtors at execution sales, to manage the properties, and to dispose of the properties. The Idaho Supreme Court held that by joining in such an enterprise, the county loaned its credit to the other participants. The court's concern seemed to be that the county might not protect its own judgments as well through this joint arrangement as it might were it to proceed separately. In *City of Port Allen, Louisiana v. Louisiana Municipal Risk Management Agency, Inc.*,[110] the statute establishing a joint risk management pool for Louisiana cities made each participating city liable for all claims against the pool. The Louisiana Supreme Court held that one city's possible liability for claims against other cities violated that state's constitutional credit provision. In *Sampson v. City of Cedar Falls*,[111] the city jointly owned an electrical generating plant with a private power company. The Iowa Supreme Court held that the joint ownership did not loan the city's credit because the city received an ownership interest equal in percentage to its contribution to the project and was liable only for its own obligations. Finally, in *Doane v. City of Oak Ridge*,[112] the city entered into a set of transactions with a company for development of a city-owned golf course, a privately owned practice facility adjacent to the golf course, and a residential subdivision surrounding the golf facilities. The city eventually was to gain title to the practice facility, and it sold the land for the subdivision to the developer under terms that guaranteed the city a share of any appreciation in the land's value because of the golf facilities. The Tennessee appellate court rejected the argument that the full arrangement constituted a loan of the city's credit to the private company because the arrangement had "no provisions for the sharing of profits or liabilities for losses pursuant to the initial pooling of investment capital."[113]

The law of joint ventures itself is not well developed,[114] probably reflecting the many different structures that carry the label of joint venture. Frequently, however, courts hold members of a joint venture jointly and severally liable for the obligations of the joint venture and for the tort liabilities incurred by the joint venture.[115]

The four cases described above and the liability aspect of the law of joint ventures suggest that the danger of a joint venture under a credit provision is that a local government might find itself responsible for obligations of the venture itself or of one or more other parties to the venture rather than just for its own obligations. Understood in that way, a joint venture structured to impose such liability on a governmental participant is a variation on a governmental guarantee of another's obligations, a clear loan of credit. Additionally, if the joint venture is structured so that the governmental participant is barred from effective participation in decision making, so that the government's invested resources are at significant risk but beyond its control, that too might be thought of as a loan of the government's credit (or at least its assets) to a private entity. On the other hand, if an arrangement characterized as a joint venture is structured so that a government cannot be held liable for others' obligations and so that the government is adequately involved in decision making, the constitution's credit provision should not deter governmental participation.[116]

Notes

1. In a number of cases the North Carolina Supreme Court has applied the public purpose doctrine to expenditures that were funded by sources other than taxation. *E.g.*, City of Greensboro v. Smith *ex rel.* City of Greensboro, 241 N.C. 363, 85 S.E.2d 292 (1955), and Dennis v. City of Raleigh, 253 N.C. 400, 116 S.E.2d 293 (1960).

2. *E.g.,* Wood v. Oxford, 97 N.C. 227, 2 S.E. 653 (1887); Briggs v. City of Raleigh, 195 N.C. 223, 141 S.E. 597 (1928). The court never cited a specific provision in the pre-1936 constitution as the source of the public purpose limitation; rather it characterized the limitation as an inherent attribute of the power of taxation.

3. Wood v. Oxford, 97 N.C. 227, 2 S.E. 653 (1887).

4. 342 N.C. 708, 467 S.E.2d 615 (1996).

5. Mitchell v. North Carolina Indus. Dev. Fin. Auth., 273 N.C. 137, 144, 159 S.E.2d 745, 750 (1968).

6. *See Dennis v. City of Raleigh*, 253 N.C. 400, 116 S.E.2d 923 (1960), in which the court upheld public expenditures for industrial advertising.

7. Mitchell v. North Carolina Indus. Dev. Fin. Auth., 273 N.C. 137, 159 S.E.2d 745 (1968); and Stanley v. Department of Conservation and Dev., 284 N.C. 15, 199 S.E.2d 641 (1973).

8. Industrial revenue bonds, under the current state program, are discussed in more detail in Chapter 2, beginning on page 48.

9. N.C. CONST. art. V, § 9.

10. 342 N.C. 708, 467 S.E.2d 615 (1996).

11. The dissenting opinion lists the twenty-four projects and the incentives that were offered to the companies. *Id.* at 736-37, 467 S.E.2d at 632–33.

12. *Id.* at 720, 467 S.E.2d at 623.

13. 342 N.C. at 724, 467 S.E.2d at 625. Actually, the statute's public hearing requirement applies only to activities undertaken pursuant to Subsection (b) of the statute. Given the importance the court accorded the hearing, however, local governments proceeding pursuant to Subsection (a) are well advised to comply with the public hearing requirement as well. The different authorizations of subsections (a) and (b) are discussed throughout Chapter 2, while the public hearing requirement is discussed in Chapter 3, beginning on page 95.

14. N.C. CONST. art. V, § 9. The amendment allows industrial revenue bonds to be issued only by county authorities organized for that purpose. It does not allow the state or cities to establish such authorities and does not allow counties or other governments to issue industrial revenue bonds directly rather than through these authorities.

15. N.C. CONST. art. V, § 10.

16. N.C. CONST. art. V, § 11.

17. N.C. CONST. art. V, § 13.

18. Grants are used in other states. *See, e.g.,* IOWA CODE ANN. § 15A.1 (1995), which expressly permits local governments to make grants to private companies in furtherance of economic development. The statute was upheld in *Brady v. City of Dubuque*, 495 N.W.2d 701 (Iowa 1993). In addition, Oklahoma provides cash grants that are based on a percentage of new payroll created by the recipient company; this program is described in Gorin, *Incentives Project: Oklahoma Quality Jobs Bill*, ECON. DEV. REV. 29–34 (Fall 1994). Cash grants are particularly effective incentives because of their flexibility to the company. Bradley C. Grogan, *Attracting Business*, URBAN LAND 40 (May 1998).

19. 4 NCAC 1I (1998).

20. 276 N.C. 576, 174 S.E.2d 551 (1970).

21. 277 N.C. 29, 175 S.E.2d 665 (1970).

22. In *Minnesota Energy and Economic Development Authority v. Printy*, 351 N.W.2d 319 (Minn. 1984), the Minnesota Supreme Court held that a state loan program to assist small businesses served a public purpose.

23. Mitchell v. North Carolina Ind. Dev. Fin. Auth., 273 N.C. 137, 156, 159 S.E.2d

745, 758 (1968). *See also Nash v. Town of Tarboro*, 227 N.C. 283, 42 S.E.2d 209 (1947), in which the court held it was not a public purpose for a town to own and operate a hotel.

24. *E.g.,* ALA. CONST. art. IV, § 94; and DEL. CONST. art. VIII, § 8. In *Utah Technology Finance Corp. v. Wilkinson*, 723 P.2d 406 (Utah 1986), the court relied upon such a clause as grounds for invalidating an authorization to the finance corporation to make equity investments in new companies.

25. Cecil K. Brown, *A State Movement in Railroad Development* (Chapel Hill, N.C.: The University of North Carolina Press, 1928), details North Carolina's purchase of stock in the North Carolina Railroad, the Wilmington & Weldon Railroad, the Raleigh & Gaston Railroad, the Atlantic & North Carolina Railroad, and the Western North Carolina Railroad. It also discusses the purchase of stock in some of these roads by counties and cities along their routes and mentions the state's pre–Civil War purchase of stock in navigation companies and plank road companies. Local governments' purchase of railroad stock was upheld by the state supreme court in *Caldwell v. Justices*, 57 N.C. 323 (1858).

26. In addition, G.S. 147-69.2 (1998 Cum. Supp.) permits the state treasurer to invest a number of funds under the treasurer's control in the common stock of companies listed on national stock exchanges or the NASDAQ. Of course these investments are subject to the fiduciary responsibilities of the treasurer and are not speculative in nature. That cannot be said, though, of the additional authorization in that statute to the treasurer to invest limited amounts of money in venture capital partnerships and in the North Carolina Enterprise Corporation. Those investments are understood to carry risks to capital. It might be argued, finally though, that the pension moneys from which such investments are made belong beneficially to state employees and retired state employees and not to the state.

27. David L. Birch, *Job Creation in America: How Our Smallest Companies Put the Most People to Work* (New York: Free Press, 1987).

28. Loan and loan subsidy programs are discussed more fully in Chapter 2, beginning on page 46.

29. "[T]he pressure to induce responsible corporate citizens to relocate to or expand in North Carolina is not internal only, but results from the actions of other states as well. . . . [I]t would be unrealistic to assume that the State would not suffer economically in the future if the incentive programs created pursuant to N.C.G.S. § 158-7.1 are discontinued. . . . The potential impetus to economic development [from incentive programs], which might otherwise be lost to other states, likewise serves the public interest." Maready v. City of Winston-Salem, 342 N.C. 708, 725–27, 467 S.E.2d 615, 626–27 (1996).

30. For example, Connecticut Innovations, Inc., is a quasi-public agency of the state of Connecticut that makes investments in emerging high-tech companies in Connecticut using state bond proceeds. One investment vehicle used by the agency is purchase of equity in assisted businesses. (This information is drawn from the agency's site on the Internet: http://www.cii.rocky-hill.ct.us/.)

31. 1991 N.C. Sess. Laws ch. 390 (Duplin County, for a specific parcel of property).

32. For example, in *Charlotte v. Heath*, the court wrote, "In the exercise of the right of eminent domain, private property can be taken only for a public purpose and upon just compensation. But in any proceeding for condemnation under the power of eminent domain, what is a public purpose, or, more properly speaking, a public use, is one for the court" 226 N.C. 750, 754, 40 S.E.2d 600, 603–4 (1946) (citations omitted). *See also,* Nash v. Town of Tarboro, 227 N.C. 283, 287, 42 S.E.2d 209, 212 (1947) ("A municipal corporation, in the exercise of a proprietary right, just as in the exercise of a governmental power,

cannot invoke the power of taxation or the right of eminent domain except for a public purpose.").

33. Redevelopment Comm'n v. Security Nat'l Bank, 252 N.C. 595, 605, 114 S.E.2d 688, 695 (1960) [citing Wells v. Housing Auth., 213 N.C. 744 (1938)].

34. 273 N.C. 137, 159 S.E.2d 745 (1968).

35. *Id.* at 158, 159 S.E.2d at 760. The court used the congruence to make a similar argument in *Foster v. North Carolina Medical Care Commission*, in which the question was whether it served a public purpose for the Medical Care Commission to issue revenue bonds in order to finance improvements to privately owned hospitals. 283 N.C. 110, 195 S.E.2d 517 (1973). In deciding that question in the negative, the court noted that "if the General Assembly may authorize a State agency to expend public money for the purpose of aiding in the construction of a hospital facility to be leased to and ultimately conveyed to a private agency, it may also authorize the acquisition of a site for such facility by exercise of the power of eminent domain." *Id.* at 126, 195 S.E.2d at 528.

36. 339 A.2d 278 (Md. 1975). *See also, Atwood v. Willacy County Navigation District,* 271 S.W.2d 137 (Tex. Civ. Ct. App. 1954), which upheld a port district's condemnation of land for lease to industrial facilities.

37. 304 N.W.2d 455 (Mich. 1981).

38. Detroit later did the same thing for a Chrysler plant. The condemnation was upheld in *City of Detroit v. Vavro*, 442 N.W.2d 730 (Mich. Ct. App. 1989), but the appellate court was deeply unhappy at having to follow the earlier precedent, calling the use of eminent domain for such a purpose "unconscionable." *Id.* at 731. The story of the Poletown condemnations is told in Jean Wylie, *Poletown: Community Betrayed* (Urbana, Ill.: University of Illinois Press, 1989).

39. 390 N.W.2d 757 (Minn. 1986).

40. Earlier, in *City of Minneapolis v. Wurtele*, 291 N.W.2d 386 (Minn. 1980), the Minnesota court upheld condemnation of downtown properties that were found to be underdeveloped in order to assemble land for a project that developed the properties in a way more to the city's liking.

41. 552 N.W.2d 365 (N.D. 1996).

42. In *New Jersey Housing and Mortgage Finance Agency v. Moses*, 521 A.2d 1307 (N.J. Super. Ct., App. Div. 1987), the court upheld condemnation of land for transfer to a private company that would operate a grocery store that would serve several public-assisted housing projects; in *City of New Haven v. Town of East Haven*, 402 A.2d 345 (Conn. Super. Ct. 1977), the court accepted without question the constitutionality of eminent domain for an industrial park; and in *City of Kansas City v. Hon*, 972 S.W.2d 407 (Mo. Ct. App. 1998), the court upheld condemnation of eight tracts near an airport, to be used for airport-related industrial projects, such as an aircraft manufacturing plant.

43. In *City of Owensboro v. McCormick*, 581 S.W.2d 3 (Ky. 1979), the court wrote that "naked and unconditional power to compel a citizen to surrender his productive and attractive property to another citizen who will use it predominantly for his own private profit just because such alternative private use is thought to be preferable in the subjective notion of governmental authorities is repugnant to our constitutional protections." *Id.* at 5.

44. *Mitchell*, 273 N.C. at 159, 159 S.E.2d at 760.

45. 411 S.W.2d 486 (Ark. 1967).

46. 247 S.E.2d 342 (S.C. 1978).

47. *Id.* at 345. *See also, Wilmington Parking Authority v. Land with Improvements*, 521

A.2d 227 (Del. 1987), in which the court rejected condemnation for expansion of an existing newspaper plant; *Baycol, Inc. v. Downtown Development Authority*, 315 So.2d 451 (Fla. 1975), in which the court rejected condemnation for a downtown mall; *Southwestern Illinois Development Authority v. National City Environmental, L.L.C.*, 710 N.E.2d 896 (Ill. Ct. App. 1999), in which the court rejected condemnation of one business in order to convey land to a second business for surface parking; *City of Owensboro v. McCormick*, 581 S.W.2d 3 (Ky. 1979), in which the Kentucky Supreme Court rejected condemnation by the city for an industrial park; *Merrill v. City of Manchester*, 499 A.2d 216 (N.H. 1985), in which the court rejected condemnation for an industrial park; *Hogue v. Port of Seattle*, 341 P.2d 171 (Wash. 1959), in which the Washington Supreme Court rejected condemnation by the port authority for an industrial park; and *Petition of City of Seattle*, 638 P.2d 549 (Wash. 1981), in which the same court rejected condemnation by the city for a project much like that rejected by the South Carolina court in *Karesh*.

48. 131 A.2d 904 (Me. 1957).

49. *Id.* at 907.

50. 455 A.2d 1 (Me. 1983).

51. The Florida court also has turned away from an earlier decision that equated public purpose and public use and held that public purpose encompasses a wider sweep. In *Department of Transportation v. Fortune Federal Savings and Loan Association*, 532 So.2d 1267 (Fla. 1988), the court rejected the identification of public use and public purpose made in *Baycol*, 315 So.2d 451.

One forceful presentation of the possible distinction between public purposes and public uses is found in the dissenting opinion of Justice Ryan, of the Michigan Supreme Court, in *Poletown Neighborhood Council v. City of Detroit*, 304 N.W.2d 455 (Mich. 1981). That case, as noted in the text at notes 7 and 8, approved Detroit's use of eminent domain to acquire a site for a Cadillac assembly plant. In arguing against the majority, Justice Ryan wrote:

> As a general proposition then, in the realm of aid to private corporations, "public purpose" (taxation) has been construed less restrictively than "public use" (eminent domain). The distinction is fully justified. The character of governmental interference with the individual in the case of taxation is wholly different from the case of eminent domain. The degree of compelled deprivation of property is manifestly less intrusive in the former case: it is one thing to disagree with the purposes for which one's tax money is spent; it is quite another to be compelled to give up one's land and be required, as in this case, to leave what may well be a lifelong home and community. (*Id.* at 474)

52. Other courts that have distinguished between public purpose and public use include the Arkansas Supreme Court, which in *City of Little Rock v. Raines*, 411 S.W.2d 486 (Ark. 1967), noted "that a project is one for which public funds may be expended is not a sufficient basis for finding that use of the property is a public use justifying the taking of private property," *id.* at 494; and the Kentucky Supreme Court, which in *City of Owensboro v. McCormick*, 581 S.W.2d 3 (Ky. 1979), noted that the "opportunity for tyranny, particularly by the self-righteous, exists in condemnation of private property to a vastly greater degree than in the levying of taxes and the expenditure of public funds," *id.* at 7.

53. N.C. GEN. STAT. § 105-275(33) (1997). Hereinafter the General Statutes are abbreviated as G.S.

54. G.S. 105-275(34) (1997).

55. G.S. 105-275(37) (1997).

56. G.S. 105-275(31)(31a)(31b)(31c) (1997).

57. G.S. 105-275(40) (1997).

58. G.S. 105-275(24) (1997).

59. The constitution does not speak specifically of abatements, but it is likely that the constitutional policy on exemptions, discussed in this section, includes abatements as well.

60. Article V, Section 2(1), of the constitution states that the "power of taxation . . . shall never be surrendered, suspended, or contracted away." This provision seems intended to deny the state and its local governments the power to grant exemptions (or abatements) by contract, thereby relinquishing the legislative power to repeal an exemption at any time. During the nineteenth century the General Assembly enacted a number of railroad charters that gave to the newly chartered company a perpetual or multiyear exemption of its property from tax. In *Raleigh & Gaston R.R. Co. v. Reid*, 64 N.C. 155 (1870), and *Wilmington & Weldon R.R. Co. v. Reid*, 64 N.C. 232 (1870), the North Carolina Supreme Court held that charter provisions granting tax exemptions of the sort described *did not* bind a later General Assembly. The United States Supreme Court disagreed, however, and held that the charter exemptions were binding. Wilmington & Weldon R.R. Co. v. Reid, 80 U.S. (13 Wall.) 264 (1871), and Raleigh & Gaston R.R. Co. v. Reid, 80 U.S. (13 Wall.) 269 (1871). The latter Court did suggest, however, that a state constitution could stop the legislature from ever enacting such an exemption. The current constitutional language might be thought a response to that history. In other states, courts have so interpreted comparable language. *E.g.*, Switzer v. City of Phoenix, 341 P.2d 427 (Ariz. 1959); Opinion of the Justices, 152 A.2d 81 (Me. 1959). In a recent case, however, the North Carolina Supreme Court seemingly did not agree with such a reading of the provision. In *Bailey v. State of North Carolina*, 348 N.C. 130, 500 S.E.2d 54 (1998), the court was deciding whether the state could constitutionally change the tax treatment of pension payments to retired state employees. The state argued that the constitutional provision quoted in this note prohibited a permanent exemption of retirees' pensions from taxation, but the court disagreed. "[I]t is clear that the State may make contracts for exemptions without contracting away the 'power' of taxation as long as the contract is for a public purpose." *Id*. at 148, 500 S.E.2d at 64.

61. In 1997 the attorney general's office issued an advisory opinion to the attorney for a city considering whether to adopt a program such as those being discussed in this section. Letter from North Carolina Attorney General to Robert B. Smith (Aug. 29, 1997) (on file with author). The letter concluded that such a program would not violate the constitutional requirement that property be taxed only by uniform rule. It did not consider, however, whether the program constituted an invalid attempt to grant a tax abatement.

62. The arguments for and against such grants being considered as unconstitutional abatements are set out more fully in WILLIAM A. CAMPBELL & DAVID M. LAWRENCE, *Economic Development Grants Linked to Property Taxes: Constitutional Concerns*, 84 LOC. GOV'T L. BULL. (June 1998).

63. There is a vigorous scholarly debate as to whether various tax incentives offered by states and local governments violate the federal Constitution's Commerce Clause. *See e.g.*, WALTER HELLERSTEIN & DAN T. COENEN, *Commerce Clause Restraints on State Business Development Incentives*, 81 CORNELL L. REV. 789 (May 1996); PETER D. ENRICH, *Saving the States from Themselves: Commerce Clause Constraints on State Tax Incentives for*

Business, 110 HARV. L. REV. 377 (Dec. 1996). As part of this debate it has been suggested that cash and other subsidies to business, as opposed to tax credits and abatements, are constitutional, and the difference in form between tax break and cash payment is central to the distinction. *See especially,* DAN T. COENEN, *Business Subsidies and the Dormant Commerce Clause,* 107 YALE L. J. 965, 985–97 (Jan. 1998).

64. This alternative measure of incentives, as well as other alternatives, is discussed in greater detail in the section on cash incentives in Chapter 2, beginning on page 65.

65. G.S. 105-380(a) (1997).

66. G.S. 105-164.4(a) (1997).

67. G.S. 105-164.7 (1997).

68. The State of North Carolina is subject to a parallel constitutional restriction on loaning or giving its credit. N.C. CONST. art. V, § 3(2).

69. In many states the courts have created a public purpose exception to their constitutional prohibitions on loans or gifts of credit. That is, even if a transaction constitutes a loan or a gift of credit, it will not be invalidated if it serves a public purpose. These states typically prohibit all loans or gifts of credit without regard for whether there has been voter approval. For example, Article XI, Section 2, of the Minnesota Constitution states that the "credit of the state shall not be given or loaned in aid of any individual, association or corporation [with exceptions that are not here relevant]." In *Minnesota Energy & Economic Development Authority v. Printy,* 351 N.W.2d 319 (Minn. 1984), that state supreme court upheld a program under which the state insured loans made by private lenders to Minnesota businesses. One reason given by the court was that the loan insurance program served the public purpose of economic development. Similarly, Article VIII, Section 8, of the Pennsylvania Constitution states that the state's credit "shall not be pledged or loaned to any individual, company, corporation or association . . . ." In *Tosto v. Pennsylvania Nursing Home Loan Agency,* 331 A.2d 198 (Pa. 1975), that state supreme court upheld an issue of state general obligation bonds, the proceeds of which were loaned to private nursing homes, because the program served a public purpose. Both the Minnesota loan insurance program and the Pennsylvania nursing home loan program would be loans of credit under the North Carolina constitution. That the respective programs served a public purpose would be the starting point toward validity, not the basis for it.

70. The Local Government Study Commission was developing its proposal for a new Article V of the constitution at the same time that the State Constitution Study Commission was proposing a modernization of the entire constitution. The latter commission proposed a version of Article V that reorganized its provisions and modernized the language but that purported to make only two substantive changes in meaning, neither of which affected the basic meaning of the credit provision. REPORT OF THE N.C. STATE CONST. STUDY COMM'N (Raleigh, N.C.: 1968), pp. 31–33. The Local Government Study Commission then used the other commission's proposals on loans and gifts of credit as the bases of its own recommendations on those provisions. In its comment to the proposed Article V, Section 3(2), establishing the limit on loans or gifts of the state's credit, the Local Government Study Commission wrote that the "subsection is taken from the Revised Constitution recommended by the State Constitution Study Commission." REPORT OF THE LOCAL GOV'T STUDY COMM'N, 1968 (Raleigh, N.C.: 1969), p. 22. Then, in its comment on the proposed limitation on local government loans or gifts of credit, the commission wrote that the subsection "is a new paragraph which adds a prohibition against loans of credit to private organizations parallel to the prohibition against State loans of credit in Sec. 3(2)." *Id.* at 26.

71. N.C. CONST. art. V, § 4(5).

72. Martin v. Housing Corp., 277 N.C. 29, 175 S.E.2d 665 (1970) (Housing revenue bonds do not create a loan of credit because the "Corporation has no authority to incur any debt which would obligate the General Assembly to make appropriations."). *Id.* at 54, 175 S.E.2d at 679; Foster v. Medical Care Comm'n, 283 N.C. 110, 195 S.E.2d 517 (1973) (Hospital revenue bonds do not create a loan of credit because use of the word credit "implies the imposition of some new financial liability upon the State or a political subdivision which in effect results in the creation of a State or political subdivision debt for the benefit of private enterprises. In order to have a gift, loan or use of the public credit, the public must be either directly or contingently liable to pay something to somebody."). *Id.* at 121, 195 S.E.2d at 525 [quoting Nohrr v. Brevard County Educ. Facilities Auth., 247 So.2d 304 (Fla. 1971)].

73. Wayne County Citizens Ass'n v. Wayne County, 328 N.C. 24, 399 S.E.2d 311 (1991).

74. "The statute [G.S. 160A-20] could hardly be clearer in barring the pledging of the taxing power to secure moneys due under a contract covered by the statute." *Id.* at 31, 399 S.E.2d at 316. "Under the plain language of the contract, the Board [of county commissioners] cannot be forced to appropriate amounts for payment of the contract in any year." *Id.* at 28, 399 S.E.2d at 314.

75. *E.g., Nash v. Town of Tarboro*, 227 N.C. 283, 42 S.E.2d 209 (1947), in which the court held it was not a public purpose for a town to issue bonds to construct (and then operate) a hotel.

76. N.C. CONST. art. V, § 4(1).

77. N.C. CONST. art. V, § 4(2) and G.S. 159-49 (1994). Several cases decided by the supreme court under the pre-1973 credit provisions demonstrate that the voter approval otherwise required for general obligation debt satisfied the voter approval requirement for loans or gifts of credit. Hudson v. City of Greensboro, 185 N.C. 502, 117 S.E. 629 (1923) (city issues general obligation bonds after voter approval and lends proceeds to railroad to build passenger terminal); Hinton v. Lacy, 193 N.C. 496, 137 S.E. 669 (1927) (state issues general obligation bonds after voter approval and lends proceeds to veterans of World War I).

78. N.C. CONST. art. V, § 4(2)(f).

79. N.C. CONST. art. V, § 4(5).

80. In *Galloway v. Jenkins*, 63 N.C. 147 (1869), all of the judges agreed that such an exchange of bonds would constitute a loan of credit. Chief Justice Pearson's opinion describes the state's practices before the loan of credit provision was added to the constitution. *Id.* at 162.

81. In three cases decided during the 1920s, the court reviewed transactions under which either the state or a local government borrowed money and then loaned the proceeds. In each case the court upheld the transaction because it had been approved by the voters. The implication is clear, however, that the transactions did constitute loans of credit by the government issuing the bonds and loaning the proceeds. Lacy v. Bank, 183 N.C. 373, 111 S.E. 612 (1922) (state loans proceeds of voter-approved state bonds to counties for school construction); Hudson v. City of Greensboro, 185 N.C. 502, 117 S.E. 629 (1923) (city loans proceeds of voter-approved city bonds to railroad for construction of passenger terminal); and Hinton v. Lacy, 193 N.C. 496, 137 S.E. 669 (1927) (state loans proceeds of voter-approved state bonds to veterans for housing construction or farm acquisition or improvement).

82. *E.g.*, State v. Washington County Dev. Auth., 178 So.2d 573 (Fla. 1965) (borrow-

ing and making loans to home buyers); Opinion of the Justices, 268 N.E.2d 149 (Mass. 1971) (borrowing and making pollution control loans to companies); State *ex rel.* Saxbe v. Brand, 197 N.E.2d 328 (Ohio 1964) (borrowing and making economic development loans to companies).

83. State Industrial Development Fund, which makes grants and loans to local governments for reloan to industrial companies (G.S. 143B-437.01; 4 NCAC 1I.0202); local government loan programs authorized by the community development statute [G.S. 160A-456(a)(1)].

84. Engelking v. Investment Bd., 458 P.2d 213 (Idaho 1969) (state invested school endowment fund moneys in private securities and stock; no loan of credit because loan of credit involves imposition of new liability on government); Fairbank v. Stratton, 152 N.E.2d 569 (Ill. 1958) ("The transaction in question involves only a purchase or loan. [The state was buying bonds issued by an authority.] There is a loan of State funds, not of State credit. The State is not undertaking to become a surety or guarantor of payment of the bonds. It would be in the position of a creditor, rather than that of a debtor which arises upon a loan of credit." *Id.* at 573); Utah Tech. Fin. Corp. v. Wilkinson, 723 P.2d 406 (Utah 1986) (state makes loans to new businesses; not a loan of credit because money used for loans comes from appropriation rather than borrowing).

85. 63 N.C. 147 (1869).

86. "It will be found that most of the [state's pre–Civil War] public debt was incurred in three modes: (1) by subscribing for stock in railroad and navigation companies and issuing bonds to pay for the stock, the State becoming a member of the corporation; this is the heaviest item and amounts to, say, eight millions of dollars; (2) by issuing bonds of the State and exchanging such bonds for a like amount of the bonds of the corporation, the State not becoming a stockholder and taking collateral security of more or less value; this is the next heaviest item and amounts to about three millions of dollars; (3) by endorsing the bonds of corporations and taking a mortgage or some other collateral security; this item amounts to about two millions." *Id.* at 153–54.

87. It should be noted that a century ago the Tennessee Supreme Court read that state's credit provision differently. In *City of Johnson City v. Charleston, C. & C.R. Co.,* 44 S.W. 670 (1897), the court held that the provision did not bar a city from issuing bonds and using the proceeds to buy stock in a railroad.

88. N.C. Const. art. V, § 4(5).

89. Although the common law distinguishes between a *guaranty*, a *suretyship*, and an *insurance* relationship [New Amsterdam Casualty Co. v. Waller, 233 N.C. 536, 64 S.E.2d 826 (1951); 38 Am. Jur. 2D *Guaranty* §§ 12–17], it is unlikely that the constitutional reference to *guarantees* is meant to be technical. Rather, any time that a government assumes potential liability for private obligations, it probably is a loan of credit under the constitution.

90. This interpretation, which seems clear from the constitutional language, constitutes a change from the court's interpretation of the pre-1973 credit provision. In *Commissioners of Bladen County v. Boring,* 175 N.C. 105, 95 S.E. 43 (1918), the state supreme court held that a county's guarantee of bonds issued by a township, without voter approval, violated the then-existing constitutional provision on loans of credit.

91. The exact definition reads: "A debt is incurred within the meaning of this Section when a *county, city or town, special district, or other unit, authority, or agency of local government* borrows money" (emphasis added). N.C. Const. art. V, § 4(5).

92. In *E.F. Solomon v. Department of State Highways and Transportation,* 345 N.W.2d 717 (Mich. Ct. App. 1984), the Michigan Court of Appeals rejected the argument that the

state, by prequalifying the subcontractors used by the plaintiff-contractor on a public works project, had guaranteed that the subcontractors would not fail financially. The court rejected that argument because such a guarantee would constitute a grant of state credit to the subcontractor, which is barred by the Michigan Constitution. A number of other cases extend loan of credit restrictions to guarantees of nonloan obligations, but in each case, the state constitutional provision explicitly includes such an obligation. For example, in *Board of County Commissioners of County of Arapahoe v. Humes*, 356 P.2d 910 (Colo. 1960), the Colorado Supreme Court invalidated a statute that made a county responsible for liabilities, other than loans, incurred by unsuccessful proponents of municipal incorporations within the county. The Colorado constitutional provision, however, expressly prohibits local governments from becoming "responsible for any debt, contract, or liability" of a private person or entity. COLO. CONST. art. XI, § 1.

93. *See supra* note 86.

94. In *Lovering v. Beaudette*, 572 N.E.2d 591 (Mass. Ct. App. 1991), a community college had entered into a contract to rent a well driver, with operator, and the standard rental contract provided that the renter would hold the rental company harmless from suit because of any injury incurred while the equipment was in use. The operator was injured and sued the rental company. Although it won, the company incurred $77,000 in legal fees and therefore demanded indemnification from the college. The court found that the college did not assent to the indemnification agreement and interpreted a statute so as not to allow such agreements. The court wrote:

> [The college] is an agency of the Commonwealth, and its obligations are obligations of the Commonwealth. Taylor Rental is privately owned and managed. The indemnity clause at issue, unlimited in amount and pledging payment of others' obligations, is arguably a pledge of the credit of the Commonwealth in aid of a private individual or corporation. . . . It follows that there is, at least, reason to doubt that the indemnity clause could validly be incorporated in a [college] contract. (*Id.* at 594)

Another case that suggests that indemnification clauses are covered by loan of credit provisions is *Texas & N.O.R. Co. v. Galveston County*, 161 S.W.2d 530 (Tex. App. 1942), 169 S.W.2d 713 (Tex. 1943). The county had contracted with the railroad for the latter to operate a drawbridge on a county-owned causeway. The contract included a provision under which the county agreed to indemnify the railroad for any liability it incurred in carrying out the contract; but when the railroad's negligence led to such liability, the county refused to pay. The court upheld the county's refusal to pay, holding that the indemnification clause violated a provision in the Texas Constitution that prohibited the legislature from authorizing "any county, city, town or other political corporation or subdivision of the State to lend its credit or to grant public money or thing of value in aid of, or to any individual, association or corporation whatsoever." Tex. CONST. art. III, § 52. In its opinion, however, the appellate court emphasized the prohibition on the county lending *aid* to the railroad more than lending *credit*. Nevertheless the state supreme court (which affirmed on a different ground) characterized the appellate court as having held that the indemnity agreement was a loan of the county's credit.

95. 84-103 Op. Atty. Gen. (Fla. 1984); 96-7 Op. Atty. Gen. (Okla. 1996).

96. Board of Trustees of Univ. of Ky. v. Commonwealth *ex rel.* Stephens, 625 S.W.2d 867 (Ky. Ct. App. 1981) (state provides insurance to pay medical malpractice awards that exceed regular insurance coverage, thereby guaranteeing private obligations; no loan of credit because state insurance was funded by current state appropriations and there was

no future obligation to continue such appropriations); Minnesota Energy and Econ. Dev. Auth. v. Printy, 351 N.W.2d 319 (Minn. 1984) (state insures private loans to businesses; not a loan of credit because insurance is covered by appropriations and there can be no future liability of the state); and Jefferson County v. Board of County and Dist. Rd. Indebtedness, 182 S.W.2d 908 (Tex. 1944) (state takes over payment of county and district indebtedness on roads taken over by state; not a loan of credit because state appropriates fund to make payments rather than actually assuming legal responsibility for debt).

97. 209 N.C. 61, 182 S.E. 733 (1935).

98. *E.g.*, Clinton v. School Dist. No. 14 of Russellville, 90 S.W.2d 508 (Ark. 1936); Downing v. School Dist. of City of Erie, 147 A. 239 (Pa. 1929); Burton v. School Dist. No. 19, 38 P.2d 610 (Wyo. 1934).

99. In *Button v. Day*, 158 S.E.2d 735 (Va. 1968), the Virginia Supreme Court invalidated an industrial loan guarantee program, even though the money supporting the guarantee was funded solely by state appropriation of current revenues and there was no obligation of the state to appropriate any additional moneys. The court wrote:

We have noted with interest and given attention to the Attorney General's argument that there is no extension of credit involved in a 'one shot' appropriation of cash unattended by an obligation to appropriate further funds. In a proper case, that might be a valid argument. We know here, however, that any money that is appropriated by the legislature to the guaranty fund, whether initially or in subsequent appropriation acts, is to be used, under the express terms of the Act, for nothing but the granting of credit, and that simply is constitutionally impermissible. (*Id.* at 741)

100. *E.g.*, Garland v. Board of Revenue of Montgomery County, 6 So. 402 (Ala. 1889) (county uses borrowed funds to build bridge for use primarily by railroad); Lord v. City and County of Denver, 143 P. 284 (Colo. 1914) (city uses borrowed funds to build tunnel for railroad tracks); Brandes v. City of Deerfield Beach, 186 So.2d 6 (Fla. 1966) (city uses borrowed funds to construct spring training facility for lease to major league baseball team); Carothers v. Town of Booneville, 153 So. 670 (Miss. 1934) (city uses borrowed funds to build factory for lease to industrial company); and State *ex rel*. Ryan v. City Council of Gahanna, 459 N.E.2d 208 (Ohio 1984) (city uses borrowed funds to develop industrial park and lease spaces in park at favorable rate).

101. O'Grady v. City of Hoover, 519 So.2d 1292 (Ala. 1987) (city uses borrowed funds to build baseball stadium, which is leased to minor league team; court finds lease commercially fair); Miller v. Greater Baton Rouge Port Comm'n, 74 So.2d 387 (La. 1954) (port commission uses borrowed funds to construct facilities leased to private operators; lease at fair market rent); and Sullivan v. Andrews County, 517 S.W.2d 410 (Tex. App. 1974) (county uses borrowed funds to purchase medical clinic, which it then leases to physicians; lease at fair market rate).

102. Village of Moyie Springs, Idaho v. Aurora Mfg. Co., 353 P.2d 767 (Idaho 1960) (city uses borrowed funds to construct industrial facility); Murphy v. Dever, 150 N.E. 663 (Ill. 1926) (city uses borrowed funds to construct elevated railroad tracks); and State *ex rel*. Beck v. City of York, 82 N.W.2d 269 (Neb. 1957) (city uses borrowed funds to construct industrial facility).

103. City of Cincinnati v. Harth, 128 N.E.2d 263 (Ohio 1920) (city borrows and uses the proceeds to improve tracks owned by street railroad company).

104. Opinion of the Justices to the Senate, 660 N.E.2d 652 (Mass. 1996) (state borrows money and uses proceeds to improve privately owned railroad lines; because improvements will lead to increased shipping through state ports, court finds adequate consideration for expenditures).

105. Davidson v. County Comm'rs of Ramsey County, 18 Minn. 432 (1872) (county borrows money and gives proceeds to railroad). *See,* Colburn v. Chattanooga Western R. Co., 28 S.W. 298 (Tenn. 1894) (city turns city bonds over to railroad company, which in turn builds railway bridge). *But see,* Johns Hopkins Univ. v. Williams, 86 A.2d 892 (Md. 1952), in which the court distinguishes between exchanging bonds with private entity and issuing bonds and giving proceeds to private entity.

106. Gout v. Kendall, 192 N.W. 529 (Iowa 1923) (state borrows money and pays bonus to Iowa veterans of World War I; state owes a "recognized obligation" to the veterans). It is not clear whether a company's promise to construct a manufacturing facility or to create a set number of new jobs would constitute adequate consideration; in the public purpose context, it clearly does. Maready v. Winston-Salem, 342 N.C. 708, 467 S.E.2d 615 (1996).

107. Village of Brewster v. Hill, 190 N.E. 766 (Ohio 1934) (city purchased electrical equipment on time, with title remaining with seller; because title was with seller, city electrical system became joint and common pool between city and seller, which constituted loan of city's credit); State *ex rel*. Wilson v. Hance, 159 N.E.2d 741 (Ohio 1959) (city and electrical cooperative own generating facility in common; uniting public and private property constitutes loan of city credit); State *ex rel*. Eichenberger v. Neff, 330 N.E.2d 454 (Ohio 1974) (state university leases land to shopping center developer, which will finance improvements and subject them to lien senior to university interests; joining public and private interests in this fashion constitutes loan of credit); and State *ex rel*. Ryan v. City Council of Gahanna, 459 N.E.2d 208 (Ohio 1984) (city develops industrial park and leases space at favorable rates; this is joint venture and therefore constitutes loan of credit).

108. Giles v. City of Biloxi, 112 So.2d 815 (Miss. 1959) (joint venture between city and landowner for development of latter's property, with city taking title to 70 percent of land).

109. 23 P.2d 723 (Idaho 1933).

110. 439 So.2d 399 (La. 1983).

111. 231 N.W.2d 609 (Iowa 1975).

112. 898 S.W.2d 728 (Tenn. Ct. App. 1995).

113. *Id.* at 731.

114. "All of the aspects of the law of joint ventures are not completely settled, either in North Carolina or in other jurisdictions." Cheape v. Town of Chapel Hill, 320 N.C. 549, 560, 359 S.E.2d 792, 799 (1987).

115. 46 AM. JUR. 2D *Joint Ventures* §§ 41–42.

116. *See Lehi City v. Meiling*, 48 P.2d 530 (Utah 1935), a case testing the constitutionality of a newly formed water district. One statutory provision allowed the district to join with other corporations, public and private, in carrying out its powers and to obligate itself jointly or severally with other corporations in financing operations and to become surety for the obligations of its partners. The court read the statute in order to save its constitutionality and therefore assumed that the district would receive full consideration if it did in fact have to act as surety; it would not be required to pay for something it did not get.

2

SUBSTANTIVE ECONOMIC DEVELOPMENT PROGRAMS

• • •

2

Substantive Economic Development Programs

• • •

Many activities that local governments engage in as part of their everyday responsibilities have important effects on economic development. This section briefly reviews some of the more important of these general functions and programs.

Government Activities That Affect and Encourage Economic Development

Public education. When the executives of private companies are asked what their most critical need is, they most often cite a qualified and capable workforce—employees with good work habits, oral and written communication skills, and basic mathematical skills who are capable of operating the kinds of sophisticated machinery that are more and more common to modern production.[1] North Carolina's strategic plan for economic development, prepared by the Economic Development Board, identifies the state's first priority for competing in the modern economic world as "education and workforce development."[2] Local governments can assist in workforce development most fundamentally by providing their residents with good public education, especially at the elementary and secondary levels. In North Carolina, the state, county governments, and local boards of education have labored for many years to improve public education, recognizing the many benefits that a good education provides. The message from employers simply emphasizes the important consequences of education for economic development. Indeed, a local government's expenditures on public education might well be the most important economic development expenditures it can make.

In addition to helping provide a qualified workforce, a good public education system is crucial to economic development in another respect. A company that is considering locating in a community will bring with it at least some of its current managerial employees. If those employees are to accept the move, they will have to be satisfied that their children will receive a good education in their new home. If they lack confidence in the local school system, their resistance might cause the company to locate elsewhere.

"Quality of life" functions and programs. Economic development professionals also recognize that the quality of life within a community, the amenities it offers to its residents, affects the location decisions of companies and entrepreneurs, especially if a company is transferring a significant number of existing employees to a new community.[3] A critical part of this quality of life is the local education system, as discussed above. In addition, quality of life includes housing costs and availability, recreational opportunities, the local library system, cultural activities, availability of medical care, and even such matters as traffic congestion and the general sense of public safety within the community. To the extent that government can influence any of these matters, local government is in the best position to do so. A government's efforts to reduce crime, provide stable and attractive neighborhoods, improve transportation, support the arts, support a local hospital, provide a strong public library and good recreational opportunities—all add to a community's attractiveness as a location for new or expanded business investment.

Day care. Many families depend on day care to allow both parents to work, and working single parents almost always need assistance with day care. To the extent that a local government is a provider of day care,[4] it is helping its citizens find and hold jobs, a basic goal of economic development.

Water and sewer systems. Many manufacturing companies have special needs for water or sewer. A community without available water supply or sewer treatment capacity will not make the first cut on many economic development projects. Local government most often provides water and sewer services within a community, and therefore the government's policies and performance with respect to those utilities are crucial to economic development.

Transportation. Good transportation facilities are essential to economic development. Of greatest importance is good access to and from a community over the highway system, which is a state government responsibility within North Carolina. But the local street system also needs to work, as does the traffic control system; and these are largely city government responsibilities. In addition, many local governments, particularly counties, support local general aviation airports, which also help attract and retain companies.

Land use and permitting processes. It is useful to economic development if a local government has already zoned prime sites for industrial use. If a site needs to be rezoned, the time necessary to do so and the potential for community opposition can be enough to cause a company to look elsewhere. In addition, companies frequently complain about the complexity of obtaining all of the governmental permits necessary to siting and constructing their facilities and then to carrying on their businesses. Many local governments have reengineered their permitting processes in response to such complaints and as a way of providing better service to their residents in general. The kinds of changes that are useful include expediting permitting procedures, establishing a single, central location for seeking permits (so-called *one-stop permitting*), and assigning a staff person to assist with compliance and forms.[5]

General Economic Development Activities

This section describes economic development activities that generally are available to individuals and companies. Incentives—economic development activities that offer specific benefits to a single company, in order to cause that company to locate or expand within the community—are treated in the next section. For each of the activities discussed in this section, the activity is described, the statutory authority cited, and any specific legal issues identified and discussed. Chapter 3 of this book discusses the procedural requirements for economic development transactions.

Basic Activities Undertaken Pursuant to G.S. 158-7.1(a)

The principal statutory authority for local government economic development programs is Section 158-7.1 of the North Carolina General Statutes. (Hereinafter the General Statutes are abbreviated as G.S.) Subsection (a) of Section 158-7.1 offers counties and cities broad authority to engage in economic development, and many economic development activities trace their statutory authority to this subsection. [Subsection (b) authorizes a number of specific economic development actions, including several kinds of incentives. These authorizations are discussed below.] The relevant language in Subsection (a) reads as follows:

> Each county and city in this State is authorized to make appropriations for the purposes of aiding and encouraging the location of manufacturing enterprises, making industrial surveys and locating industrial and commercial plants in or near such city or in the county; encouraging the building of railroads or other purposes which, in the discretion of the governing body of the city or of the county commissioners of the county, will increase the population, taxable property, agricultural industries and business prospects of any city or county.

This subsection authorizes several activities, as described below.

Economic development planning. In order to establish a coherent economic development program, a local government must engage in economic development planning. To do so, the government undertakes or commissions studies of its current economic base, current employment structure and needs, the demographics of its population, its physical attributes and limitations affecting economic growth, current community service levels affecting economic growth, and so on. From the information gathered through such studies, the government develops goals for the economic development program and strategies for reaching those goals. No special statutory procedures condition these activities.

Business recruitment and promotion. This basic economic development activity includes developing an inventory of business sites and available buildings (and sharing that information with the North Carolina Department of Commerce for entry into the department's statewide database); responding to inquiries from business prospects, consultants, and state economic development officials; hosting site visits from these groups; and placing advertisements about the community and otherwise marketing it to companies and their location consultants. Again, no special statutory procedures are associated with these activities.

Development of existing and new businesses. This second basic economic development activity includes such measures as counseling and providing technical assistance to persons starting new businesses or operating small businesses, offering classes on starting businesses, assisting new businesses in obtaining financing, operating small business loan funds (see the discussion on financing, below), assisting existing businesses with marketing, publishing directories that list products or services provided by local businesses, conducting regular visits or surveys of existing businesses, and otherwise monitoring and ministering to the needs and concerns of existing businesses. No special statutory procedures condition any of these activities.

Construction and Marketing of Shell Buildings

G.S. 158-7.1(b) authorizes several specific economic development activities, one of which is a shell building program. Subsection (b)(4) provides that a "county or city may acquire or construct one or more 'shell buildings', which are structures of flexible design adaptable for use by a variety of industrial or commercial businesses." (Shell buildings are sometimes referred to as "speculative buildings.") Under a shell building program, a local government or its agent acquires or constructs a building (or buildings) that is usable for a variety of manufacturing activities or, if its ceilings are high enough, for warehousing and distribution activities. Having one or more available industrial buildings in a community is an important economic development tool. As many as eighty percent or more of companies interested in locating in North Carolina begin their search by looking for an existing building. Even if a company decides to construct a new facility in a community, as they often do, the company might never have visited the community to begin with had the community not had a shell building available.

Subsection (b)(4) is broad enough to authorize a government's purchase and adaptive reuse of a variety of existing buildings. For example, a county might acquire an old school building or a city an older downtown building and then renovate the building for resale for a wide range of commercial activities. Although these are not shell buildings in the typical sense of *industrial* recruitment, they do fit the statute's definition of shell buildings—"structures of flexible design adaptable for use by a variety of . . . commercial businesses."

G.S. 158-7.1 requires a county or city governing board to hold a public hearing before expending any money to acquire or construct a shell building, and to hold an additional hearing before selling or leasing the building to a company. Chapter 3 details these procedural requirements.

Business Incubators

G.S. 158-7.1 authorizes local governments to operate or support business incubators. Subsection (b)(4) permits direct operation, through leases in a shell building as defined in that paragraph, while subsection (a) permits support of a facility operated by another entity, such as a nonprofit economic development organization. A business incubator is a program intended to encourage and support new businesses. Typically it is housed in a building with flexible space, rented on a monthly basis to new businesses. The incubator furnishes a variety of services to the businesses in the incubator (and often furnishes some of these services to nontenant businesses as well). The services might include administrative services, such as a receptionist, secretarial or word processing assistance, bookkeeping, and mail services; business equipment, such as computers (perhaps with Internet access), facsimile machines, and copiers; business counseling, such as help in developing a business plan or in securing financing; mentor support from established businesses; networking among the assisted businesses; seminars and other training programs; and a business library and conference room. An incubator assists new businesses during the critical early stages, when they are most vulnerable to failure. The usual intention is that businesses "graduate" from the incubator after two to four years.

Although the authority to own and lease a shell building is clearly adequate authority for a county or city to own and operate a business incubator, most North Carolina business incubators are owned and operated by entities other than local governments.[6] One reason for this may be the procedural and substantive requirements that a county or city must follow in order to lease space to incubator tenants. G.S. 158-7.1(d) requires that a local government's governing board hold a public hearing before any lease of space in a shell building, including an incubator. This requirement would be cumbersome for most incubators. In addition, if the rentals are at a below-market rate (which they frequently are), G.S. 158-7.1(d2) requires that the lessee make improvements to the property sufficient to create property tax liabilities that will, when added to actual lease payments, reach a market rental rate. This requirement simply makes no sense in an incubator. For these reasons, it is more practical for a county or city to provide financial support, pursuant to G.S. 158-7.1(a), to a privately operated incubator than to operate one itself.

Land Banking and Options on Land or Buildings

A basic business recruitment strategy is maintaining an inventory of available industrial sites in the county or city. Sometimes a local government goes further and buys a site that is on the market, holding it for future conveyance to a business prospect, thereby ensuring the continued availability of the site for economic development. (A local government also might buy a site identified by a specific company for conveyance to the company; that form of incentive is discussed in the incentives section of this chapter.) Purchasing industrial sites is authorized by G.S. 158-7.1(b)(2), which permits a county or city to "acquire, assemble, and hold for resale property that is suitable for industrial or commercial use." The statute permits a county to acquire a site anywhere within the county (although apparently not in another county); a city may acquire a site inside the city or, if the property will be used by a business providing jobs for city residents, anywhere within the county or counties in which the city is located.

Land banking under the community development statute. In addition to the authority granted by G.S. 158-7.1(b)(2), cities are allowed to acquire and hold industrial or commercial land pursuant to the community development statutes. G.S. 160A-457 authorizes cities to acquire real property that is, among other purposes, "appropriate for . . . the economic development of the community." The statute goes on to allow the city to convey this property to private interests by private sale, although any conveyance needs to be at fair market value. (G.S. 153A-377 grants comparable authority to counties, but its usefulness to economic development is seriously marred by the statutory requirement that all conveyances be effected by public, competitive sales.) A local government that acquires or conveys property pursuant to G.S. 160A-457 must follow different standards and procedures from one acquiring or conveying property pursuant to G.S. 158-7.1. Those differences (which are discussed in Chapter 3) may cause a local government to select one statute over another.

Acquiring options. Instead of buying land or an available building (and thereby tying up public resources in real estate), a local government might wish to acquire only an option for the land or building. Such a step protects the site for economic development, at least for the time period of the option, but at a much-reduced cost to the local government. Later, the government can exercise the option itself or convey it to a private company, which can exercise the option and acquire the property. G.S. 158-7.1(b)(3) authorizes this use of options.

G.S. 158-7.1 requires a county or city governing body to hold a public hearing before expending any money to acquire a site or an option. (A hearing is not required if a city is acquiring the property pursuant to G.S. 160A-457.) The governing body must hold an additional hearing before selling or leasing a site to a company and perhaps before conveying an option to a company. Chapter 3 details these procedural requirements.

Industrial Parks

G.S. 158-7.1(b)(1) permits a county or city to "acquire and develop land for an industrial park, to be used for manufacturing, assembly, fabrication, processing, warehousing, research and development, office use, or similar industrial or commercial purposes." The statute permits a county to own and develop an industrial park anywhere in the county, whereas a city may do so anywhere in the county or counties in which it is located. Local government development of an industrial park may include the installation of utilities, drainage facilities, street and other transportation facilities, street lighting, and the like; the demolition or rehabilitation of existing structures; and the physical preparation of the site for industrial or commercial uses.

Local governments may combine their authority to develop industrial parks with their authority to own and lease shell buildings. The result is one or more government-owned and -operated industrial or commercial buildings divided into a number of separately leased spaces. Although no North Carolina local government currently operates such a facility, local governments in other states have had good success in doing so,[7] and the North Carolina statutes are broad enough to allow it here as well.

If a local government develops an industrial park, it will want to prepare, adopt, and record covenants that guide the private development and operation of sites within the park. Industrial park covenants typically include such matters as land uses that are permitted or prohibited in the park, design guidelines or rules for construction on park sites (perhaps with some requirement for architectural review of construction plans by the park developer), maintenance assessments for upkeep of common areas in the park, and perhaps support of an owners' association once some or all sites have been sold. Covenants sometimes also include provisions giving the local government the option to repurchase tracts in the park that are not developed within a reasonable time (such as eighteen or twenty-four months) after they are sold to a company. The exact content of industrial park covenants differs from one park to another, depending on the market within which the park operates and the sort of industrial mix desired by the park developer.[8]

G.S. 158-7.1(b) requires a county or city governing body to hold a public hearing before expending any money to acquire land for or otherwise to develop an industrial park. The governing body must hold an additional hearing before selling or leasing sites within the park. These procedural requirements are detailed in Chapter 3.

Financing Private Businesses

Local governments are allowed to assist private businesses in borrowing money in a variety of ways. This section summarizes three ways: government-operated loan pools, government subsidies to bank loans, and industrial revenue bonds.

Government-operated loan programs. New and small businesses tend to find it difficult to raise cash to begin and expand their operations. Because they are too small to attract venture capitalists, they must look instead to banks and to nonbank lenders. Banks, however, accustomed to minimizing risks, either refuse to extend loans to such businesses or impose terms that these businesses usually cannot meet. Some local governments, seeking to fill the resulting gap, have developed their own loan programs, creating a pool of money from which to make loans and replenishing the pool with revenues generated by the repayment of earlier loans. Government loan programs might target new and small businesses that are shut out of private lending sources; or they might make loans to companies that can contract with private lenders but on terms that are more favorable to the borrower than are those of private lenders. For example, a local government loan program might offer such subsidies as below-market interest rates (or no interest rates at all), extended amortization schedules, or lack of collateral.

Although no North Carolina statute explicitly authorizes such loan programs,[9] G.S. 158-7.1(a) is adequate legal authority for a loan program. The lack of specific statutory mention of loan programs means that the details of the program are entirely at the discretion of the local government creating it. (A caveat: One potential source of funding for a local government loan program is community development block grant proceeds from the federal government. If grant funds of that type are used, federal regulations will impose conditions that may limit a government's flexibility somewhat in determining the contours of the program.) The local government may determine, without statutory restriction, such matters as the purposes for which loans will be made, the eligibility criteria for borrowers, the amount of any fees charged to potential borrowers, the minimum and maximum amounts of loans, collateral requirements and other terms of loans, and the procedures to be followed in approving loan applications.

If a local government does establish a loan program, the records of the program are presumptively open to public access under the public records law. Certainly this holds true for the basic financial records of the program: amounts loaned, repayment histories, and actual notes given by businesses evidencing loans. Some information furnished by a business as part of a loan application, however, may be off-limits to public access. G.S. 132-1.2 protects business trade secrets that are submitted to a local government in connection with such an application. Financial statements probably qualify as trade secrets, and it may be that other information included with an application will also.[10] (If the application includes *personal* financial information about the business owner, however, that is not a *business* trade secret and would therefore be open to public access.[11]) In order for trade secret protection to attach to this information, the business must designate the information as a trade secret or as confidential at the time the business submits the information to the local government. Therefore, a local government may wish to include on its application form a space for a business to indicate whether and which information submitted is confidential.

Government subsidies to bank loans. Instead of establishing its own loan program, a local government may decide to encourage local banks to make more loans to small businesses by subsidizing certain types of bank loans. Subsidy programs do not entice banks into making bad loans, but they do encourage banks to loan to businesses that otherwise would appear too weak to be approved for a loan. Subsidy programs, in contrast to government-operated loan programs, permit the government to rely on the expertise of bankers in analyzing a borrower's credit and, in addition, reduce the government's own exposure to loss from defaulted loans.

A variety of government subsidies might expand the willingness of banks to make loans. A local government could agree to make grants to a business to be used to pay the principal or interest on a bank loan; it could make its own loans to a business on terms that are subordinate to the bank's loan; it could place funds on deposit with a bank, thereby increasing the bank's reserves, in return for which the bank would agree to increase its small-business-loan activity.

One measure that a North Carolina local government may not be able to take is to formally guarantee loans made by banks to small businesses. Under such a program, a local government typically sets aside a sum of money and agrees to guarantee repayment of private loans up to the amount set aside. The government faces no liability beyond those moneys that it sets aside. Loan guarantee programs efficiently leverage bank lending and are in place in a number of other states. As was discussed in Chapter 1, however, a loan guarantee program in North Carolina, even one based on and limited to a current appropriation, may run afoul of the state constitution's ban on lending public credit.[12]

As with government-operated loan programs, G.S. 158-7.1(a) provides the statutory authority for subsidizing bank loans.

Industrial revenue bonds. Industrial revenue bonds are issued when a governmental entity borrows money and uses the loan proceeds to finance a manufacturing plant or other facility for a specific private company. In the typical transaction, the governmental entity borrows money and loans the proceeds to a private company, the company constructs its plant, and the governmental entity uses the company's loan repayments to retire the bonds. The loan repayments are the sole security for the bonds. The governmental entity serves as a conduit between the private company and the bond market; the bonds are sold on the credit of the company, not the governmental entity. These bonds are creatures of the federal (and to a much lesser extent, state) tax code. If certain requirements of the Internal Revenue Code are met,[13] the interest on industrial revenue bonds is treated as interest on the obligations of a government borrower and is exempt from federal income tax. Thus these bonds offer a way for companies to finance their capital needs at a tax-exempt interest rate, giving them less expensive money than they could borrow on their own.

The Internal Revenue Code places two important restrictions on this form of financing. First, it limits the principal amount of any industrial revenue bond issue to $10 million.[14] In determining the amount of the bonds, the code counts not only the actual amount of the bond issue but also all capital expenditures made by the company in the same local government jurisdiction during the three years just before and the three years just after the date of bond issuance. In addition, the code directs that the outstanding amount of any other industrial revenue bonds that financed other facilities in the same local government jurisdiction on behalf of the same company be included. If the bond amount, calculated in this manner, is larger than $10 million, the interest on the bonds is taxable under the code. North Carolina entities occasionally issue industrial revenue bonds exceeding the $10 million limit, with the result that the interest on the bonds is taxable under federal tax law. Taxable financing can be slightly less expensive to a company than a direct loan because the interest, though taxable under the federal tax code, remains exempt from North Carolina income tax. To be worth doing, however (given transaction costs), taxable industrial revenue bonds need to be much larger than $10 million—as much as $100 million.

Second, the code limits the use of the proceeds of such bonds to constructing manufacturing facilities. At one time federal law also allowed the proceeds to be used for the construction of freight terminals; research, development, or laboratory facilities for industrial companies; and distribution facilities for industrial companies, and the North Carolina enabling act still authorizes that larger list of projects.[15] But industrial revenue bonds for anything other than manufacturing facilities generally will not be tax-exempt under current federal law.[16]

The North Carolina enabling act[17] for industrial revenue bonds also imposes a number of other limitations on the use of such bonds. First (though subject to waiver by the secretary of commerce), the company must agree to pay high enough wages at the financed facility so that its average weekly manufacturing wage is either above the average weekly manufacturing wage paid in the county in which the facility will be located or at least ten percent above the statewide average weekly manufacturing wage.[18] Second (subject to certain exceptions), the project must either save or generate at least one job per $250,000 of bond financing.[19] Third, the project may not cause or result in abandonment of an existing facility of the same company elsewhere in North Carolina, unless the other facility is obsolescent or suffers from lack of available labor or from site limitations. Finally, the project must not have an adverse impact upon the environment, as certified to the secretary of commerce by the Department of Environment, Health, and Natural Resources.

In North Carolina, industrial revenue bonds are issued by county agencies called the (blank) County Industrial Facilities and Pollution Control Financing Authority.[20] At this writing, almost every county has established such an authority. Each authority is governed by a seven-member board of commissioners appointed by the board of county commissioners. The authority's board members are appointed to staggered six-year terms but serve at the pleasure of the county commissioners.

The authority begins the formal process of issuing industrial revenue bonds by entering into an *inducement agreement* with the company. Among other things, this agreement evidences that the industrial revenue bonds will be an important factor in causing the company to locate or expand in the county whose authority will issue the bonds. The agreement also enables the company to begin expending its own moneys on the proposed project, these expenditures to be reimbursed later from the proceeds received at the issuance of the industrial revenue bonds.

After the inducement agreement is entered into, the project must be the subject of a public hearing, usually before the board of county commissioners, although the commissioners may delegate this task to the authority board. Once the hearing has been held, the board of county commissioners must adopt a resolution approving the proposed project and the issuance of the bonds for the project.

After local approval has been given, two state agencies must approve the financing, the Department of Commerce and the Local Government Commission. The Department of Commerce's role is to ensure that the bond-financed project meets the state's economic development goals, that is, that the project qualifies under the specific North Carolina requirements summarized above. The Local

Government Commission's role is to satisfy itself that the company will be able to make the payments necessary to retire the debt. One way the commission does this is by requiring the company, unless it enjoys an investment grade bond rating, to obtain a letter of credit from an investment-grade bank under which the bank agrees to provide back-up funding for the company's obligations under the financing. The authority and the company should retain bond counsel at the beginning of proceedings to issue industrial revenue bonds, and that person or firm can guide both entities through the entire process.

The Internal Revenue Code imposes a limit on the amount of industrial revenue bonds (and other "private activity" bonds) that can be issued in each state. In 1998 the North Carolina volume cap was $371 million; as is shown below, less than one-half of this cap was used on industrial revenue bonds (although the balance was or will be used by the North Carolina Housing Finance Agency in its bond programs to finance home ownership for first time homebuyers). In calendar year 1997, thirty-five industrial revenue bond issues were closed in North Carolina, totaling about $164 million. In calendar year 1998, there were thirty industrial revenue bond issues that closed, and these issues totaled about $126 million.[21]

Providing Equity for Private Businesses

A final method by which local governments can financially help new or small businesses is providing equity capital. Small businesses often lack the financial resources to attract commercial lenders and the cash flow to repay loans made by a government loan pool. If the business is to attract financial assistance, the assistance must come through equity investments, with the investors taking an ownership share in the company. (For certain sorts of businesses, investors might provide what some call *quasi-equity*. Instead of taking an ownership position in the company, a provider of quasi-equity receives the right to receive royalties on company patents or licenses. Obviously, though, not all companies are engaged in businesses that will generate such sources of income.) There has not been much governmental experience with this form of business assistance in North Carolina, although at least one local government has approved a small venture capital program and the state treasurer is authorized to invest limited amounts of money in venture capital.

The basic constitutional issue of whether North Carolina local governments may invest directly in private companies as an economic development tool is discussed in Chapter 1 (see pages 8–9), and the reader is referred to that discussion. Assuming that such a program is constitutional, the statutory authority is G.S. 158-7.1(a). As with government loan pools, the lack of specific statutory mention of equity programs means that the details of any program are within the discretion of the local government. A government establishing an equity investment program should consider the purpose of the program. Is it to provide venture capital to firms that might become outstanding successes, or is it to provide assistance to smaller firms that are likely to remain small but that serve other governmental goals, such as providing business opportunities within minority communities?

The government should decide on the eligibility criteria for assisted companies and the nature of its investment. A government might become a common shareholder, a preferred shareholder, or a lender holding rights to acquire equity at a later date.

The government should consider how it might cash out its investment. Most venture capital firms expect at best twenty percent of their investments to result in highly successful companies. If a governmental equity program is to be self-supporting, the government must be sure to reap its rewards when they arise.

In addition, the government should decide on program administration. Equity programs often use advisory boards whose members possess business skills that might not be found in government, such as entrepreneurship or investment banking.

As with a local government loan program, the records of an equity investment program are presumptively open to public access under the public records law. Also like a loan program, however, some of the information furnished by the business as part of its application may be exempt from public access. G.S. 132-1.2, as has been noted, protects business trade secrets that are submitted to a government as part of such an application. A business's financial statements probably qualify as trade secrets, and it may be that other information included with an application will also.[22] (If the application includes *personal* financial information about the business owner, however, that is not a *business* trade secret and would therefore be open to public access.[23]) In order for trade secret protection to attach to such information, the business must designate the information as a trade secret or as confidential at the time the information is submitted to the local government. Therefore a local government may wish to include on its application form a space for a business to indicate whether and which information submitted is confidential.

Incentives

Although in a broad sense incentives include any activity that subsidizes a private company as part of a local government's economic development program,[24] this chapter uses the term in a narrower sense. Here an *incentive* is anything of value that is offered to a private company for one of the following purposes: to cause the company to locate a facility in the community (referred to in brief as *locations*); to cause the company, already located in the community, to expand its operations there (referred to in brief as *expansions*); or to cause the company not to close or reduce in scale a facility that is already located in the community.

Incentive Policies

Local governments have for many years had formal incentive policies regarding water and sewer extensions. These policies have established the conditions under which the government would extend water or sewer lines to an industrial, commercial, or residential development and at whose cost. More recently, many local governments have adopted broader incentive policies, setting out the conditions under which they will offer financial incentives and, in some policies, the nature and amount of incentives the local government will offer for various levels of investment or job creation. Not all local governments have adopted formal incentive policies, however, especially policies that detail the incentives that the government will offer. Some governments have preferred to negotiate each package of incentives separately, without explicit reference to earlier deals. This section briefly describes the advantages and disadvantages of adopting formal incentive policies.

There are several possible advantages. First, formulating a policy can cause a local government to think systemically about its goals for economic development and to establish the steps it is willing to take to reach those goals, which is always good practice. The policy can then identify the kinds of projects for which the government will offer incentives and perhaps promise enhanced incentives to those projects that meet specific economic development goals. In addition, if the policy sets minimum conditions for awarding incentives, a local government can easily refuse requests for incentives for projects that fall below the minimums. Second, a formal policy can set the limit on what a government will do for a particular company. An established limit gives the government an anchor in the event it finds itself in a bidding war for a company. Third, a formal policy gives greater assurance of fair treatment among assisted projects. All projects are eligible for the same set of incentives, and the incentives are set out in written form. This may be a particularly important element in gaining support for incentive policies from existing businesses, because it shows them that they can qualify for incentives if they expand.

Formal policies, particularly those that set out the nature and amount of incentives that a government is willing to offer, suffer from at least two potential disadvantages. First, while the policies are usually careful not to create an entitlement to incentives for companies that locate or expand within the jurisdiction, they probably do create an expectation that incentives will be offered pursuant to the policy. As a result, a government might find itself giving incentives that are not necessary to attract a business to a particular location or to encourage a business to expand. Second, having its incentives position spelled out in written policies might weaken the government's bargaining position, inasmuch as its end offer appears to be on the table at the beginning of negotiations.

Content of Incentive Policies

This section discusses the kinds of provisions that local governments might want to consider for inclusion in an incentive policy. The discussion is based on actual policies that have been adopted by North Carolina counties and cities.

Eligibility Requirements

Investment and job creation. Most local governments that plan to offer incentives establish thresholds that projects must meet to be eligible for incentives. These thresholds are most commonly stated in terms of a minimum capital investment by the private company, and the policy often requires that a minimum number of permanent new jobs be created through the company's project.

Wage levels. Some local governments require that the jobs created at the project pay at least the average weekly manufacturing wage paid in the county. Occasionally local governments require that projects receiving incentives pay wages at some level above the county's average weekly manufacturing wage, for example at 110 percent.[25]

Public payback period. Some policies, especially when incentives are paid at the front end of a project, establish a maximum time in which the taxes paid by the company will repay the local government's incentive. For example, a local government may want to recover its incentive through taxes within three years. A payback guideline limits the value of incentives that can be offered to each project, depending on the size of the company's taxable investment.

Locations versus expansions. Some policies offer more favorable incentives for expansions by existing employers than for locations by new companies. The threshold investment requirement might be lower, the wage level requirement might be lower, or the incentive might be higher. Offering more favorable incentives for expansion recognizes that most new jobs in a community are created by expansion of existing companies and seeks to reward companies that are already paying local taxes and otherwise contributing to the community.

Kinds of businesses. Local governments usually offer incentives to certain kinds of businesses only—most often manufacturing companies, sometimes

warehouse or distribution companies, occasionally a broader group of companies. A formal policy usually sets out the kinds of businesses for which incentives will be available, often citing the range of North American Industry
Classification System (NAICS)* numbers that will be eligible for incentives. This
is a well-recognized classification system, and a local government can rely on
the Employment Security Commission for properly determining a company's
NAICS number.

Other criteria. Some cities require that projects receiving incentives be located within the city or, if they are not already so located, that the project
owners petition for annexation to the city. Alternatively, a city might require
that projects located outside the city be close enough that city annexation will
be possible within a few years. Similarly, cities that operate electric systems
often require that any assisted project purchase power from the city rather than
a competitor. Occasionally a local government is particularly interested in developing certain neighborhoods or areas and therefore limits incentives (or offers
greater incentives) to projects located in those neighborhoods or areas.

Contract Requirement

It is becoming more and more common for local governments to enter into
contracts with the companies to which incentives are offered. These contracts
set out the company's reciprocal obligations and provide for recouping or reducing incentives if the company does not keep its commitments. As a result,
incentive policies often specify that a contract is a required condition for receiving incentives. (Contract provisions are discussed beginning on page 67.)

Kinds of Incentives Offered

Many formal incentive policies include only the kinds of provisions discussed above. Others, however, proceed to set out the kinds of incentives that
the local government intends to offer to companies. In general the incentives fall
into three groups. They are discussed below.

Public infrastructure. Some local government incentives center upon the
provision, at no cost to the project or at a reduced cost, of public infrastructure,
especially utility lines or roads. In the absence of this incentive, the project
would be expected to pay these costs.

Payment of specific company costs. Other local government incentive policies identify specific costs that normally the company would incur but that the

---

* This system is replacing the older Standard Industrial Classification (SIC) system.

local government pays for instead. The most common of these costs are for land or building acquisition; site preparation, such as grading or stormwater management; equipment acquisition; and employee training.

Direct cash incentives. In recent years, a number of local governments have adopted policies under which the government will make one or, more commonly, several annual cash payments to a company, based on some measure set out in the policy. Originally the usual measure was the amount of property taxes paid by the company, but local governments have since begun to use other measures, such as the amount of capital investment made by the company or the number of permanent jobs created.[26] If the payments are to be made over several years, the policy normally specifies the number of years.

These forms of incentives are discussed in greater detail beginning on page 59.

If a local government's incentive policy specifies the kinds of incentives that the government will offer, it is important that the policy make plain that it does not create any entitlement to incentives for companies that meet the thresholds set out in the policy. Rather, the governing board must consider and agree to each incentive arrangement.

Business Activities Eligible for Incentives

Business locations or expansions that have already taken place. After a local government has adopted a formal incentives policy or given incentives to a particular company, it is not unusual for an existing company that has recently located or recently expanded, without incentives, to approach the local government and ask that it too be given incentives, arguing that fairness demands that it receive a benefit comparable to that being offered to the other company.[27] Can the local government give an incentive, after the fact, to such a company?

The answer is no. Although local governments do not always enter into written incentive contracts with companies, the incentive arrangement is essentially contractual. The local government gives the company an incentive, and in return the company promises to make a capital investment, create jobs, or both. The North Carolina Supreme Court has identified these actions of the company as the public benefit that sustains the constitutionality of incentives: "work and economic opportunity for those who otherwise might not have it [and] . . . a broader tax base from which the State and its local governments can draw funding for other programs."[28] Thus the promise from the company is the *consideration* that supports the incentive, both constitutionally and contractually. If the company cannot offer the local government some consideration of that kind, the incentive becomes a mere gift of public assets, with the public receiving nothing in return for its expenditure. When the jobs already exist and the investment has already been made, the company no longer has anything to offer the local government in consideration for the incentive.

Incentives to retain existing companies. Sometimes a local government is approached by an existing company that is considering relocating or threatening to relocate to another community and asked to provide incentives so that the relocation will not take place. Can incentives be offered in such a situation?

The statutory authority for incentives to retain a company (referred to in brief as a *retention*) is ambiguous but probably adequate. G.S. 158-7.1(a) authorizes a county or city to make appropriations "for the purposes of aiding and encouraging the *location* of manufacturing enterprises . . . or other purposes which . . . will increase the . . . business prospects" of the county or city (emphasis added). Although the use of the word "location" might suggest a new location or an expansion more than a retention, an incentive that has the effect of avoiding a plant closing certainly will increase the business prospects of the community. So the statutory language can be made to fit retentions as well as new locations and expansions.

Such an interpretation accords with the statutory and constitutional policies that support economic development incentives, which are intended to bring in good jobs and to increase the tax base of a community. The notion is that but for the incentives, a company would not locate or expand its facility in the community, and thus neither the jobs nor the tax base would be created. Failure to offer an incentive for retention would lead to fewer jobs and a reduced tax base. To remedy those losses, the statute and the constitution clearly permit a local government to offer incentives to a new company that proposes to locate or expand in the community. So why not allow the same money to be spent to protect the existing jobs and tax base and thereby make it unnecessary to offer incentives to replace them?

Incentives to projects located in other counties. May a county or city provide incentives to encourage the location of a new facility in a neighboring county? In one example, a county wanted to help a new agricultural processing plant locate in a neighboring county because the plant would provide an important market for many agricultural producers located in the first county. Clearly such assistance serves a public purpose for the first county even though the project is located elsewhere,[29] but is there statutory authority for such assistance?

The matter has not been fully resolved, but G.S. 158-7.1(a) appears to support extraterritorial incentives. Some of the provisions in G.S. 158-7.1 limit expenditures to projects located in the same county as the local government: For example, Subsection (b)(1) does this for constructing industrial parks, and Subsection (b)(2) does this for acquiring individual industrial sites. But the general language of G.S. 158-7.1(a) authorizes any expenditure that "in the discretion of the governing body of the city or of the county commissioners of the county, will increase the population, taxable property, agricultural industries and business prospects of any city or county." Returning to the example cited at the beginning of this section, support of the processing plant in the next county will no doubt increase the agricultural industries and business prospects of the county offering the incentive, and so the incentive fits the statutory language.

Incentives to residential developments. May a local government offer incentives, as defined here, to attract new residential development? It has long been common for some local governments to offer small subsidies to residential developers through the extension of water and sewer lines, and the authority for such incentives has been the authority to operate water and sewer enterprises rather than the economic development statutes. G.S. 158-7.1, the basic economic development statute, refers consistently to industrial and commercial projects and facilities (including agriculture and probably tourism within those terms), but it stretches the statute considerably to include residential developments within its terms. There is a fundamental difference as well in the kinds of jobs created by residential development as opposed to commercial and industrial development. All jobs in a residential project are in construction and by nature are temporary, whereas industrial and commercial projects normally result in permanent jobs. Therefore, it seems more likely than not that there is no statutory authority for offering incentives—beyond public infrastructure—to residential developments.

Incentives to governmental projects. In *Carter v. Stanly County*,[30] taxpayers challenged the authority of the county to purchase land and convey it to the state in order to induce the state to construct a prison in the county. The court of appeals held that G.S. 153A-158 (which authorizes counties to acquire land for their own purposes) and G.S. 160A-274 (which authorizes conveyances of land by one governmental unit to another) did not authorize the county to acquire land for the purpose of giving it to the state and thereby attracting the state prison. (The court held that a local act of the General Assembly gave the county the necessary authority, however.)

The appeals court made no mention of G.S. 158-7.1, however, and did not discuss whether that statute might be broad enough to allow such a purchase and conveyance by a county. Although the specific authorizations in G.S. 158-7.1(b) concerning the purchase of land refer to industrial and commercial projects, the language in G.S. 158-7.1(a) is broader, allowing expenditures that increase the "business prospects" of the county. A state prison (or other state or federal facility) will provide good jobs and thereby increase the business prospects of a county. Furthermore, a governmental facility is much more like a commercial project than is a residential one, especially in the type of jobs created, so the concerns expressed about assisting residential projects do not apply as clearly. Therefore there is support in G.S. 158-7.1(a) for that statute granting a county the authority to give land to the state for a state facility, but the matter remains in doubt.[31]

Tying Incentives to Hiring Local Residents

A recurrent theme of this book is that an important purpose of economic development programs in general, and incentives in particular, is the creation of good jobs for a local government's residents. A current reality, however, is that we live in a mobile society and that thousands of North Carolinians live in one county and work in another. Indeed, many North Carolina jobs are held by residents of Virginia, Tennessee, and South Carolina. Therefore one local government's economic development programs may lead to jobs that benefit residents of several other local governments. The local government will benefit directly from increases in its tax base, but its residents might not be the only, or even the principal, beneficiaries of the new jobs. Recognizing this, some local governments have considered tying their incentives not simply to the creation of jobs, but to the creation of jobs that are filled by residents of the local government. Is such a policy legally permissible?

If such a policy were challenged, it probably would be held to violate the Privileges and Immunities Clause of the Fourteenth Amendment to the United States Constitution and possibly the Commerce Clause as well.[32] Although the relevant case law is somewhat indecisive, the clear trend of the cases is against preferences for local employees.

The foundational case is the United States Supreme Court's decision in *United Building & Construction Trades Council of Camden County and Vicinity v. Mayor and Council of the City of Camden*.[33] The city of Camden, New Jersey, had adopted an ordinance that required contractors and subcontractors on city-funded construction projects to seek to hire Camden residents for at least forty percent of the jobs on each project. The ordinance was challenged by the local construction unions. The New Jersey Supreme Court upheld the ordinance against a privileges and immunities attack, arguing that the ordinance discriminated against New Jersey residents not living in Camden as much as residents of other states and therefore did not result in special discrimination against the latter group.

The United States Supreme Court reversed. The Court first held that in-state discrimination did not protect the ordinance against a privileges and immunities challenge; the ordinance also discriminated against nonresidents of New Jersey. The Court then went on to hold that the opportunity to seek employment with private employers is a fundamental right of national citizenship and thus protected by the Privileges and Immunities Clause. Camden sought to justify the ordinance because of the city's severe unemployment rate, and the Supreme Court remanded the case to the New Jersey courts to judge the adequacy of these justifications. There are no reported further actions in the case. Subsequently, though, numerous lower courts have reviewed comparable state and local programs that favored local residents for jobs in public works projects and have consistently invalidated the programs under the Privileges and Immunities Clause.[34] State and local governments have been unable to convince courts that serious unemployment is a constitutionally sufficient justification for such programs.

More recently public works preference cases have been the basis of challenges to economic development incentive programs that require companies receiving incentives to try to hire residents of the jurisdiction offering the incentive. In *Hudson County Building and Construction Trades Council, AFL-CIO v. City of Jersey City*,[35] construction unions challenged a Jersey City, New Jersey, ordinance that required recipients of economic development incentives from the city to make a good faith effort to hire city residents for at least fifty-one percent of the construction and permanent jobs associated with the assisted projects. (The incentives offered by Jersey City included property tax abatements, grants and loans, and gifts of property.) The reported decision involves only plaintiffs' motion (made before trial) for summary judgment, a motion based largely on the Supreme Court decision in *Camden*. Although the court denied the motion in order to give the city a chance to justify the program, it noted that it was highly unlikely that the city would be able to do so. There are no further reported decisions in this case. The next year, however, the Fifth Circuit Court of Appeals entered a final decision in an incentives case, holding that preferences for residents were unconstitutional. *Pelican Chapter, Associated Builders & Contractors, Inc. v. Edwards*[36] involved a Louisiana tax abatement program that required recipient companies to give preference to Louisiana residents in acquiring both goods and services; agency regulations required that eighty percent of jobs go to in-state residents. The trial court enjoined the program as a violation of the Commerce Clause, and the federal court of appeals affirmed. Thus the few cases that have been decided suggest that these kinds of preferences are susceptible to successful constitutional attack.[37]

Types of Incentives

The following section describes the kinds of incentives that local governments offer to companies. The listing and discussion attempt to be complete, but the absence of a particular incentive does not necessarily mean that a local government may not use it. Unless an incentive is described as clearly improper, it probably is permitted by statute and the state constitution.

Public Infrastructure

A traditional kind of incentive is to provide public infrastructure to a project in a way in which the infrastructure would not normally be provided. The local government might pay certain costs that it normally does not; or it might install public facilities that it would otherwise have no reason to install or that it might otherwise have installed at a later date.

Water and Sewer Facilities

System extensions. A common and traditional public infrastructure incentive is to extend water or sewer lines to a new facility at no cost to the company owning or operating the facility or at a cost lower than that normally paid. This sort of incentive is often set out in a formal policy, under which the incentive is offered to any project that meets threshold capital investment requirements.

The statutory scheme for utility line extensions is somewhat curious. First, there appears to be an overabundance of statutory authority. G.S. 158-7.1(b)(5) authorizes a local government to "construct, extend or own utility facilities or . . . provide for or assist in the extension of utility services to be furnished to an industrial facility, whether the utility is publicly or privately owned." Although this clause seems entirely adequate authority for a local government to pay for the extension of lines from its own water or sewer system to an industrial facility, the next clause in the statute, G.S. 158-7.1(b)(6), more specifically authorizes a local government to "extend or . . . provide for or assist in the extension of *water and sewer* lines to industrial properties or facilities" (emphasis added). The reason for the redundancy appears to be the different treatment accorded to expenditures under the two clauses with regard to the statutory limitation on the amount of expenditures and investment a local government may have in incentives at any one time. Expenditures under Subsection (b)(6) are not counted against the limitation; those under Subsection (b)(5) are. (This limitation is discussed in detail below.)

Second, both statutory clauses offer explicit authority to pay for extensions to *industrial* properties, whereas other provisions in G.S. 158-7.1 explicitly allow incentives for commercial as well as industrial projects. Does this mean that a local government is barred from paying for extension of water or sewer (or other utility) lines to an office park, a shopping center, or other commercial projects? Probably not. Given the expansive reading of G.S. 158-7.1(a) by the state supreme court in the *Maready* decision (discussed more fully below), that subsection is probably adequate authority for offering utility line extensions as incentives to commercial projects.

Third, because water and sewer line extensions to industrial projects are specifically authorized by G.S. 158-7.1(b), the public hearing requirement of G.S. 158-7.1(c) attaches to any such incentive offered to an industrial project. Although this statutory hearing requirement does not extend to incentives offered under G.S. 158-7.1(a), it is a good idea constitutionally to hold such a hearing. (This point is discussed fully in Chapter 3.) Therefore the differing statutory authority for utility extensions to industrial and commercial projects probably has no important practical consequence.

Extension fees. In addition to financing the capital cost of extending water or sewer lines to a new facility, many local governments agree to pay, on behalf of the facility's owners, the fees normally charged to new users. These fees might include connection charges, acreage charges, impact fees, and other development charges. G.S. 158-7.1(a) is the most appropriate authority for such an incentive.

Special facilities. Somewhat less common but nonetheless clearly permissible is the construction or installation, at government expense, of special water or sewer facilities or their components for the particular benefit of an industrial or commercial project. A city might install a new water tank in order to provide higher water pressure or greater water capacity to a new industrial facility. A city might install a booster for its water system to facilitate the installation of sprinklers in a new shopping center. A county or city might install and operate an industrial sewerage pretreatment plant on the grounds of a new industrial facility. In each case, the cost of these facilities or components might normally be charged to users of the system. G.S. 158-7.1(b)(5), which authorizes a county or city to "construct . . . utility facilities" for an industrial project, is the most appropriate authority for the water tank or sewerage pretreatment facility; G.S. 158-7.1(a) is the better authority when the assisted project is commercial rather than industrial.

Special rates. One form of incentive that is not legally permissible is to exempt a company from paying some or all of its water or sewer rates. Such an incentive runs afoul of a local government's obligations as the operator of a public utility; its rates must be uniform within classes of customers, and differences among classes cannot be arbitrary. As the North Carolina Court of Appeals put it some years ago, "the statutory authority of a city to fix and enforce rates for its services and to classify its customers is not a license to discriminate among customers of essentially the same character and services."[38] One industrial customer cannot be charged one rate and another industrial customer, receiving comparable amounts of service, a different rate. Of course a local government might try to achieve the same outcome by agreeing to give a company cash incentives, which the company could then use to pay its water or sewer bills.

Electric and Natural Gas Facilities

G.S. 158-7.1(b)(5) explicitly permits a local government to pay for the extension of utility systems other than water and sewer to an industrial property. Obviously this applies to the seventy-five or so North Carolina cities that operate electric distribution systems and the six that operate natural gas distribution systems. But the statute also permits cities and counties to pay for extension of electric or natural gas systems owned by others, including investor-owned companies. Because G.S. 158-7.1(b) is the direct statutory authority for financing electric and natural gas extensions or facilities, a local government must hold a public hearing before appropriating or expending funds for such purposes. Chapter 3 details the requirements for public hearings.

Streets and Roads

Another incentive is to construct road improvements that serve a new or expanded facility. The incentive might lie in constructing improvements that otherwise would not be built, constructing improvements earlier than they might otherwise be built, or paying for improvements that otherwise might be charged to the property owner. Although the state Department of Transportation has a formal program for such incentive-driven road projects (which is described in Chapter 5), local government incentive policies rarely include specific mention of street or road improvements, probably because such improvements are considerably less common than water and sewer extensions. Rather, such incentives are much more likely to be negotiated in each case. The most appropriate statutory authority for such improvements is G.S. 158-7.1(a).

County construction of or payment for street or road improvements; city construction or payment for extraterritorial roads. Cities have authority to construct, improve, and maintain streets inside cities, but counties lack any authority for street expenditures. Given that circumstance, may counties make or pay for road improvements as an economic development incentive? May cities do so for projects located outside their boundaries? The answer to both questions appears to be yes, as long as neither the county nor the city assumes any responsibility for maintaining the street or road after it is constructed. A county or city may, under G.S. 158-7.1(a), pay for many kinds of projects or facilities that it has no other independent authority to fund. In the *Maready* litigation, for example, Winston-Salem paid for interior modifications in a privately owned office building. That a local government, therefore, has no specific authority to pay for particular street or road construction should not be a barrier to its doing so as an economic development incentive.

Railroad Spurs

Occasionally local governments are asked to assist in the cost of extending railroad lines to a specific industrial or commercial site. G.S. 158-7.1(a) specifically authorizes counties and cities to expend money to encourage the building of railroads, and, as was noted in the introduction, North Carolina has a long history of local assistance in railroad construction. Therefore there appears to be adequate authority for this sort of infrastructure expenditure.

Payment of Specific Company Costs

A second major group of incentives involves a local government paying a specific business expense that otherwise would be borne by the company. Although the local government sometimes makes the expenditure directly, the more common practice is for the company to make the expenditure initially and then be reimbursed by the local government.[39] Typically the local government agrees to reimburse the company up to a specific maximum amount based on the company's actual expenditures. If the expenditures are below that maximum, so is the reimbursement.

There are at least two reasons why the reimbursement model is favored. First, it allows the company to control the project and associated expenditures; it is, after all, the company's project. Second, it appears to allow the local government to avoid having to follow the public bidding and contracting laws for the project. If the local government were to make the expenditure directly, the project might have to be formally bid, pursuant to G.S. 143-129, even though a private company is the eventual beneficiary of the project. That is because G.S. 143-129 applies to any construction project or purchase contract involving the expenditure of *public* money, without regard for the eventual ownership of the project or purchased goods. If the reimbursement model is followed, however, the company is the entity contracting for construction or purchase; there is no public money being spent under the contract. Although the point is not beyond argument, because no public money is paid directly to the contractor or vendor and because the final product is owned by the company, the general practice is to assume that following the reimbursement model avoids any need to follow public bidding and contracting procedures for the basic project.

The following is a list of the kinds of company expenditures that local governments commonly make as economic development incentives.

Land or building acquisition or construction. G.S. 158-7.1(b)(1) permits a local government to develop an industrial park and convey sites in the park, G.S. 158-7.1(b)(2) permits a local government to acquire and convey individual industrial or commercial sites, and G.S. 158-7.1(b)(4) permits a local government to acquire or construct and then convey shell buildings. When the conveyance of a site or building is for less than full monetary consideration, G.S. 158-7.1(d2) imposes additional requirements, which are discussed in Chapter 3.

G.S. 158-7.1(b) contemplates a local government acquiring property for the purpose of conveying it to an industrial or commercial company. But sometimes local governments already own property, which they no longer need for the purpose for which it was acquired, that is suitable for industrial or commercial use. Although there is no general bar to using such property as an economic development incentive, some local governments have first had the governing board adopt a resolution that specifically states that the property is now held for economic development. Then there is no question but that the property may be conveyed as an incentive pursuant to G.S. 158-7.1(b), (d), and (d2).

Site preparation. G.S. 158-7.1(b)(7) specifically permits a local government to provide site preparation for industrial properties or facilities. [G.S. 158-7.1(a) would be authority for comparable expenditures for commercial properties or facilities.] Among the kinds of expenditures included in the term *site preparation* are excavating and grading, demolishing existing structures, installing drainage facilities, relocating on-site utilities, and channeling or piping natural streams.

Training. Local governments often pay for the training of employees at new or expanded facilities, training that supplements that provided by the state through the community colleges' industrial training program. (Several of the incentive grants at issue in the *Maready* litigation included on-the-job training.) The authority for such expenditures is G.S. 158-7.1(a).

Other. Although the kinds of expenditures listed above are the most common examples of incentives that pay for specific company costs, many other sorts of company costs have been met by local governments in specific instances. Among the specific costs met by Winston-Salem or Forsyth County, as listed and approved in the *Maready* decision,[40] were:

- financing the purchase of land by a company;
- paying a portion of a company's rent payments;
- paying a portion of the company's costs for employee parking in a public garage;
- paying relocation costs for employees and their spouses;
- upfitting space in a private office building for a new tenant and relocation costs of the existing tenant;
- upgrading existing industrial facilities for a new tenant or owner.

Other North Carolina local governments have paid for such company costs as upgrading existing industrial facilities for expansion by the current owner and acquiring new equipment or machinery. With these sorts of expenditures, the specific nature of the expenditure is negotiated and depends on the costs for which the company seeks assistance. The key point is that the state supreme court has made it clear that G.S. 158-7.1(a) authorizes local government payment for just about any kind of cost otherwise borne by a company if the incentive will in fact cause the company to locate or expand within the local government's jurisdiction.[41]

Cash Grants to a Company

In recent years many North Carolina local governments have offered companies cash grants as incentives, either at the beginning of a project or over several years after the project has begun or been completed. Although there has been no judicial review of cash grants, their general constitutionality seems unassailable. (The constitutional issue is discussed in Chapter 1, beginning on page 14.) The statutory authority for these grants is G.S. 158-7.1(a).

The amount of such grants and whether they are paid at the beginning of the project or over several years are matters that many local governments negotiate for each project. That a county or city makes cash grants to one company in no way indicates that it is willing to do so for other companies. A number of local governments, however, have adopted incentive policies that establish cash grants as their basic incentive, with the amount of the incentive increasing with the size of the company's investment or the number of new, permanent jobs that the company creates. These policies usually set out the measure on which the amount of any particular incentive will be based. One such measure used by a number of local governments has raised serious constitutional questions. This measure bases the amount of cash grants to be paid to any company on the amount of property taxes paid by that company, and the constitutional question involves whether such an incentive system amounts to an unconstitutional abatement of the company's taxes. The arguments on each side of the constitutional issue are set out in Chapter 1 (see pages 12–15) and will not be repeated here. Rather, the following paragraphs describe three alternative measures that local governments have used as the basis for establishing the amount of cash grants in order to avoid the constitutional issue.

Cash grants tied to capital investment. A major purpose of governmental economic development programs is to increase the value of taxable property within the unit of local government. Therefore offering cash grants that are tied to the amount of a company's new capital investment (including machinery and equipment) directly connects the incentive to this governmental goal. The new capital investment made by a company can be measured either by the new value added by the company to the local property tax base or by the company's actual capital expenditures. (At least one local government requires that the investment be in property that becomes part of the local tax base, although the amount of the investment is measured by the company's actual capital expenditures.) If a county or city decides to measure capital investment by the amount of value added to the tax base, the local government should remember that private investment that includes significant expenditures for machinery and equipment will show significant decreases in tax value each year because of depreciation on the machinery or equipment. For that reason, a local government that is using taxable value as the measure of capital investment may want to measure that value separately for each year in which grants are being given. In that way, if the company's taxable value decreases, so will the amount of the grant.

Although cash grants structured in this way can be awarded and paid at the beginning of an economic development project, in anticipation of the promised investment by the company, they are better offered over several years, with each year's payment reflecting the current value of the company's investment.

Cash grants tied to jobs created. A second major purpose of governmental economic development programs is to increase individual wealth by creating good jobs for a local government's citizens. Therefore offering cash grants that are tied to the number of permanent jobs created by a new location or an expansion directly connects the incentive to this governmental goal. The amount offered for each job might be tied to wage levels or, indeed, to a company's capital investment. That is, the amount offered per job could increase as wage levels increase or as the amount of capital investment increases.

Cash grants tied to permanent jobs created probably work much better as a series of grants given over several years, as jobs are actually created and filled, although it is possible to award a single grant at the project's beginning, based on company projections.

Cash grants tied to payroll. Governments increasingly are not interested simply in creating jobs but in creating good jobs, jobs that offer higher pay to the government's citizens. Rather than measuring cash grants simply by reference to the number of jobs, a local government might measure them as a percentage of a company's local payroll (or payroll for hourly workers). Such a measure rewards job creation, but it also directly rewards the creation of better jobs.[42]

Prohibited Incentives

Chapter 1 (beginning on page 12) describes the constitutional difficulty in North Carolina of offering direct property tax abatements or refunds to companies that locate or expand in the state. That same chapter (see pages 21–23) describes the constitutional bar to guaranteeing obligations of a private company.

To repeat that chapter's conclusions, these two possible forms of incentives—tax abatements and loan guarantees—are constitutionally unavailable in North Carolina.

There is at least one other potential incentive that is sometimes asked for but that cannot be given under current North Carolina law: an enforceable promise from a city not to annex a specific parcel of property. The North Carolina Supreme Court has held that local governments may not make certain sorts of contractual promises: "Where governmental discretionary powers are involved a board can make no contract which would bind its successors in office with respect to the exercise of the discretion. . . . The true test is whether the contract itself deprives a governing body, or its successor, of a discretion which public policy demands should be left unimpaired."[43] One example of the sort of contractual promise that this doctrine bars is one whereby a city agrees not to annex a specific parcel of property.[44] A property owner could not enforce such a promise if the city later went against the promise and annexed the parcel after all.

Incentive Contracts

As has been noted, local governments increasingly are recording their incentive arrangements with companies in written contracts or agreements.[45] This increased use of contracts evidences the desire of local governments that recipient companies meet the commitments they have made for capital investment and job creation. If those commitments are not met, local governments often expect and demand the return of some or all of the incentives already paid. If a company is to be obliged to refund some or all of an incentive paid to it, that obligation must be created by contract. This section discusses the normal subject matter of such contracts with special attention to the mechanisms used to recapture incentives paid to companies after they have been unable to meet their investment or job commitments.

Basic Contract Provisions

Incentive contracts normally contain at least three basic sets of provisions, and a fourth is highly desirable. First, the contract sets out the incentives that the local government has agreed to provide to the recipient company. Second, the contract sets out the commitments that the company has made in consideration of receiving the incentives. Typically these commitments are expressed in terms of the dollar amount of new investment the company will make within a specified time period; they usually also include some number of promised new permanent jobs, again within some specified time period. The company may make a commitment also as to the pay level for the new jobs, particularly in comparison to the current county average weekly manufacturing wage. Third, the contract sets out the rights and obligations of the parties if the company does not meet its contractual commitments. A fourth provision that frequently is found in such contracts and that is desirable, although it usually is boiler-plate, is a statement to the effect that but for the offer of incentives, the company would not be locating or expanding its facility within the local government's jurisdiction. Such a statement supports the constitutionality of the incentives; if the incentives were unnecessary to attracting the location or ex-pansion, a court might consider them a gift rather than an appropriate expen-diture of public assets.

Clawbacks

Incentive contract provisions that control what happens when a company does not meet its investment or employment commitments are known generi-cally as *clawbacks*. The term is most appropriate, however, when applied to requirements that companies return incentives already paid.[46] The kind of clawback provision included in any particular incentives contract depends on the nature of the incentives awarded through that contract.

The discussion that follows focuses on three kinds of incentives and the possible clawback provisions associated with each: upfront payments, cash payments made over several years, and gifts of real property.[47] In general these provisions are matters to be negotiated and agreed upon by the parties. Except with gifts of real property, neither the statutes nor the constitution require any particular contractual provisions. (The statutes do require a form of clawback when real property is conveyed to a company for less than full cash consideration. This requirement is discussed later in this section.) Fur-thermore, if an incentive is not paid until the company has met its commit-ment, the need for a clawback evaporates.

Clawbacks for upfront payments. If a local government has made a cash payment to a company at the beginning of the project or has paid specific costs on behalf of the company before the facility has been constructed or opened or employees hired, the usual clawback is to require the company to refund some or all of the initial payment. If for some reason the project does not go forward, the clawback requirement is a full refund. If, however, the company has con-structed some part of the intended project but not the full amount promised, the usual clawback requirement is a partial refund. For example, if the amount in-vested is only 70 percent of the amount promised, the contract may require the company to refund a proportionate share—30 percent—of the initial payment. Sometimes the contract requires that the company make some threshold percentage of the promised investment—for example, 25 percent—before the proportionality provision comes into play; if the threshold percentage is not reached, the company must refund the full amount of the initial incentive. Some contracts require the company to pay interest on any amount refunded.

The company's target might be expressed as a final investment total or job total that is to be reached after a specific number of years, or it might be expressed as a set of annual numbers that increase over time and demonstrate that the company is making progress toward meeting its final commitments. If the latter method is used, the contract sometimes divides the amount of the initial cash incentive by the number of target years and provides for a possible clawback for each year. For example, if at the beginning of a contract a local government gave a $240,000 cash incentive to be used for site preparation, the contract might specify that the company is to have invested $5 million by the end of the first and second years, $10 million by the end of the third year, and $18 million by the end of the fourth year. Each of those four annual targets would be subject to a possible clawback of as much as $60,000, one-fourth the initial cash payment. If the company then met the first two annual targets but had only $8 million invested at the end of year three, it would have to return to the local government some percentage of the $60,000 at issue for that year.

When a company's commitments are limited to making minimum levels of capital investment, it is simple to state clawback requirements as the percentage of the promised investment actually made. If the commitments also include job targets, however, it is possible that a company will have a shortfall in investment but not jobs (or vice versa) or differing percentages of shortfall in the two categories of targets. The contract must then specify how clawback requirements will be determined. One common choice is to focus only on investment and to tie clawbacks entirely to the amount of any shortfall in that category. The company's performance on job creation is then irrelevant to its refunding obligations. If both targets are to be included in the clawback calculation, the simplest method is to determine the shortfall in each category and then average the numbers. For example, if the company is 10 percent short in investment and 20 percent short in jobs, the average shortfall is 15 percent and the company must refund that percentage of the payment at issue.

A potential problem with this usual clawback provision—a contractual requirement that the company make a full or partial refund of the initial incentive payment—is that the company might resist making the refund or, indeed, be unable to. If the company resists making the payment, arguing in some fashion that the contract does not require it to, litigation might be necessary if the local government is to recover its incentive payment. Many incentives are small enough that such litigation would not be productive. Even if the company agrees on its liability, it might have failed to meet its commitments because of a more general failure in its business, and it might not have the resources to make the refund. The local government would then be just one more unsecured creditor of a failing company.

Recognizing this, some local governments have required some form of security to support the company's contractual obligations. The most direct form of security is a lien upon the land and facilities of the company used in the project, given by the company as part of the incentives contract with the local government. It would secure the company's agreement to refund incentives if the company does not meet its contractual commitments. North Carolina law recognizes such a security interest as an equitable lien,[48] and the case law appears to support enforcement of the lien against subsequent owners of the property who have notice of the lien.[49] In one variant to this sort of arrangement, the local government characterizes its payment to the recipient company as a loan, which can be fully or partially changed to a grant if specific targets are reached. That is, a portion of the loan could be forgiven for each job created, taxes paid by the company might be credited against loan repayment, or the loan could be forgiven if the targeted investment was reached. The basic transaction begins and is characterized as a loan, and the contract creates a lien on the company's real property to secure its obligations to repay the loan should it fail to meet its commitments.

Clawbacks for annual payments. If a local government's incentive will be paid over several years, the contract typically sets out annual targets that the company commits to meet. If the company does not meet those targets, the contract provides for a proportionate reduction in the required incentive. Obviously not paying an incentive is far simpler than trying to force a refund of one already paid.

Clawbacks when real property has been conveyed as an incentive. If a local government conveys real property to a company and takes as consideration property taxes or other revenues to be received by the local government because of improvements the company makes to the property, G.S. 158-7.1(d2) requires a clawback of the property itself in certain circumstances. The statute provides that the unit must contractually bind the acquiring company to construct, within five years or less, improvements on the property that will generate the tax revenue to be counted as consideration. "Upon failure to construct the improvements specified in the contract, the purchaser shall reconvey the property back to the county or city." There are a number of ways that the reconveyance requirement can be structured in an incentives contract.

Deed restrictions: possibility of reverter or right of re-entry. The deed conveying the real property to the company could convey a fee simple determinable or a fee simple subject to a condition subsequent. With the former, if the improvements are not made within the specified time period, title to the property automatically reverts to the granting local government. With the latter, if the improvements are not made, the local government enjoys a right to re-enter the property and assume ownership and possession. Because the statute seems to require reconveyance, the fee simple determinable appears to meet its demands more closely.

Contractual requirement to reconvey. The incentives contract might simply impose the obligation on the company to reconvey the property if the improvements are not constructed. If the company does not do so, however, the unit would need to bring suit to enforce the contract.

Deed of trust. Although it is possible to structure the requirement to reconvey using a deed of trust, doing so is cumbersome and offers no clear advantage over including a possibility of reverter in the deed. The standard deed of trust used in North Carolina gives the trustee a power of sale to be exercised if the property owner does not fulfill its obligations owed to the beneficiary under the deed of trust. Having the trustee sell the property, however, does not meet the statutory requirement that the recipient company reconvey the property to the grantor local government, and there is no guarantee that any sale under the power of sale will return the full value of the property to the government. A property owner who has defaulted or is about to default on the obligations secured by a deed of trust may initiate a sale in lieu of foreclosure, in which the deed is returned to the beneficiary under the deed of trust in return for cancellation of any remaining obligations owed to the beneficiary. Presumably an incentives contract could require the property owner to take that step if the improvements are not constructed, but again this is so cumbersome that it is hard to see why it might be used in lieu of either of the first two methods.

Each of these mechanisms that ensure reconveyance of the property to the local government is subject to an important practical difficulty. If the company needs to finance the improvements it makes on the property, the financing institution will almost certainly demand its own security interest in the property and probably will demand that that interest take priority over other security interests. Therefore, the local government will need, as a practical matter, to subordinate its rights in the property to any financing lien. If that is done, however, and the company does not construct the required improvements, chances are that the local government will not get the property back or that it will get the property back subject to the lien of the financing institution. For that reason, the local government may want to include in the incentives contract a requirement that the company make payments to make the government whole should the property not be reconveyed or be conveyed subject to the financing institution's deed of trust.

A final point involves the possibility of allowing a company that has not constructed all of the required improvements to make special payments to the local government so that the government receives the fair market value of the property through a combination of taxes and other government revenues generated by the improvements plus the special payments. This alternative may be particularly attractive if the company has made some improvements to the property but not enough to satisfy its contractual obligations. Because the government receives the full consideration for the property, this option seems to accord with the statutory purpose. A company can make a partial payment for the property at the initial closing of the conveyance, with its tax payments calculated to bring in the difference. Allowing a company to make payments later in the contract period, when it becomes evident that the tax payments will be insufficient to cover the value of the property, is not very different. If the public hearing on the original conveyance takes note of this possibility, the statute appears to permit allowing this option to the grantee company.

Incentives Machinery

Often the parties to an incentives contract find it useful to define important terms and set out the machinery under which incentive payments will be made. Some of these provisions are as follows.

Capital investment. If the company commits to a specific total capital investment, or if the contract includes annual capital investment targets, the parties need to be clear about how the capital investment will be measured. One common way is to define it in terms of taxable capital investment—that is, what amount of new investment is reflected in county tax records. Other contracts define the term by the actual capital expenditures of the company and typically require the company to provide some form of documentation of those expenditures.

New jobs created. Incentive contracts include a number of provisions concerning the company's commitment to create a specific number of new full-time, permanent jobs. Two initial questions are (1) whether the parties will count only jobs that are filled or will also count jobs for which the company is actively recruiting and (2) what qualifies as a *full-time* job (such as a person who works at least 2,000 hours in one year). Once those matters are settled, the parties frequently set out how the company will document its job creation. The most common method is to require the company to certify as to the number of jobs it has created or filled, following any guidelines set out in the contract. A second method is to allow the local government to review the payroll records of the company.

Timing of incentive payments. If a local government agrees to make incentive payments over several years, with payments triggered by company investment, the contract should specify when the payments will begin. If the incentive payments are to be measured by property taxes paid by the company, normally the first payment is not made until the company's investment is complete. If the incentive payments are to be measured by the amount of investment made by the company, the contract must specify whether the first payment will be made in the year that the company begins construction or in the year that it completes construction.

Miscellaneous. An incentives contract normally includes the standard boilerplate of contracts: that the contract is the entire contract between the parties, that North Carolina law will govern the contract, that any modifications must be agreed to by both parties, that illegal provisions are severable, and so on. One such provision that might require some thought is assignability. Frequently local governments wish to limit the assignability of an incentives contract (perhaps requiring local government approval), but contracts are assignable unless they provide otherwise.[50] Therefore any limitation on assignment needs to be specified in the contract.

Incentive Investment and Expenditure Limitations

G.S. 158-7.1(f) limits the amount of certain economic development expenditures made pursuant to that section. For many local governments, however, the limit is neither effective nor particularly limiting because economic development practice has evolved in ways not contemplated by the limit's authors. The limit applies only to expenditures made pursuant to G.S. 158-7.1(b) and not to all expenditures made pursuant to that subsection. It makes no reference to expenditures made pursuant to Subsection (a), and therefore cash incentives and other expenditures made pursuant to that subsection are not subject to the limit or used in its calculations. As a practical matter, the limit probably most often restricts a local government that has made a large investment in an industrial park and has not yet sold off any or much of the land in the park.

A local government's position under the statutory limit is calculated by adding, at the end of each fiscal year, the following amounts:

- The local government's investment in any industrial park it currently owns. This amount includes the cost of land, site preparation, and any improvements made to the park, including utility lines.
- The local government's investment in industrial or commercial sites that it currently owns. In most cases this is the cost of land and perhaps of site preparation.
- The amount a local government has paid for any options that it currently holds on industrial or commercial property.
- The local government's investment in any shell buildings it currently

owns. This includes the purchase cost of existing buildings and the construction cost of new buildings.

- The local government's expenditures during the fiscal year to construct or extend electric or natural gas services to an industrial facility or to construct or acquire water and sewer facilities other than collection or distribution lines for industrial projects.
- The local government's expenditures during the fiscal year on site preparation for industrial properties or facilities. Amounts expended on site preparation and already counted from the above paragraphs are not counted a second time.
- The amount of tax revenue received and counted during the fiscal year. This applies if the local government has conveyed property to a company and has counted as consideration tax revenue to be received over several years from improvements the company makes to the property.

Note that the limit may count expenditures made in several fiscal years, because it counts a local government's current investment in an industrial park, industrial or commercial sites, and shell buildings. The total of the above amounts may not exceed one half of one percent (0.5%) of the local government's property tax base, the amount of property subject to ad valorem taxation by the local government.

An example may help in understanding this statutory limit. A local government has made the following economic development expenditures:

1. Four years ago, the local government purchased 125 acres for an industrial park, spending $22,500 an acre for the land. Since then, the local government has sold 65 of the acres, leaving 60 acres still in governmental ownership. At $22,500 an acre, this is a current investment of $1,350,000.
2. At the industrial park, the local government did some site preparation at the sites it has sold; it extended water and sewer lines to the park, and it constructed a road giving access to the sites it has sold. The portion of these expenditures attributable to the remaining land totaled $135,000.
3. Two years ago, the local government constructed a shell building at the industrial park, which it has not yet sold. The cost of construction was $625,000.
4. A 40-acre conveyance of land at the industrial park was made for no current cash consideration; rather, the local government counted as consideration the property tax revenues it expected to receive over the next ten years from the new industrial facility to be constructed at the site. The

Table 1
Economic Development Expenditures under Statutory Limit

Project	Amount under Limit	Amount Not under Limit
Industrial park	$1,350,000	
Site preparation	135,000	
Shell building	625,000	
Taxes received	232,375	
Water/Sewer payment		$235,000
Training		45,000
Cash incentive		130,000
TOTAL	$2,342,375	

plant has been built and equipped and has a tax value of $35,750,000. The local government's tax rate is $.65, and during the fiscal year the local government received property taxes on this facility in the amount of $232,375.

5. During the fiscal year the local government reimbursed one company for the cost of extending water and sewer lines to its facility. The total of this incentive was $235,000.

6. During the fiscal year the local government supplemented community college training as an incentive for three plant expansions. The total amount expended for such training was $45,000.

7. During the fiscal year the local government made a cash payment as a negotiated incentive to one new plant that located within its jurisdiction. This cash incentive was in the amount of $130,000.

In determining the economic development expenditures subject to the statutory limit, this local government counts only those expenditures listed in the first four numbered paragraphs above. The expenditures made in the final three paragraphs—water and sewer extensions, training, and a cash incentive—do not count against the limit. The total, then, of the expenditures that do count—investment in an industrial park and site preparation at the park, construction of a shell building, and receipt of tax revenues that are being counted as consideration for a land conveyance—comes to $2,342,375. (These figures are summarized in Table 1.)

This local government has a property tax base of $1,256,000,000. One half of one percent of that tax base is $6,280,000, and therefore this local government is within the statutory limit.

The statute places enforcement of this expenditure and investment limitation on the Local Government Commission (LGC), the agency in the office of the state treasurer that has general supervision of local government finance. The statute directs the LGC to review local government financial statements each year to determine if a local government has exceeded its limitation. There is a section of the Annual Financial Information Report (AFIR) that local governments submit each fall to the LGC that asks for the information necessary for the LGC to make the statutory determination. If the LGC determines that a local government has exceeded its limit, the statute requires that the LGC approve each expenditure made pursuant to any provision of G.S. 158-7.1 that the local government intends to make during the next three fiscal years. The LGC may not give that approval, and thus the expenditure may not be made, if the expenditure would cause a county or city to exceed the limit. Through the 1998 fiscal year, no government had exceeded this statutory limit since it was first imposed in 1986.

Downtown Development Programs

Much of what has been said about the authority of local governments to engage in economic development applies as much to downtown development efforts as to industrial development or other sorts of commercial development. A city may establish a loan pool to make loans to downtown businesses, and cities have done so, especially to assist downtown property owners in improving the street facades of their buildings. A city may purchase for resale available commercial sites in a downtown under the general economic development authority to acquire land suitable for commercial buildings or to acquire shell buildings. A city may provide public infrastructure that supports private development by improving downtown streets or sidewalks or by constructing parking facilities for the particular use of new office or retail facilities. And a city may negotiate creative incentives with companies in order to attract them to downtown sites. Several of the incentive arrangements at issue in the *Maready* litigation involved downtown projects—rent subsidies and partial payment of employee parking costs to one company, refitting office space to facilitate rental to a second company, and special parking facilities for a third company.

The purpose of this section is to discuss two statutes that provide authority for economic development efforts that are specific to downtowns: (1) the creation of business improvement districts (or, in North Carolina statutory parlance, municipal service districts) in the downtown and (2) entering into joint public-private downtown development projects. In addition, the section summarizes one final statute that, though not restricted to downtown, probably is most useful in downtowns if it is to be a mechanism for economic development; that statute is the urban redevelopment law.

Business Improvement Districts (BIDs)

A popular tool of downtown development efforts throughout the United States are business improvement districts (BIDs). In essence, such a district draws a line around some or all of a downtown area, raises extra revenues from property owners or businesses in the enclosed area, and uses those revenues to undertake a potentially wide variety of activities that are intended to increase the economic vitality of the defined area. These activities range from provision of special public services within the area, such as special street cleaning or concentrated security services; to special capital improvements in the area, such as street or sidewalk improvements, unique street lighting, or new parking facilities; to more direct economic development efforts, such as coordinated retail campaigns or specialized efforts to attract new commercial construction.[51] In North Carolina the statutory authorization for creation of BIDs is the Municipal Service District Act, G.S. 160A-535 through 160A-544. This statute permits municipal service districts to be established for a number of purposes, the most important of which is *downtown revitalization*. As of 1999 there were forty-five municipal service districts in North Carolina, all but two of which had been set up for the purpose of downtown revitalization. Thus BIDs are found throughout the state. The cities with downtown service districts range from Charlotte (which actually has three in its downtown area) and Fayetteville to such smaller cities as Maxton, Whiteville, and Hendersonville (which has two districts).

Creation. It is relatively simple for a city to establish a municipal service district or BID. The city must prepare a report, which is the basis of a public hearing before the city council; after the hearing, the council may establish the district. In practice, cities establish BIDs because downtown businesses or property owners want them to. The statutory procedure, which is summarized below, is set out in G.S. 160A-537.

The first step is preparing a report, which contains a map of the proposed district, showing its boundaries; a demonstration that the district needs the proposed services or projects to "a demonstrably greater extent than the remainder of the city"; and a plan for providing the proposed services or projects within the district. This plan could indicate whether the city will provide the service directly or through a contractor, approximately how long it will take before the district's services or projects begin, and whether the district will be open-ended in duration or expire after a specific number of years.

The second step is to file a copy of this report with the city clerk at least four weeks before the hearing; the report is available for public inspection once it is filed. Often copies of the report are distributed to downtown businesses and property owners, although the statute does not require this.

Third, the city prepares and publishes a notice of the public hearing. The notice must give the date, time, place, and subject of the hearing and state that the report is available at the clerk's office. It must also include a map of the proposed district. A typical notice might read as follows:

NOTICE OF PUBLIC HEARING

The Xboro city council will hold a public hearing at 7:30 P.M., Monday, December 18, 2000, in the council chambers at City Hall. The hearing is to consider definition of a municipal service district for downtown revitalization in the downtown area of Xboro, pursuant to the Municipal Service District Act of 1973, G.S. 160A-535 *et seq.* If the district is so defined, property therein will be subject to taxation as necessary to finance the proposed services and projects of the district. A report on the proposed district, prepared pursuant to G.S. 160A-537, is available for public inspection in the office of the city clerk. A map showing the boundaries of the proposed district is attached to this notice.

The statute requires that this notice be published at least once not less than one week before the hearing and that a copy of it be mailed to each owner of property within the district at least four weeks before the hearing.

Fourth, the city council holds the public hearing.

Fifth, at any time after the hearing, the council may adopt a resolution defining and establishing the district.

Boundaries. The Municipal Service District legislation implements a constitutional provision[52] that allows a city to define special service areas in order to provide services within such areas that are additional to the services provided citywide. Therefore, as a constitutional matter, such a district should include only properties that will benefit from the additional services provided through the district. In some cases, this may suggest that, if at all possible, residential properties should be excluded from a BID because the purpose of the district is to enhance the *commercial* life of the downtown.

Funding. Although nationally properties within business improvement districts are assessed in a variety of ways,[53] in North Carolina such a district is a *property tax district.* It exists in order to enable the city to levy an additional property tax within the district, the proceeds of which finance additional services or projects provided to the district. This district property tax is additional to the citywide property tax. The tax is levied on the same tax base, within the district, on which the regular city tax rate is levied.[54] That property tax base includes real and personal property, and the same exemptions apply to the district tax as apply to citywide taxes. Therefore property owned by governments and churches is exempt from the district tax, as is any other tax-exempt property. In addition, the tax rate must be uniform throughout the district. If differential rates are desired for different parts of the downtown, different service districts must be established.

Nationally some BIDs have their own borrowing power. A North Carolina BID, however, has no independent borrowing power; it is simply a part of city government. The Municipal Service District Act contains a mechanism for issuing city bonds that are retired only from service district revenues,[55] but that mechanism has yet to be used.

Business Improvement District activities. The Municipal Service District Act authorizes a city to expend the proceeds from a downtown service district tax on a wide variety of activities. Among the common BID services that are permitted by the statute are enhanced maintenance of streets, sidewalks, and other public facilities; provision of extra security to augment regular police services; downtown marketing and promotion; presentation of special downtown events; management of downtown parking; promotion of downtown business location and expansion; and construction of capital improvements. Many smaller North Carolina cities use some or all of their service district tax revenues to support the city's participation in the North Carolina Main Street program.

In some states cities enter into "base-level-of-services" agreements with BIDs (which are separate legal entities in those states) or with a private organization that manages the BID. In such an agreement, the city agrees to continue providing existing city services with existing city revenues; BID revenues will not displace the existing revenues. While it would be possible for a North Carolina city council to state its *intention* that those city services provided to downtown at the time the BID is established will continue to be provided within the district and funded by citywide revenues, it is doubtful that a city could bind itself by contract not to reduce that level. The entire constitutional purpose of a service district, however, is to finance services that are additional to those provided citywide. It probably is beyond a city's authority to use district tax proceeds to provide services within the district that are not additional to the services provided elsewhere in the city.

District governance. In North Carolina a service district is a part of city government, and the city council must appropriate district tax proceeds, just as it must appropriate other revenues of city government. The Municipal Service District Act permits the city to provide services within the district with city forces or through a contract with a private organization. Thus a city could follow the common pattern nationally of contracting with a management firm to operate a BID.

Nationally many BIDs are, as a practical matter, governed by boards made up of owners of and tenants in downtown property. These boards decide how the resources of the district are to be used. The North Carolina Municipal Service

District Act makes no mention of a citizen board for a district; it neither requires nor forbids the council to establish such a board. If a board is established for a North Carolina BID, it would have whatever powers the city council granted to it, but it could not be granted final authority over use of district resources. The council could accede to the board's recommendations as the council sees fit, but it would not be possible to bind the council to following those recommendations.

Public-Private Development Projects

G.S. 160A-458.3 provides special authority for a city to cooperate with one or more private parties in the construction and operation of new capital projects in the downtown area. The statute is intended to allow a city to participate with one or more private partners in projects that mix public facilities, such as parking decks or city offices, with private commercial facilities. The statute itself gives one example of such a project: "a single building comprising a publicly owned parking structure and publicly owned convention center and a privately owned hotel or office building."

The statute offers two specific advantages to cities entering into such projects. First, it permits the city to delegate construction of the entire project, including the city-owned portion, to the private participants. As long as no more than fifty percent of the total cost of the project is paid for with city funds, none of this delegated construction is subject to the normal bidding or contracting requirements of G.S. Chapter 143, Article 8. (If a project involves federal funds that are loaned to the private developer, such as through an Urban Development Action Grant, those funds are not considered city funds for purposes of this statute.)

Second, the statute permits a city to contract with a private party to operate the entire project, including the city-owned portions. If that is done, the contract must include provisions that ensure that the city-owned facilities are operated for the public's benefit.

Urban Redevelopment

G.S. Chapter 160A, Article 22, is the urban redevelopment law. The General Assembly enacted the statute in 1951 to permit cities (and later, counties) to participate in the federal urban renewal program. The statute permits local governments to define redevelopment areas, to prepare redevelopment plans for those areas, and to carry out the plans. During the time when the federal program was in existence, many cities defined portions of their downtown (and other business areas) as redevelopment areas to take advantage of the federal moneys and special municipal powers available in redevelopment areas. Even though the federal government has since terminated the urban renewal program, the state enabling authority continues, and cities may continue to define redevelopment areas and plan for and carry out redevelopment projects within those areas.

The redevelopment statute offers two unique tools for economic development in a downtown area. First, if a city properly defines a redevelopment area, the city may use the power of eminent domain to assemble property within that area. The city can then convey the property to private parties for construction of redevelopment projects in conformity with the redevelopment plan. It should be noted, however, that G.S. 160A-514(c) requires that any conveyance of property in a redevelopment area must be by competitive sale. If a city wishes to convey property by private negotiation, it must obtain local legislation for that purpose from the General Assembly.

Second, G.S. 160A-512(8) includes a special grant of authority for cities to borrow money in order to carry out redevelopment projects. During the 1970s and early 1980s a number of cities borrowed money to establish loan pools from which they made loans to downtown property owners, especially to improve the street facades of their properties. The statute's signal advantage was its procedural simplicity: a city could borrow money simply by going to the bank and signing a note. As long as there was no pledge of the city's taxing power, the city needed neither voter nor Local Government Commission approval. After the 1986 federal tax act, interest paid by local governments on the original loans setting up the loan pools was no longer exempt from federal taxable income,[56] and loan pools became much less attractive. But the state legislative authority remains, and a local government's taxable borrowing rate, which it would pass through to downtown property owners through a loan pool, is in many cases better than the rate such owners could obtain on their own direct bank loans. So this authority remains a useful downtown development tool.

Notes

1. In 1997 one experienced economic developer wrote that "the No. 1 economic development issue is the quality of the work force. States and communities that do not focus and commit resources to the changing nature of work and the increasingly high educational requirements are headed down a dead end street." J. Mac Holladay, *Trends That Strengthen Economies, State Government News*, Aug. 1997, at 6, 7. Holladay has run economic development programs for three southern states: Georgia, Mississippi, and South Carolina.

Similarly, the final report of the North Carolina Alliance for Competitive Technologies (NC ACTs) noted that the "defining factor of the growth of our economy may be the capacity of our workforce to meet the demands of employers. In focus groups and surveys across the state, NC ACTs repeatedly heard from industry leaders that one of the most significant barriers to expanding or modernizing was the lack of sufficiently skilled workers." NC ACTs FINAL REPORT, Strategy 6, p. 1. The report can be found on the World Wide Web at www.ncacts.state.nc.us/strategy.

2. Making North Carolina a High Performance State, Executive Summary, p. 2. (This report can be found on the Internet at www.commerce.state.nc.us/commerce/econbd.)

3. *E.g.*, "One of the most important factors influencing location decisions for new private sector investment is the attractiveness or amenity of a particular area or city. This form of attractiveness or amenity is more commonly referred to as *quality of life.*" Edward J. Blakely in *Planning Local Economic Development: Theory and Practice* (Newbury Park, Cal.: Sage Publications, 1989), p. 75. "Amenities have become more important because many industries, particularly in high-tech sectors, have become more 'footloose' or freed from traditional, cost-oriented locational pulls. A locational decision maker may choose a site with more amenities or a better quality of life if other direct-cost factors are about equal, and many firms will select amenity-rich environments even when other things are not equal." John P. Blair in *Local Economic Development: Analysis and Practice* (Thousand Oaks, Cal.: Sages Publications, 1995), p. 51.

4. N.C. GEN. STAT. §§ 153A-376(a)(2) (1991) & 160A-456(a)(2) (1994) authorize counties and cities to provide day care for families of low or moderate income. Hereinafter the General Statutes will be abbreviated as G.S.

5. A one-stop permitting office and other mechanisms to help business in dealing with government are seen as indications of a good business climate, which "has been identified as an important locational factor [which includes] the less tangible aspects of a community's attitude toward business." John P. Blair in *Local Economic Development: Analysis and Practice* (Thousand Oaks, Cal.: Sages Publications, 1995), p. 53.

6. The North Carolina Technological Development Authority, a nonprofit corporation sponsored by state government, has provided assistance to incubators in North Carolina since 1985. The location of its assisted incubators and descriptions of their operation can be found on the Internet at www.nctda.org/incubators.

7. The Boston (Mass.) Economic Development and Industrial Corporation, an agency of the city of Boston, operates at least three such facilities. Matt Kane & Peggy Sand, *Economic Development: What Works at the Local Level* (New York: National League of Cities, 1988), pp. 74–76.

8. Local governments can be creative with such covenants. One set of covenants for a local government-developed industrial park in North Carolina requires site owners to make an annual contribution to the local school system of $25 per employee.

9. The community development statutes—G.S. 160A-456(a) (1994) & 153A-376(a) (1991)—authorize cities and counties to make loans to businesses for building rehabilitation, but that is a far narrower purpose than a typical small business loan program.

10. See the discussion of what is a trade secret in David M. Lawrence, *Public Records Law for North Carolina Local Governments* (Chapel Hill, N.C.: Institute of Government, The University of North Carolina at Chapel Hill, 1997), pp. 133-136, 192.

11. *Id.* at 192.

12. See the discussion on pages 21–23.

13. The principal relevant provisions are Sections 141 & 144.

14. If the bonds are issued for pollution-control facilities for a company, the $10 million limit does not apply. I.R.C. § 142.

15. G.S. 159C-3(11)(1996).

16. I.R.C. § 144(a)(12) (West 1998).

17. G.S. Chapter 159C.

18. G.S. 159C-7(b)(1)a (1998 Cum. Supp.). This section permits the secretary of commerce to waive this wage requirement if unemployment in the county is especially severe and the board of county commissioners has requested the waiver. The Department of Commerce's regulations define especially severe unemployment as either (1) a current county unemployment rate of at least 5 percent, coupled with an unemployment rate during the preceding six months that averaged at least 10 percent or at least 125 percent of the state average, or (2) the recent or imminent closing of a major facility that will cause the loss of either 300 jobs or the jobs of at least 5 percent of the county's workforce. 4 NCAC 1E.0303 (1998).

19. 4 NCAC 1E.0306 (1998). The exceptions permit the secretary of commerce to waive this requirement because of the wage scale at the new facility, the economic condition of the county in which the project is located, the effect of the project on the county's tax base, or the project's spin-off effects.

20. G.S. 159C-4 (1996).

21. Annual summaries prepared by the North Carolina Department of Commerce and sent to the author by Jane Goswick, finance officer, on March 2, 1999.

22. See the discussion of what is a trade secret in David M. Lawrence, *Public Records Law, supra* note 10, pp. 133–36, 192.

23. *Id.* at 192.

24. A business incubator involves incentives because it typically offers a company space at a below-market rental rate. A revolving loan program, or any kind of loan assistance program, involves incentives because such programs provide financing to companies at rates below those available on the private credit markets or to companies that cannot borrow at all elsewhere. Even a program that provides assistance to new companies in developing business plans is an incentive because it provides a service that the company would otherwise have to pay for.

25. These policies are consistent with the state's economic development goals. The state's economic development plan, *supra* note 2, comments that "[a]s growth in the state's labor force slows, the quality of jobs becomes more important than the number of jobs created. Targeting industries and firms that have the capacity to generate large numbers of sustainable high-wage jobs is thus a key to improving the state's quality of life." "Goals and Objectives," p. 3.

26. The constitutional concerns associated with cash grants based on property taxes paid are discussed in Chapter 1, at pages 14–15.

27. Such a company is arguing political, not legal, fairness. The competitors of companies that receive incentives do not suffer constitutional harm simply because they themselves do not also receive incentives. Norfolk Fed'n of Bus. Dists. v. Department of Hous. & Urban Dev., 932 F. Supp. 730 (E.D. Va. 1996), *aff'd without reported opinion,* Norfolk Fed'n of Bus. Dists. v. City of Norfolk, 103 F.3d 119 (4th Cir. 1996); Coast Materials Co. v. Harrison County Dev. Comm'n, 730 So.2d 1128 (Miss. 1998).

28. Maready v. City of Winston-Salem, 342 N.C. 708, 727, 467 S.E.2d 615, 627 (1996).

29. The state supreme court has made it clear that a public purpose is served when expenditures benefit a county's citizens, even when the expenditure is made in another county. Morgan v. Spindale, 254 N.C. 304, 118 S.E.2d 913 (1961) (city could support construction of armory outside city); Martin County v. Wachovia Bank and Trust Co., 178 N.C. 26, 100 S.E. 134 (1919) (county could pay three-fourths of construction cost of bridge, even though most of bridge in neighboring county).

30. 125 N.C. App. 628, 482 S.E.2d 9 (1997).

31. In *Burks v. City of Licking,* 980 S.W.2d 109 (Mo. Ct. App. 1998), the court held

that extending incentives (land and utility lines) to a state prison was a legitimate economic development activity. The city's statutory authority allowed it to take actions to "benefit trade and commerce."

32. The Privileges and Immunities Clause prohibits states and local governments from "abridg[ing] the privileges and immunities of citizens of the United States." U.S. CONST. amend. XIV, § 1. The Commerce Clause prohibits states and local governments from discriminating against interstate commerce. U.S. CONST. art. 1, § 8, cl. 3.

33. 465 U.S. 208 (1984).

34. *E.g.*, A.L. Blades & Sons, Inc. v. Yerusalim, 121 F.3d 865 (3d Cir. 1997); W.C.M. Window Co., Inc. v. Bernardi, 730 F.2d 486 (7th Cir. 1984).

35. 960 F. Supp. 823 (D.N.J. 1996).

36. 128 F.3d 910 (5th Cir. 1997).

37. It perhaps should be noted that each of the cases discussed was brought by construction unions. If an incentives program gives preferences for hiring residents for permanent jobs only, it may be difficult to find a plaintiff to bring an action challenging the preferences.

38. Town of Taylorsville v. Modern Cleaners, 34 N.C. App. 146, 149, 237 S.E.2d 484, 486 (1977). *See also Wall v. City of Durham*, 41 N.C. App. 649, 255 S.E.2d 739 (1979), in which the court made it clear that comparable customers receiving comparable services cannot be placed in different rate classes.

39. There is little doubt that the reimbursement model is authorized by statute. G.S. 153A-449 (1991) for counties and G.S. 160A-20.1 (1994) for cities authorize local governments to "contract with and appropriate money to any person, association, or corporation, in order to carry out any public purpose that the [county or city] is authorized by law to engage in." G.S. 158-7.1 (1994) authorizes counties and cities to engage in a wide variety of economic development incentives; and these two statutes then authorize the local governments to contract with private companies and reimburse the companies for carrying out these authorized purposes on behalf of the local governments. It is worth noting that many of the incentive arrangements approved in *Maready v. City of Winston-Salem*, 342 N.C. 708, 467 S.E.2d 615 (1996), followed the reimbursement model.

40. A list of the specific incentives at issue in that case is found in the dissent, 342 N.C. 708, 736–37, 467 S.E.2d 615, 632–33 (1996).

41. *Maready*, 342 N.C. 708, 467 S.E.2d 615. The dissent in this case suggested that one possible incentive that could now be granted was the payment of country club memberships for company executives. Although the dissenters intended this to be a horrific example of the wrongheadedness of the majority's decision, their conclusion appears to be correct. If membership costs are an expense that the company itself would otherwise pay, on the ground that such memberships serve the business needs of the company, there is no principled way to distinguish them from the other business expenses that the court approved as incentives in *Maready*.

42. I know of no North Carolina local government currently using payroll as the measure for cash grants, but the state of Oklahoma gives cash grants on that basis. Carolyn D. Guniss, "Quality Counts," *Plants Sites and Parks* (Sept.-Oct. 1994), p. 225.

43. Plant Food Co. v. City of Charlotte, 214 N.C. 518, 519, 520, 199 S.E. 712, 713, 714 (1938). This limitation on local government contracting is discussed more fully in David M. Lawrence, "Contracts That Bind the Discretion of Governing Boards," *Popular Government* 56 (Summer 1990): 38–42.

44. Thrash v. City of Asheville, 95 N.C. App. 457, 383 S.E.2d 657 (1989).

45. Incentive contracts have become common only in the last decade or so. A 1985

book on incentives characterized such contracts as rare. William Hamilton, Larry Ledebur, & Deborah Matz, *Industrial Incentives: Public Promotion of Private Enterprise* (Washington, D.C.: Asland Press, 1985), p. 7.

46. One article on the subject distinguishes between *clawbacks*, which are recoveries of incentives already paid; *rescissions*, which are cancellations of promised incentives; *penalties*, which are fines or charges for nonperformance; and *recalibrations*, which are adjustments of promised incentives. Larry C. Ledebur & Douglas Woodward, *Adding a Stick to the Carrot: Location Incentives with Clawbacks, Recisions and Recalibrations*, 4 ECON. DEV. Q. 221, 227 (1990).

47. A single contract might include incentives from two or all three categories.

48. "[E]very express executory agreement in writing, whereby the contracting party sufficiently indicates an intention to make some particular property, real or personal, or fund, therein described or identified, as security for debt or other obligation . . . creates an equitable lien upon the property so indicated, which is enforceable against the property in the hands not only of the original contractor, but of his heirs, administrators, executors, voluntary assignees and purchasers or encumbrancers with notice." Winborne v. Guy, 222 N.C. 128, 131–32, 22 S.E.2d 220, 222 (1942).

49. In *Stanley v. Cox*, 253 N.C. 620, 117 S.E.2d 826 (1961), the state supreme court held that a separation agreement and subsequent consent decree of divorce between husband and wife created an equitable lien in the husband's share of a tract of land held by them as tenants in common. The husband agreed to make certain payments with respect to the property, and the separation agreement and consent decree created a lien upon his share of the property to secure this obligation. In *Stanley v. Cox*, the court enforced this lien against subsequent purchasers from the husband. See also, L. JONES, I A TREATISE ON THE LAW OF LIENS, 3d ed., rev. by E. White (1914), § 30, in which the authors state that an equitable lien can be created by agreement and "will be enforced in equity, not only against such [creating] owner, but also against third persons who are either volunteers, or who take the estate on which the lien is given, with notice of the stipulation."

50. *E.g.*, State *ex rel.* Boney v. Central Mut. Ins. Co. of Chicago, 213 N.C. 563, 197 S.E. 122 (1938).

51. A recent review of business improvement districts, from a national perspective, is International City/County Management Association, *Business Improvement Districts: Tool for Economic Development*, 29 MIS REPORTS (Mar. 1997).

52. N.C. CONST. art. V, § 2(4).

53. *See, e.g.*, McGowan v. Capital Ctr., Inc., 19 F. Supp.2d 642 (S.D. Miss. 1998), which involved a BID financed by assessments on downtown property based on gross square footage of buildings and unimproved real estate.

54. G.S. 160A-544 (1994) creates an exception to this statement. It exempts from service district taxation the personal property of public service corporations. Thus if a telephone company has switching equipment in a downtown area, that equipment would not be subject to district tax.

55. G.S. 160A-543 (1994).

56. The loans were considered private activity bonds, a federal tax characterization that is explained in Chapter 4 at pages 141–44.

3

ECONOMIC DEVELOPMENT PROCEDURES

• • •

3

ECONOMIC DEVELOPMENT PROCEDURES

• • •

ECONOMIC DEVELOPMENT activities involving private companies require secrecy. Companies that are locating or expanding commonly demand confidentiality as a condition of considering a community as the location for a particular facility. Companies often hire consultants to help identify and narrow the list of possible communities in which to invest, and in many instances, the consultant's discussions with local economic development officials never reveal the company's name. Even after the identity of the company has become known to local officials, the company will often continue to demand that its identity and plans remain confidential. If either becomes public before the company would like, the company might well drop the community from its search.

There is an additional pressure for secrecy—from the local government itself. It is engaged in negotiations with the company. As in any negotiation, the local government strengthens its negotiating ability if it can shield its position from the other party, in this case the company.

The North Carolina General Assembly has recognized these practical needs for confidentiality in the open meetings and public records laws. These statutes allow public bodies to discuss some economic development matters in closed session and allow economic development officials to shield some economic development records from public access. In general, the open meetings and public records statutes permit secrecy to continue until a local government and a company have reached tentative agreement on an incentive package or, if no incentives are being offered, until the company is ready to announce its plans publicly.

After the point of protected secrecy is past, however, the economic development statute requires exceptional openness, particularly before final commitments are made. Section 158-7.1 of the North Carolina General Statutes (hereinafter abbreviated as G.S.) requires a public hearing before a local government may appropriate or expend money on a range of incentives authorized by the statute; it requires a second public hearing before a local government may convey property to a company pursuant to the statute.

This chapter discusses and details these contrasting policies of initial secrecy and eventual openness under North Carolina's open meetings and public records laws. It also explains the procedures that a local government must follow when conveying real property as an incentive and concludes with a description of two additional authorizations to convey property. Sample forms for use in economic development transactions are presented following the discussion.

The Open Meetings Law

North Carolina's open meetings law permits a public body (such as a board of county commissioners, a city council, or an economic development commission) to meet in closed session "to discuss matters relating to the location or expansion of industries or other businesses in the area served by the public body."[1] In the paradigm case, this authorization permits a public body to meet in closed session and discuss the incentives it might offer a company that is considering locating or expanding within the public body's jurisdiction. As the paradigm shifts, however, three questions arise regarding this authorization for closed sessions.

Subjects That May Be Considered

Retention of a Company

May a public body meet in closed session to discuss measures it might take to *retain* a company within its jurisdiction? Suppose a manufacturing company with a plant within a county approaches the county economic development director and announces that it is going to close one of two facilities, one of which is the facility within the county. The company asks what incentives the county might offer to keep the local facility open. May the board of county commissioners meet in closed session to discuss the county's response?

The need for confidentiality that underlies the closed session authorization applies to this situation. One reason companies demand confidentiality when they investigate whether to locate a new facility within a community is that they may be planning to close an existing facility elsewhere and do not want it known in that community or by the employees of that facility. Whatever we may think of this as a matter of company policy, it is often company practice, and the open meetings law recognizes the realities of business practice. If a company approaches a local government and reveals that it may be closing a facility within the community, this information may not be publicly known, and the company may expect local officials to respect the company's request for continued confidentiality. Of course this sort of news has a way of getting out, so any reasonable expectation of confidentiality is probably less when plans call for closing a plant than when a company is considering locating a new facility or expanding an existing one.

The other reason for the closed session authorization is the local government's own need for confidentiality as it prepares for negotiations with the company. That need is as strong when the government is seeking to retain a facility as when it is seeking to attract one. In sum, the policy justifications for the closed session authorization generally still apply when the issue is what measures might be taken to retain a business facility.

Even so, is the statutory language itself broad enough to allow a closed session? To repeat the language, the statute permits closed sessions on matters relating to "the location or expansion of industries or other businesses in the area served by the public body." Obviously discussing how to keep a plant open has nothing to do with business *expansion*; can it be said, though, to involve business *location*? One meaning of the word *location* is the act or process of locating ("the company president is devoting his time to the location of a new facility"), and that meaning seems to suggest that the statute's concern is with discussions about attracting new facilities to the community. But another meaning of the word is the fact or condition of being located ("the company representative described the location of its plant"), and that meaning may be broad enough to encompass discussions about companies currently located within the community and how to keep them there. Because such discussions fit within the policy justifications for closed sessions, it is reasonable to read the statutory language broadly enough to allow them.

Government Facilities

May a public body meet in closed session to discuss how to attract a facility of another government, such as a state prison or a federal post office? Here the argument in favor of closed sessions is considerably weaker. The state simply does not enjoy the same expectations of confidentiality about its locational process for a prison that a company does for its locational process for a manufacturing plant. The state facility has been authorized through a very public budget process, and the North Carolina public records law contains no shield denying public access to state documents relating to locating a new facility. Therefore the facility owner's demand for confidentiality is absent when a local government is seeking to attract a governmental facility.

Admittedly a local government seeking a governmental facility may need to bargain with the government placing the facility and thus may wish for confidentiality in developing its bargaining position, but that need alone is probably inadequate to support a closed session. After all, the statute speaks of location or expansion by "industries and other businesses." A state or federal facility is neither an industry nor a business in common parlance. Given the lack of a need for secrecy on the state's or the federal government's part, it is unlikely that the statutory language can be stretched to include a state or federal facility.

Industrial Site Selection

May a public body meet in closed session to select among the possible sites for an industrial park or a single industrial property? Until 1994 the open meetings law included a specific authorization for closed sessions to select sites any time a public body was acquiring real property. In that year, however, the General Assembly amended the law and deleted that specific closed session authorization.[2] As a general matter, then, a public body may not hold a closed session to select among sites for purchase. But does the separate closed session authorization for discussions of industrial location or expansion offer independent authority for a closed session on site selection?

The state attorney general's office considered this question in an advisory opinion issued in 1995.[3] The opinion concluded that, subject to two exceptions, a public body may not hold a closed session to discuss site selection, even if the site is for an industrial park or industrial facility. It argued "that the authority for closed session discussions on property site selection has [not] been subsumed under the authority for closed session discussions on industrial expansion. The intent of the [1994 amendment affecting site selection] was to eliminate the authority to hold closed sessions for general discussions of site selection."[4]

The opinion's first exception arises when site selection itself is a matter to be negotiated with the property owner. The open meetings law does allow closed sessions to establish a public body's negotiating position on "the price and other material terms of a contract or proposed contract for the acquisition of real property."[5] If the specific acreage to be acquired is a matter of negotiation with the seller, then the statute clearly permits a closed session to develop the public body's position on that issue.

The second (and quite narrow) exception arises if the property is being acquired for potential reconveyance to a specific company and that company has its own preferences as to sites. Recognizing that the open meetings law intends to protect company secrecy, the opinion allows that "a closed session may be held for the limited purpose of discussing which businesses prefer which sites. We caution that such a closed session may be held solely to discuss the preferences of particular businesses, and that the location of a site or sites under consideration by a public body may not be kept confidential."[6] That is, during a generally open discussion of sites, the public body may hold a brief closed session for the sole purpose of learning the preferences of specific businesses for specific sites. Once that information has been disclosed, the open session must resume.

There is a third possible exception not mentioned by the attorney general's opinion letter (and possibly not acceptable to the authors of the opinion). To revert one last time to the statutory language, the open meetings law permits a closed session to discuss "matters relating to the location or expansion of industries or other businesses." The opinion letter appears to read the quoted language as referring to specific industries or businesses, which is its usual application, but it might also refer to location or expansion of industry or business in general. Such a broader reading would allow a public body to consider in closed session not only the site preferences of particular businesses but also the suitability of various sites to industrial or business uses in general. That one site was quite hilly and therefore would need grading, that another might contain environmental liabilities, that a third was served by rail transportation, all are factors affecting the general suitability of a tract to industrial or business development and therefore are matters relating to industrial or business location or expansion. A public body's judgment that presentation or discussion of these specific factors would best be done in closed session is a reasonable reading of the statutory language.

Closed Session Negotiations

The closed session authorization for business location or expansion recognizes that the most common occasion for its use will be when a public body is negotiating an incentives arrangement with a company. Therefore the statute specifies that while in closed session the public body may reach "agreement on a tentative list of economic development incentives that may be offered by the public body in negotiations. The action approving the signing of an economic development contract or commitment, or the action authorizing the payment of economic development expenditures, shall be taken in open session."[7]

The practical effect of the language quoted above, which was added to the open meetings law in 1997,[8] is that a public body may consider incentives in closed session and may reach tentative agreement with the company in closed session as long as no legally binding commitments are made. That is, the public body may reach consensus on the incentives it will offer, may hear the company's response to that offer, may adjust its own consensus and offer in light of the company's response, and so on until both parties are ready to sign an agreement. The public body must approve the actual contract or other commitment in open session, but it may take all earlier steps in closed session.

So understood, the language added in 1997 confirms the state supreme court's interpretation of the statute in *Maready v. City of Winston-Salem*.[9] The governing boards of the two defendant governments in that case had held closed sessions to discuss and develop incentive packages to be offered to particular companies. The trial court found that, while in closed sessions, the boards' "'[s]taff was given instructions as to further negotiations and the Board members did, in nine cases, indicate their informal approval regarding certain economic development incentives.' Any company receiving notice of a preliminary approval was also advised, however, that final approval at a public meeting would be required before any contract could be signed or any funds expended."[10] After noting that the public hearing requirement in G.S. 158-7.1(c) (discussed on pages 95–100) directs that the notice of any hearing concerning acquisition of economic development property indicate the governing board's intention to acquire the property, the court concluded that "it logically follows that the intent to approve the acquisition which is the subject of the hearing may be formed in a closed session."[11]

The Public Records Law

Expansion and Location Projects

Public records relating to general economic development activities are always open to public inspection, though the public records statute [G.S. 132-6(d)] does allow "public records relating to the proposed expansion or location of specific business or industrial projects in the State [to] be withheld [from public inspection] so long as their inspection, examination or copying would frustrate the purpose for which such public records were created." The kinds of records that might relate to specific business or industrial projects include correspondence with a company or its consultants, internal memoranda about the project, appraisals of land or buildings that might be conveyed to the company, draft contracts with the company, and the minutes or general accounts of closed sessions held concerning the project.

Retention of a Company: Government Facilities

The preceding discussion of the open meetings law suggested that closed sessions of a public body might be permitted to discuss measures to retain an existing facility under threat of closure but probably not to discuss comparable measures to attract a government facility. How do the records relating to such projects fare under the public records law provision?

The policy justifications for denying public access to records associated with efforts to retain an existing facility mirror those for allowing closed sessions to discuss such efforts; they generally accord with policies underlying the public records exception. The language in the exception, however, is harder to fit to facility retention. The language permits a government to deny public access to records concerning the proposed expansion or location of specific *projects*. Because it is difficult to characterize the closure of a facility as a project, the language does not easily extend to records of facility retention efforts.

Records of efforts by a public body to attract governmental facilities fare no better under the public records provision than under the open meetings provision: The exception to public access appears not to include such records.

Trade Secrets

Both government-operated loan pools[12] and government purchase of equity interests in companies were discussed in Chapter 2.[13] In each of those types of programs, the government might receive financial statements from applicant companies that contain information probably constituting trade secrets. Thus if the applicant for assistance notes that the statements are confidential or are trade secrets, the statements are not subject to the public records law. An economic development office might receive financial statements or other trade secrets in other contexts as well. If the submitter states that these materials are confidential, then these materials also are not subject to the public records statute.[14]

When Do Records Become Public?

The public records statutes exempt trade secrets from public access for as long as they remain trade secrets, which might be permanently. The statutes do not, however, permanently exempt other economic development records from public access. Rather the exemption continues only "so long as [the record's] inspection, examination or copying would frustrate the purpose for which such public records were created." No appellate court has considered this language, but its meaning probably is as follows. First, if a negotiation with a company results in some kind of agreement, the records associated with the negotiation become public once formal agreement is reached. Second, if a negotiation concludes without agreement and the company goes elsewhere, the records associated with the negotiation become public once it is clear that no agreement will be reached now or in the future.

The Public Hearing on Appropriations and Expenditures

Before a county or city may appropriate or expend money pursuant to G.S. 158-7.1(b), Subsection (c) of the statute requires that the governing body hold a public hearing on the proposed appropriation or expenditure, having given at least ten days of published notice of the hearing. If the proposal involves acquiring an interest in real property, the statute requires that the notice describe

- the interest to be acquired,
- the proposed cost of the interest,
- the governing board's intention to acquire the interest,
- the source of moneys to fund the acquisition,
- any other information needed to reasonably describe the acquisition.

If the proposal involves improving privately owned property through site preparation or extending water and sewer lines to the property, the statute requires that the notice describe

- the improvements to be made,
- the proposed cost of making the improvements,
- the source of moneys to fund the improvements,
- the public benefit to be derived from making the improvements,
- any other information needed to reasonably describe the improvements and their purpose.

Although the statute does not address proposals that do not fit within the above categories, the notice for hearings on other proposals should include comparable kinds of information: a description of what will be paid for, the cost, the source of funding, and anything else that will help to explain the project and the reasons for it. A set of example notices for a public hearing pursuant to this subsection are set out on pages 117–18.

The name of the private company to which an incentive is to be offered is not on the statutory list of items that must be included in the notice of public hearing. [Some public hearings required by G.S. 158-7.1(c) are for projects that are not associated with a specific private company. For example, a local government might be acquiring land for an industrial park or constructing a shell building.] In most instances the company's name will be public knowledge by the time the hearing is held, and including the name in the notice will increase the informativeness of the notice. But if the company's identity is still confidential, the statute does not seem to require that it be revealed in the notice or at the hearing itself.

Local governments have been extending water and sewer lines to industrial properties for decades under general policies adopted by city councils and boards of county commissioners. G.S. 158-7.1(b) specifically authorizes extending or providing for or assisting in extending water or sewer lines to an industrial property or facility.[15] Must a local government hold a public hearing each time an extension is made pursuant to such a general policy? Probably not. G.S. 158-7.1(b) is unnecessary as an authorization to counties and cities to adopt and implement general policies for extension of utility lines. Local government authority to own and operate enterprise systems,[16] including water and sewer systems, has long been adequate statutory authority for those actions. What

G.S. 158-7.1(b) adds is authority to extend lines to specific sites in ways not contemplated by a government's general extension policies—that is, authority to offer water and sewer extensions as a special economic development incentive. That being the case, a county or city should hold a public hearing on water or sewer line extensions only if it is offering to do more than its normal policies require. If it is only following regular extension policies, and especially if no governing body action is required under those policies, the governing body need not hold a public hearing on the extensions.

Projects That Require a Hearing

The statute specifically requires a public hearing for any project undertaken pursuant to G.S. 158-7.1(b). That subsection authorizes the following specific economic development projects:

- acquiring and developing an industrial park,
- acquiring property suitable for industrial or commercial use,
- options to acquire property suitable for industrial or commercial use,
- acquiring or constructing a shell building,
- constructing and extending utility facilities and lines to industrial properties or facilities or financing such construction or extensions,
- site preparation for industrial properties and facilities.

As was noted in Chapter 2, many local governments are no longer undertaking these kinds of projects themselves but are instead reimbursing private companies for doing so. That is, after a company buys land or grades a site, the local government reimburses the company for the costs of acquisition and/or grading.[17] When a local government reimburses a company for a project listed in G.S. 158-7.1(b), the statutory requirement of a hearing still applies; Subsection (b) remains the statutory authority for the ultimate expenditure.

The point was made repeatedly in Chapter 2 that many current economic development incentives are not authorized by Subsection (b) but by Subsection (a) of Section 158-7.1. The statute's public hearing requirement applies only to incentives listed in and authorized by Subsection (b). Does that mean that a local government need not hold a hearing when it prepares to appropriate or expend money (or enter into incentive contracts) pursuant to Subsection (a)?

Although the statute does not require a hearing, the state supreme court's reasoning in *Maready v. City of Winston-Salem*[18] suggests that a local government should hold a hearing anyway, in order to protect the constitutionality of the incentive. In the *Maready* decision, the court held that economic development incentives in general provide benefits to the larger public that outweigh any specific private benefits to the company receiving the incentives. The court admitted, however, that other cases might present particular incentives for which the public benefit does not outweigh the private; were that to be the case, the incentives would not serve a public purpose and therefore would be unconstitutional.

The court then noted that G.S. 158-7.1 requires a public hearing before expenditures are made pursuant to the statute and stated that these "strict procedural requirements . . . provide safeguards that should suffice to prevent abuse."[19] The court seems to be saying that if a local government has held a public hearing and given the public a chance to comment on a proposed incentive package, and if the government thereafter decides to go forward, the incentive carries a presumption of public rather than private benefit. In order to attain that presumption, though, a local government must have held a public hearing on the incentive at issue. For that reason, any time a local government proposes to offer an incentive or enter into an incentive contract, the local government should hold a public hearing, regardless of whether the incentive is authorized by Subsection (a) or Subsection (b) of G.S. 158-7.1.* The *Maready* opinion indicates that Winston-Salem and Forsyth County held public hearings on all of the projects at issue in that case, not just those authorized by G.S. 158-7.1(b).[20]

The Timing of the Hearing

The statute requires that the public hearing be held before any appropriation or expenditure is made on the incentive or other activity in question. In most cases there is no question as to when the hearing should be held, but occasionally questions of timing do arise. The following section discusses three timing issues.

Contract for Future Incentive Payments

Some incentive contracts obligate the local government to make certain expenditures at a future date rather than immediately after the contract is signed. A series of cash grants, for example, might not begin until the company's facility is constructed, a year or more into the future; or a reimbursement for water and sewer extension costs might not be due for some months. If the contract does not require any expenditures during the current fiscal year, the Local Government Budget and Fiscal Control Act does not require any appropriation

---

* Subsection (a) is also the authority for a broad range of general economic development activities, as noted in Chapter 2 (beginning on page 41). Because there is no doubt about the constitutionality of these more general activities, there is no need for a special public hearing before expending money on them.

for the contract in the current fiscal year.[21] When the first expenditures under a contract are some months or years away, when must the local government hold the public hearing: before entering into the contract or before making its first appropriations pursuant to the contract?

Almost certainly before entering into the contract. The contract imposes obligations on the local government to make expenditures and appropriations, if not now, in the future. The statute clearly intends that the governing body seek public comment before it commits the government to an incentive arrangement. Holding the hearing after the government is already committed by contract frustrates the statutory intention. Furthermore the open meetings provision discussed earlier in this chapter explicitly requires that the board approve the contract in open session before the contract is signed. There is neither reason nor occasion for continued secrecy once the government and company are ready to execute an incentives contract. Even if neither appropriations nor expenditures will be made immediately, a local government should hold the public hearing required by G.S. 158-7.1(c) before approving any incentives contract.

Preliminary Costs of Land Acquisition

A local government must hold a public hearing before it acquires real property pursuant to G.S. 158-7.1, whether for an industrial park, an industrial or commercial site, or a shell building. But what if the local government makes expenditures before actual acquisition as part of the process of deciding whether to acquire the site? At least two sorts of preliminary expenditures are frequently made. First, the government might pay for surveys or environmental or other testing on the site to determine if the site is suitable for industrial uses. Second, the government might acquire an option on the site, paying the owner for the option. The statute requires a public hearing before any expenditures are made pursuant to the statute. If the ultimate authority to acquire a site is G.S. 158-7.1, any preliminary expenditures related to that site also are pursuant to the statute, and the hearing should be held before the preliminary expenditures are made. Thus each of the above examples triggers the requirement of a public hearing under this reading of the statute.

A Hearing before a Site Is Selected

The two issues discussed above involve delaying the time of the hearing. Sometimes, however, a local government might wish to *advance* the hearing. For example, a local government may have decided that it will acquire land for and develop an industrial park but has not yet decided on which land. May the required hearing be held at that point, before a specific parcel, or parcels, of land to be described in the notice or at the hearing has been selected? Although such an approach might be efficient, the statute does not seem to allow it.

First, the statute requires that if the hearing is on the acquisition of real property, the notice of the hearing is to describe the interest to be acquired. Although the phrasing is a bit ambiguous, the intention seems to be that the notice must describe the property itself as well as the legal interest to be acquired. If there is no site, that statutory requirement cannot be met. Second, the statute seemingly intends that the public will comment upon the wisdom of the specific project that the board intends to approve. A hearing on the abstract idea of a county industrial park will draw a different sort of comment than will one held to consider a proposal for an industrial park at a specific site within the county. Holding the hearing at the abstract stage does not serve the full intentions of the statute.

Action after the Hearing

Beginning on page 119 of this chapter are several example resolutions authorizing a local government to expend funds or contract for incentives following the public hearing required by G.S. 158-7.1(c).

The Public Hearing on Conveyances of Real Property

If a local government has acquired real property pursuant to G.S. 158-7.1(b), before the government may convey or lease any interest in that property pursuant to that statute, G.S. 158-7.1(d) requires that the governing body hold a public hearing on the conveyance or lease with at least ten days of published notice. Once the hearing is complete, the governing body must approve the transaction.

G.S. 158-7.1 offers three advantages to a government conveying or leasing property for economic development. First, G.S. 158-7.1(d) allows a government to convey or lease property by private negotiation with the company acquiring or leasing the property, avoiding the usual statutory requirement that property be conveyed through competitive means.[22] Second, the same subsection allows a local government to subject the property to any covenants, conditions, or restrictions that the government deems to be in the public interest or necessary to carrying out the economic development goals underlying the conveyance or lease. Third, and probably most important, G.S. 158-7.1(d2) (discussed in the following section) effectively allows a local government to convey or lease the property without real cost to the company, thereby allowing the property to be used as an incentive. [G.S. 160A-457(d) offers cities a limited, alternative procedure for conveying property to private companies by private sale. It does not, however, permit the property to be given to the company. This alternative statutory authority for economic development property transactions is discussed beginning on page 110.]

Transactions Subject to the Hearing Requirement

The statutory requirement of a public hearing applies to any conveyance or lease of an interest in real property that is held or has been acquired pursuant to G.S. 158-7.1(b). Therefore the hearing must be held before a local government leases or conveys (1) part of an industrial park, (2) any single tract of land held or acquired for industrial or commercial purposes, or (3) a shell building or space in a shell building. A more open question is whether a hearing is required when a local government, having acquired an option on real property, intends to assign that option pursuant to G.S. 158-7.1(b)(3). North Carolina case law supports the notion that an option is technically not an interest in real property.[23] That idea, however, has come under some attack nationally in recent years,[24] and the General Assembly has explicitly defined an option as an interest in land in at least two contexts.[25] Given the trend of the law, it is possible that the General Assembly considered assignment of an option as a conveyance of an interest in land under G.S. 158-7.1. In general G.S. 158-7.1(d) requires a hearing whenever some kind of property-based incentive is being conveyed to a specific party, and that general purpose includes assignment of an option. For that reason, a local government probably should hold a hearing before assigning an option.

Note that the statute applies to property *held* for the purposes of G.S. 158-7.1(b) as well as to property *acquired* for those purposes. This statutory language recognizes that governments sometimes own property that has been acquired and used for some purpose other than economic development but that is no longer needed for the original purpose. If the property is suitable for industrial or commercial uses, the local government may in effect redirect the property to economic development purposes and proceed to develop or convey it pursuant to the economic development statute. When that is to be done, some governing bodies formally reassign the property to economic development uses by adopting a resolution that sets out the purposes for which the property was originally acquired and used, recites that the property is no longer needed for the original purposes, and resolves that the property is now held for economic development pursuant to G.S. 158-7.1. An example of such a resolution is set out beginning on page 121.

Notice of the Public Hearing

As noted above, the statute requires that the local government give at least ten days published notice of the public hearing. The notice must include the following details:

- the interest to be conveyed or leased,
- the value of the interest,
- the proposed consideration for the conveyance or lease,[26]
- the governing body's intention to approve the conveyance or lease.

An example of a notice for a public hearing to convey land is set out beginning on page 122.

The Wage Determination

Before a local government may convey or lease an interest in real property pursuant to G.S. 158-7.1, Subsection (d) requires the governing body to "determine the probable average hourly wage to be paid to workers by the business to be located at the property to be conveyed." The statute requires that this determination be made before the property is conveyed or leased rather than before the hearing is held, and some local governments make the determination based on testimony or documents presented at the hearing. Others, however, make the determination before the public hearing, so that the information is available to anyone wishing to comment at the hearing.

Components of Average Hourly Wage

Subsection (d) does not define which company payroll costs should be included in determining the average hourly wage at the business to be conducted on the property conveyed or leased, nor does it indicate which employees' wages are to be included in determining the average. For example, should the average wage include only direct pay to employees, or should it also include such benefits as employer-paid pension contributions or medical insurance or employer-supplied work clothing? Should the wage calculation include only hourly workers or also supervisors and facility managers?

We should start with the guidelines used by the North Carolina Employment Security Commission in its periodic determinations of companies' average weekly wage and average weekly manufacturing wage. These determinations are used for a variety of economic development purposes. If a company is to qualify for the various economic development tax credits offered by the state, the company must meet a statutory wage standard that is defined in terms of an *average weekly wage* that is based on determinations of the Employment Security Commission.[27] If a company is to qualify for industrial revenue bond financing, it must meet a statutory wage standard that is defined in terms of an *average weekly manufacturing wage* that also is based on determinations of the Employment Security Commission.[28] Indeed, there is reference to the commission's wage computations in G.S. 158-7.1 itself. Subsection (d2) permits a local government to convey real property to a company without the company having to pay direct monetary consideration for the property. For a company to be eligible for such an incentive, however, it must agree to create a substantial number of jobs that pay at or above the *median average wage* in the county. Median average wage is defined as "the median average wage for all insured industries in the county as computed by the Employment Security Commission for the most recent period for which data is available."[29] Therefore it is sensible to at least begin with the commission's guidelines in determining the probable average hourly wage to be paid by one company.

The more relevant portion of the commission's guidelines determines what company costs are included in *wages*. G.S. 96-8(13) defines wages for all of the activities of the Employment Security Commission. The definition is lengthy, but the gist of it is that a company's cash payments to employees are included in wages, but non-cash benefits are not. Thus wages include regular and overtime pay, vacation and holiday pay, year-end bonuses and profit sharing, and comparable employee pay incentives but do not include non-cash benefits, such as insurance or retirement contributions, made by a company on an employee's behalf. There is little doubt that a local government should use the same definitions in making the average hourly wage determination required by G.S. 158-7.1(d).

More problematic are the Employment Security Commission's guidelines as to which employees' wages to count. Basically the commission counts everyone who works at a particular location. It includes not only production workers but also managers, supervisors, professionals, maintenance employees, and so on. As a result the average weekly wage or the average weekly manufacturing wage states a figure higher than the average wage being paid to a company's production workers. G.S. 158-7.1(d), however, directs the local government to determine the probable average hourly wage to be paid to workers by the business. The use of *workers* may well be intended to exclude managerial and professional employees. The use of the term *hourly wage* also seems to indicate an intention to exclude salaried employees. Therefore the more likely interpretation of the statutory requirement is that the local government is to determine the probable average hourly wage to be paid to hourly employees.

Means of Making the Determination

Once *what* is to be counted has been determined, *how* does a local government go about determining the probable average hourly wage that will be paid at a facility as yet unbuilt? Obviously the company is the best source for the necessary information. Local governments have followed at least two methods for securing this information from companies. Many rely on a letter or other documents provided by the company either before or at the public hearing. This conforms to the state's policy with respect to industrial revenue bonds: Companies seeking to qualify for such financing must file a form with the state Department of Commerce listing categories of employees, the number of employees in each category, and the amount of compensation paid in each category. This form is then certified by a company official. Another method is to ask company officials to testify as to the information, most often at the hearing.

Making the Determination When No Jobs Are Immediately Expected

Local governments do not always convey industrial or commercial property to companies that have immediate plans to construct facilities that will create jobs. A local government, for example, might convey an industrial site or a site within an industrial park to a developer who intends to construct a shell building on the site. Until the developer constructs the building and then finds a client to fill the building, there will be no jobs for which an average hourly wage calculation can be made. In such a situation, how can the local government comply with the statutory requirement of determining the probable average hourly wage?

One possibility is to decide that the wage determination requirement is irrelevant, cannot be made, and therefore need not be made. That is not unreasonable, but it flies in the face of the direct statutory requirement. A second possibility is to hold a second hearing when the developer sells or leases the building and to make the determination at that time based on the type of company that actually will be in the building. The difficulty with this approach is that because the local government no longer owns the property, it is no longer part of the decision-making process, and so neither the public hearing nor the wage determination would have any effect on the conveyance by the developer. A third possibility is to make the most-educated guess possible at the time the property is sold to the developer. This guess could be based on the kind of shell building that the developer intends to build, the general level of wages in the county at present, and any agreements that might be reached between the local government and the developer as to the kinds of businesses that will be placed in the building. None of these three possibilities meets the full intentions of the statute, but the third seems to come closest.

Consideration for the Conveyance of Property: The Possibility of Gifts of Land or Buildings

The previous discussion about the notice for the public hearing on conveying or leasing real property indicated that the notice must include the value of the property interest that is being conveyed or leased. This value is determined by the governing body: G.S. 158-7.1(d) requires the governing body to determine "the fair market value of the interest, subject to whatever covenants, conditions, and restrictions the county or city proposes to subject it to." Subsection (d) concludes by requiring that the "consideration for the conveyance may not be less than the value so determined" by the governing body.

The statute does not specify the means that the governing body must use to determine the *fair market value* of the property being conveyed. One obvious method is to rely on an appraisal of the property by a qualified appraiser, but the statute does not appear to require an appraisal. Perhaps the local government has staff members, or even governing body members, experienced in local real estate who can make qualified judgments about the value of the property. However the determination is made, the governing body's resolution setting out the determination should indicate the basis for it.

As just noted, G.S. 158-7.1(d) requires that the consideration received by a local government for any conveyance of property must be no less than the fair market value of the property, as determined by the governing body. Subsection (d2) of the section states, however, that in "arriving at the amount of consideration that it receives," the governing body "may take into account prospective tax revenues from improvements to be constructed on the property, prospective sales tax revenues to be generated in the area, as well as any other prospective tax revenues or income coming to the [local government] over the next 10 years as a result of the conveyance or lease." Because a local government will receive the various tax and other revenues in any event, this language amounts to an authorization to convey the property as an incentive to a company, with the company in fact paying none or only part of the value of the property. Given the state supreme court's holding in *Maready v. City of Winston-Salem* that a company's provision of new taxable investment or new jobs is adequate public benefit to support local government incentives to the company,[30] gifts of land pursuant to Subsection (d2) clearly serve a public purpose and are constitutional. Indeed, although the statute does not allow it, the constitution probably permits a local government to convey property to a company even when it will not receive tax and other revenues within ten years in a cumulative amount adequate to pay for the property as long as the local government finds that the company's capital investment and creation of jobs is important to the community's economic health. Thus for this one form of incentive, the statute imposes restrictions that probably are narrower than what the constitution permits. The following is a detailed discussion of Subsection (d2), including the special procedural rules that apply when the subsection is used.

When Tax and Other Revenue Sources Must Be Taken into Account

Subsection (d2) is relevant only when the more standard consideration received by a local government for property is less than the property's fair market value. If the local government receives fair market value, either in cash at the closing or in a series of installment payments, the subsection does not apply. Conversely if title is transferred and the company pays nothing (or pays less than fair market value), Subsection (d2) is triggered and its requirements must be met. Other situations that trigger the subsection are presented below.

- The local government acquires property at less than market value (which allows the seller to claim a tax-deductible charitable contribution for the difference between market value and the actual amount paid) and then conveys the property to a company for what it (the government) paid. This is still a sale at less than fair market value, and the difference between real fair market value and the amount actually paid must be made up from future taxes and other revenues collected by the government.
- The company agrees to pay for the property in installments over several years, but it pays no interest or interest at a rate that is below market. The difference between the market interest rate and the interest actually paid must be made up from future taxes and other revenues collected by the local government.
- The company agrees to pay for the property but only at some date in the future, and no interest is charged for the period between closing and actual payment. The amount of the market interest rate for the period must be made up from future taxes and other revenues collected by the local government.
- The company agrees to lease the property, but the lease amount is below the fair rental value of the property. The difference between market rate rent and the rent actually paid must be made up from future taxes and other revenues collected by the local government.

Reimbursing the Company's Property Costs

As was noted in Chapter 2, it is increasingly common for local governments to reimburse a company for the company's cost in acquiring its site, rather than for the local government itself to acquire the site and then convey it to the company.[31] If that route is followed, the local government should still comply with the requirements of Subsection (d2). Even though it has not purchased and then conveyed property to a company, the local government is doing the economic equivalent, and the policy of the statute demands that the amount reimbursed be returned to the government through taxes and other revenues. The other procedural requirements of the subsection (discussed below) also should be met.

Revenues That May Be Counted as Consideration

The statute's apparent intention is that the taxes and other revenues that a local government takes into account as consideration are to reimburse the government for the value of the property it has conveyed. Therefore the local government should count only those revenues that are available for appropriation for economic development. A revenue that is available for that purpose may legally be used to replenish the funds that were used to acquire the property that was conveyed. If a revenue is restricted and therefore not available for economic development expenditures, it should not be counted. In the descriptions of revenues that follow, those that carry restrictions are noted.

Property Taxes

The revenues most commonly used in arriving at consideration are the property taxes paid on improvements constructed on the property. In the usual case, the government conveys raw land to the company (or reimburses the company for its cost in acquiring raw land) and the company constructs and equips some kind of facility on the land. The taxes on the facility and on machinery and equipment within the facility normally are adequate to recover the fair market value of the property, and the local government need look to no other revenues. (Although the statute speaks of taxes on "improvements to be constructed" on the property, any taxes generated from personal property installed on the property, such as business machinery, should be counted as well.)

Note, however, that the government may count only the taxes that are generated by the company's investment in the property. The amount of taxes attributable to the land itself, for example, may not be counted. In addition, if what is conveyed (or leased) is a shell building, the value of the building as conveyed also does not represent investment by the company, and the local government may not count the taxes attributable to that value. Rather the government may count only the taxes attributable to any improvements that the company has made to the building, or attributable to any personal property that the company has installed in the building.

Sales Taxes

The statute specifically allows a local government to count as consideration "prospective sales tax revenues to be generated in the area." (Clearly this means local government sales taxes accruing to the government conveying the property and not the total of state and local government sales taxes paid.) The statutory formulation is a little ambiguous: It certainly includes sales taxes paid by the company or its contractors during construction and equipping of its facility and sales taxes paid by the company once it begins operations, but it also may include additional sources of sales tax. For example, a new manufacturing facility may attract suppliers to the county, and the sales taxes paid by those suppliers also would have been generated in the area and because of the facility constructed by the company receiving the land. Counting sales taxes generated by any company other than the immediate grantee of the land and its construction contractors is highly speculative, however, and the local government should have a strong basis for counting more than those more direct taxes.

A portion of sales taxes received by a county is earmarked for school capital construction or debt service on school bonds.[32] These earmarked sales tax proceeds may not be expended for economic development and therefore should not be counted as consideration for any conveyance of real property.

Other Taxes

There are no other important taxes that a county might receive from a new industrial or commercial facility, but there are three taxes from which a city might receive significant amounts of new revenue because of such a facility. First, some cities measure business or privilege license taxes on the basis of the gross receipts generated at a business location;[33] for an industrial facility, this tax might generate several thousand dollars a year. Second, if a facility uses significant amounts of electric power and is served by an investor-owned electric utility or by an electric membership corporation, the city will receive state utility franchise tax payments based on the gross receipts earned by the facility's electric supplier.[34] This tax is returned to cities at a rate of roughly three percent of the gross receipts received by the electric supplier from customers inside the city. Third, if the facility uses natural gas supplied by a private supplier, it will pay the state piped natural gas tax, which is based on the monthly volumes of therms of gas used by the company. The state returns one half of that tax to the city in which the facility is located.[35]

Other Revenues: Utility Charges

The principal remaining revenues that a local government might use to arrive at the amount of consideration it has received for a conveyance are any payments made to the local government because of utility services that the government supplies to the facility. In most cases, these will be water and sewer services, but in some instances they could include electric services or, in a very few instances, natural gas services. For any utility revenues, the Local Government Budget and Fiscal Control Act requires that their first use be to pay all of the operating costs of the utility system, including any debt service on utility bonds.[36] Thus a government should count only the net amount of utility revenues, if any, as consideration for the conveyance of real property.

Procedural Requirements

If a local government decides to use the authorization in G.S. 158-7.1(d2) and take various city revenues into account in arriving at the amount of consideration received for conveyance of government property, the subsection imposes some additional procedural requirements.

Wage Determination

The governing body must first "determine that the conveyance of the property will stimulate the local economy, promote business, and result in the creation of a substantial number of jobs in the county or city that pay at or above the median average wage in the county or, for a city, in the county where the city is located." Recall that G.S. 158-7.1(d) requires a local government to forecast the probable *average hourly wage* that will be paid by the purchaser or lessee anytime it plans to convey or lease real property pursuant to G.S. 158-7.1. Subsection (d2) imposes an additional requirement that necessitates determining the *median average wage* that the company will pay and comparing that to the county's existing median average wage.

The company's forecast average wage must equal or exceed the county's current average wage. That is, if real property is to be used as an incentive, the jobs created must be at least as good as the average level of jobs already present in the county. The statute specifies that the median average wage in a county is the median average wage for all insured industries in the county as computed by the North Carolina Employment Security Commission.[37] If a city is located in more than one county, that city is to use the figures for the county in which the greatest proportion of the city population is resident. Because the statute references the Employment Security Commission determinations, presumably it intends that governments follow the commission's practice of including the wages of all employees at a location and not just hourly employees.

Contractual Commitment of Company

The local government and the company must then enter into a contract that obligates the company "to construct, within a specified period of time not to exceed five years, improvements on the property that will generate the tax revenue taken into account in arriving at the consideration." It is important that the company construct any improvements as quickly as possible because the ten-year period within which the local government must receive tax and other revenues sufficient to pay for the property begins from the time the property is conveyed and not from the time that improvements are completed. The subsection goes on to specify that if the company fails to construct the improvements pursuant to the contract, "the purchaser shall reconvey the property back to the county or city." The various mechanisms that a county or city might place in its contract with the company to enforce this statutory requirement of reconveyance are discussed in Chapter 2 (beginning on page 70).

If a local government has reimbursed a company for the latter's acquisition of real property rather than conveying the property itself to the company, the government and the company should enter into a comparable contract, binding the company to construct any improvements within the five-year period. The contract should include a clawback provision to ensure that the local government will have its reimbursement returned to it if the company does not construct the improvements pursuant to the contract.

Approval of Conveyance

An example resolution for conveying real property pursuant to G.S. 158-7.1(d) and (d2) is set out in the final section of this chapter (beginning on page 122).

An Alternative Authorization for Property Transactions: G.S. 160A-457

An earlier discussion in this chapter noted that cities enjoy a limited, alternative statutory authorization to acquire and convey real property for economic development purposes. The statute is G.S. 160A-457, and this section discusses that statute and its similarities to and contrasts with G.S. 158-7.1. (Counties are subject to G.S. 153A-377, which is similar to G.S. 160A-457, except that the

Table 2
Comparison of Authorizations for Property Transactions

Requirement	G.S. 160A-457	G.S. 158-7.1
Acquisition		
Public hearing	No	Yes
Conveyance		
In community development project area	Yes	No
Pursuant to community development plan	Yes	No
Public hearing	Yes	Yes
Publish notice of hearing	Once, 10 days before hearing	Once a week, for 2 weeks, 10 to 25 days before hearing
Wage determination	No	Yes
Value determination	Appraised value	Fair market value
Convey for no less than value so determined	Yes	Yes
Count taxes, other revenues as consideration	No	Yes

county statute does not include any authority for negotiated sales of property. For that reason, it is of little practical use for economic development.) The most significant difference between G.S. 160A-457 and G.S. 158-7.1 is that a city may not use the former statute to give property to a company. (The similarities of and differences between G.S. 160A-457 and G.S. 158-7.1 are summarized in Table 2.)

The Authority to Acquire Real Property

G.S. 160A-457 authorizes a city to acquire a broad range of properties. Those that are relevant here are as follows:

- real property that is "blighted, deteriorated, deteriorating, undeveloped, or inappropriately developed from the standpoint of sound community development and growth";
- real property that is "appropriate for rehabilitation or conversation activities"; and
- real property that is "appropriate . . . for the economic development of the community."

The statute imposes no procedural conditions on a city that acquires property pursuant to it. That is, it does not require public notice, a public hearing, or any governing body findings before the city acts.

The Authority to Convey Real Property

G.S. 160A-457 contains two basic authorizations by which a city may convey property acquired pursuant to the statute. First, it authorizes a city to convey property pursuant to G.S. Chapter 160A, Article 12. By and large that article requires competitive sales, and for that reason a city is unlikely to use its procedures for economic development conveyances. Second, the statute authorizes a city to convey property by private negotiation, pursuant to Subsection (4) of the statute. Because this second authorization does allow negotiated sales, a city might use it for an economic development project. Unlike the statute's authority to acquire property, its authority to convey is subject to a series of procedural requirements.

First, the property must be located within a *community development project area* and the conveyance must be for uses consistent with the *community development plan*. Although no North Carolina statute defines community development project area or community development plan, the phrases are terms of art in the Community Development Block Grant (CDBG) program. That fact creates some ambiguity in this authorization for private sales of property. The introductory paragraph to G.S. 160A-457 states that a city may exercise the powers authorized by the section "either as a part of a community development program or independently thereof," which suggests that the definitions of the CDBG program are not binding on activities undertaken pursuant to the section. But how else can meaning be given to the words? The statute's introductory language, quoted above, was part of the statute as originally enacted; the authorization for private sales of property was added some years later. Perhaps, given that sequence, the language in the introductory paragraph should be given less weight. At the least, in defining an area as a community development project area and in establishing a plan for the area, a city should respect the policies underlying the CDBG program, particularly its economic development component. The pervasive purpose of the CDBG program is improving the lives of persons of low and moderate income. In the program's economic development component this purpose translates to seeking either to create jobs that mostly can and will be filled by such persons or to assist businesses that provide services directly to persons of low or moderate incomes.[38] These purposes shape the areas that might reasonably be designated as community development project areas and the kinds of companies and jobs that might be assisted within such an area. Assisting a company that provides only high-skill jobs and that locates at some remove from low- and moderate-income residential areas seems incompatible with the goals of community development so understood.

Second, before a city council may approve a conveyance pursuant to this statute, G.S. 160A-457 requires that the council hold a public hearing on the conveyance. The notice of the hearing must disclose the terms of the conveyance and must be published once a week for two successive weeks; the first publication must come not less than ten days nor more than twenty-five days before the hearing. An example notice for this hearing is set out in the final section of this chapter (beginning on page 124).

Third, before the city may convey the property, G.S. 160A-457 directs that the city have the property appraised and disclose that appraised value at the hearing. The city may not convey the property for less than the appraised value. Significantly, this statute does not include any authorization by which the city may count as consideration taxes and other revenues received by the city because of improvements constructed on the property. Therefore, if the city wishes to use the real property as an incentive to a company, this statute will not work; the city will have to use G.S. 158-7.1.

An example of a resolution authorizing conveyance of property pursuant to G.S. 160A-457 is set out in the final section of this chapter (beginning on page 124).

Conveying Property to Nonprofit Economic Development Organizations

As will be discussed in Chapter 4, local governments frequently use nonprofit economic development organizations to assist in their economic development programs. One mechanism governments sometimes use is to convey property to such an organization, so that the nonprofit organization (rather than the local government itself) may develop and market an industrial park, construct and market a shell building, or simply market industrial or commercial sites. As was noted earlier, in the context of conveying land to a for-profit developer for a shell building, G.S. 158-7.1(d) is not particularly well suited to conveyances in which the buyer itself will not be operating a business on the site. It is very difficult to make the expected average hourly wage determination that Subsection (d) requires of all conveyances pursuant to the statute. With a for-profit developer, G.S. 160A-457 offers the only alternative statutory authority for conveying the property by private sale. With nonprofit economic development organizations, however, there is an additional alternative: G.S. 160A-279.

Summary of G.S. 160A-279

G.S. 160A-279 permits a county or city to convey property by privately negotiated sale to any nonprofit organization to which the county or city is authorized to appropriate funds. Two identical statutes authorize counties and cities to appropriate funds to nonprofit economic development organizations:

G.S. 153A-449 and 160A-20.1 authorize counties and cities, respectively, to "contract with and appropriate money to any person, association, or corporation, in order to carry out any public purpose that the [local government] is authorized by law to engage in." Counties and cities are authorized by G.S. 158-7.1 to carry out economic development, and therefore they may appropriate money to private organizations engaged in the same activities. Because counties and cities may appropriate funds to nonprofit economic development organizations, G.S. 160A-279 permits them to convey property by private sale to the same organizations.

Although the private organization is not technically an agent of the local government, the statute's intention is that the organization use the property to carry out some public purpose in lieu of the local government doing so. To accomplish that goal, the statute directs the local government to "attach to any such conveyance covenants or conditions which assure that the property will be put to a public use by the recipient entity."

Consideration

G.S. 160A-279 says nothing about what consideration the nonprofit entity must pay for any property conveyed pursuant to the statute; it simply permits the conveyance to be negotiated privately rather than made through competitive procedures. The amount and form of consideration that the local government must receive is left to more general principles. Those general principles, set out below, permit the government to give the property to the nonprofit organization in return for the organization's promise to use the property for public purposes.

First, the North Carolina Constitution prohibits a government from making a gift of public money or other assets, and the state supreme court has indicated that giving away public property or selling public property at well below its market price falls within that prohibition.[39]

Second, although a government may not give away its property, it need not always receive *monetary* consideration. One well-established form of nonmonetary consideration is the grantee's promise to put the property to public use. The leading North Carolina case, *Brumley v. Baxter*,[40] illustrates the principle. The City of Charlotte conveyed surplus city property, worth at least $52,500, to the Charlotte Veterans' Recreation Authority without any monetary consideration. But because the authority promised to put the property to public use—that is, recreation for veterans—the state supreme court held that the transaction did not violate the constitution.[41] Therefore if the nonprofit economic development organization promises to use the property conveyed by the county or city for an economic development purpose for which the county or city might have used it, that promise and use is constitutionally adequate consideration for the government's conveyance of the property.

Procedures

G.S. 160A-279 directs a local government conveying property pursuant to that section to follow the procedure set out in G.S. 160A-267 (which is used for private sales of surplus personal property). That procedure directs that the sale be authorized by resolution or order of the county or city governing body, which must be adopted at a *regular* meeting of the governing body. The resolution or order must identify the property to be conveyed; it also should specify the consideration (including any promise of public use) that the government will receive from the nonprofit organization.[42] Following adoption of the resolution or order, the local government must publish a notice summarizing the content of the governing body's action and then wait at least ten days before closing the sale. The statute does not require any public hearing before the governing body adopts its resolution or order, nor does it require any special notice of the meeting at which the governing body takes its action.

An example of a resolution conveying property to a nonprofit organization (that also takes account of the procedural requirements discussed in the remaining paragraphs of this section) is found in the final section of this chapter (beginning on page 125).

Procedures When the Nonprofit Organization Conveys the Property to a Private Company

Assume that a county or city has conveyed real property to a nonprofit economic development organization and that the organization has since found a company to which it will convey the property. Does the economic development statute impose any procedural requirements on this second conveyance? Not by its own terms.

G.S. 158-7.1(d) applies to counties and to cities; it makes no mention of nonprofit organizations. Normally nonprofit organizations may convey their property in any manner and under any conditions they find acceptable. But the matter is not so simple. The opening paragraphs of this chapter emphasize the special degree of openness that the statute imposes on a local government once it is ready to convey property to a company, and pages 100–105 detail the specific steps that the statute requires at that stage. It is implausible that a local government could avoid these openness requirements simply by giving the property to a nonprofit organization that then reconveys the property to a private company. Otherwise a local government could launder the property through the nonprofit organization and avoid any public scrutiny of the ultimate use of public funds. (If the conveyance to the nonprofit organization is for full monetary consideration—a relatively unlikely occurrence—the local government has recouped its initial investment and the nonprofit organization is acting entirely on its own. G.S. 158-7.1 is no longer relevant.)

Recognizing this, a number of local governments have required that the county's or the city's governing body approve any conveyance by the nonprofit organization before the conveyance is made and, at that time, have had the government's governing body follow the appropriate procedures of G.S. 160A-7.1. In that way, the statute's policy of openness at the point of decision and commitment is honored. A possible alternative is to require, as a condition of the original conveyance to the nonprofit organization, that the organization's board of directors, rather than the local government's governing body, follow the statutory procedures. That is clearly a second-best choice, however. Citizens are more likely to participate in a public hearing held by elected officials than one held by the directors of a private organization. The first alternative retains final decision making where the statute places it—with the local government's governing body.*

---

* One might wonder why a local government would convey property to the nonprofit organization if the ultimate conveyance to a private company still had to be approved by the local government's governing body. One reason is that the private organization might not be subject to the open meetings and public records statutes; see the discussion on this point in Chapter 4, at pages 154–55. Therefore the records of the organization's negotiations with private companies would never need to be made public.

FORMS FOR USE IN ECONOMIC DEVELOPMENT TRANSACTIONS

Notice of Public Hearings Pursuant to G.S. 158-7.1(c)
• • •

Public Hearing on Acquiring Land on Which to Develop an Industrial Park

NOTICE OF PUBLIC HEARING

XYZ County proposes to appropriate and expend county funds for the following economic development project pursuant to North Carolina General Statute 158-7.1. The County Board of Commissioners intends to consider acquiring fee simple title to 125 acres of land on which the County will develop an industrial park. The land is part of a larger tract owned by Michael Smith and is located along Robin's Egg Road about one-half mile south of its intersection with U.S. Highway 164. The larger tract is bounded by Hermitage subdivision on the north, property owned by the Hunter family heirs on the west and southwest, property owned by Michigan Industries, Inc., on the south, and Robin's Egg Road on the east. The County proposes to purchase the southern two-thirds of the Smith tract. The cost of the land is $6,500 per acre, for a total cost of $812,500. The County will fund the project with available revenues in the county's General Fund. The Board of Commissioners believes this project will stimulate and stabilize the local economy and result in the creation of a substantial number of new, permanent jobs in the county.

The XYZ County Board of Commissioners will hold a public hearing on the county's proposed appropriation and expenditure of funds for this project at 7:30 P.M. on Monday, March 10, 200x, in the Commissioners' Room in the XYZ County Office Building in the City of ABC. The Commissioners invite all interested persons to attend and present their views.

Public Hearing on Reimbursing a Company for Site Preparation

NOTICE OF PUBLIC HEARING

XYZ County proposes to appropriate and expend county funds for the following economic development project pursuant to North Carolina General Statute 158-7.1. The County Board of Commissioners intends to consider entering into a contract with Michigan Industries, Inc., under which the County will reimburse Michigan Industries for the cost of site preparation at the company's land on Robin's Egg Road. The costs for which the County will reimburse the company include grading the 37-acre site, installing pipes to channel an existing creek under the site, and installing underground utility conduits on the site. The cost of such activities will not exceed $630,000. The County will fund the project with available revenues in the county's General Fund. The Board of Commissioners believes this project will stimulate and stabilize the local economy and result in the creation of a substantial number of new, permanent jobs in the county.

The XYZ County Board of Commissioners will hold a public hearing on the county's proposed appropriation and expenditure of funds for this project at 7:30 P.M. on Monday, March 10, 200x, in the Commissioners' Room in the XYZ County Office Building in the City of ABC. The Commissioners invite all interested persons to attend and present their views.

Public Hearing on Contracting to Make Cash Grants to a Company

NOTICE OF PUBLIC HEARING

XYZ County proposes to appropriate and expend County funds for the following economic development project pursuant to North Carolina General Statute 158-7.1. The County Board of Commissioners intends to consider entering into an economic development incentives contract with St. Joseph Optical. Under the contract, the County will make three annual cash incentive grants to St. Joseph, pursuant to the County's industrial recruitment policy, beginning in the fiscal year in which St. Joseph completes construction of a manufacturing facility costing no less than $34,500,000 on land it owns on Berrien Springs Road. Pursuant to the County's industrial recruitment policy, the amount of each year's grant will be 0.85 percent (.85 of 1 percent) of the taxable value of the facility constructed by St. Joseph. The County estimates this amount will be about $295,000 annually. The County will fund the payments with available revenues in the County's General Fund. The Board of Commissioners believes this project will stimulate and stabilize the local economy and result in the creation of a substantial number of new, permanent jobs in the county.

The XYZ County Board of Commissioners will hold a public hearing on the County's proposed appropriation and expenditure of funds for this project at 7:30 P.M. on Monday, March 10, 200x, in the Commissioners' Room in the XYZ County Office Building in the City of ABC. The Commissioners invite all interested persons to attend and present their views.

Authorization of Economic Development Expenditures

• • •

Resolution Authorizing Purchase of Land and Construction of Shell Building

WHEREAS, North Carolina General Statute 158-7.1 authorizes a city to construct a shell building in order to further the economic development of that city; and

WHEREAS, the ABC City Council has held a public hearing to consider whether to acquire land and construct a shell building on that land; and

WHEREAS, construction of a shell building will attract private companies to the City, leading to the creation of new, permanent jobs for the City's residents and a stable and diversified economy for the City; and

WHEREAS, the ABC City Council has adopted an amendment to the City's budget ordinance appropriating the funds necessary to the project;

THE ABC CITY COUNCIL THEREFORE RESOLVES THAT:

1. The City is authorized to expend approximately $740,000 of City funds to acquire land and construct a shell building on the land.

2. The land to be acquired is more particularly described as follows:

[Description]*

3. The Mayor of the City of ABC is authorized to execute the documents necessary to acquire the land described above so that the City may construct a shell building on the land.

Adopted May 14, 200x.

---

* The description should be adequate to identify the property. If a surveyed description exists, it should be used, but other forms of description will adequately identify the property.

Resolution Authorizing Incentives Contract with a Company

WHEREAS, North Carolina General Statute 158-7.1 authorizes a county to undertake an economic development project by extending assistance to a company in order to cause the company to locate or expand its operations within the county; and

WHEREAS, the Board of Commissioners of XYZ County has held a public hearing to consider whether to participate in an economic development project with Michigan Industries, Inc., by reimbursing Michigan Industries, Inc., for the cost of site preparation at land it owns on Robin's Egg Road and for the cost of training employees at the facility to be constructed on Robin's Egg Road; and

WHEREAS, Michigan Industries, Inc., will construct a facility for manufacturing home tools on the site, making an investment of at least $14,000,000 and creating at least 120 new, permanent jobs in XYZ County; and

WHEREAS, this economic development project will stimulate, diversify, and stabilize the local economy, promote business in the County, and result in the creation of a substantial number of jobs in the County; and

WHEREAS, the Board of Commissioners of XYZ County has adopted an amendment to the County's budget ordinance appropriating the funds necessary to the project;

THE BOARD OF COMMISSIONERS OF XYZ COUNTY THEREFORE RESOLVES THAT:

1. The County is authorized to expend up to $275,000 of county funds for the Michigan Industries, Inc., project.

2. The attached contract between the County and Michigan Industries, Inc., is approved.

3. The Chairman of the Board of Commissioners is authorized to execute the contract and any other documents necessary to the project on behalf of the County.

Adopted June 7, 200x.

Miscellaneous Resolutions and Notices

• • •

Resolution Assigning Government Property to Economic Development

WHEREAS, the City of ABC many years ago acquired a site on Skidmore Road and thereafter operated a maintenance facility on the site for the City's solid waste vehicles; and

WHEREAS, the City has now consolidated all vehicle maintenance activities at a new facility, and the site on Skidmore Road is no longer needed for City activities; and

WHEREAS, the site on Skidmore Road is in an industrial area and is appropriate for private industrial use; and

WHEREAS, the City desires to hold the site for conveyance to a private company for such use;

THEREFORE, THE ABC CITY COUNCIL RESOLVES THAT:

The site of the City's former solid waste vehicle maintenance facility on Skidmore Road, more particularly described below, is now held by the City for economic development purposes pursuant to North Carolina General Statute 158-7.1.

[Description]*

Adopted September 12, 200x.

---

* The description should be adequate to identify the property. If a surveyed description exists, it should be used, but other forms of description will adequately identify the property.

Notice of Public Hearing Pursuant to G.S. 158-7.1(d)

NOTICE OF PUBLIC HEARING

XYZ County proposes to convey land in the Eastside Industrial Park, owned by the County, for an economic development project pursuant to North Carolina General Statute 158-7.1. The County Board of Commissioners intends, subject to public comment at the public hearing for which notice is hereby given, to approve conveyance of a fee simple interest in a 17-acre tract of land at the industrial park. This tract is Parcel 6 at the industrial park, as shown on a plat of the park that is available at the offices of the County Department of Economic Development, Room 241, XYZ County Office Building in the City of ABC. [The conveyance will be made to Michigan Industries, Inc., which will construct a surgical instrument manufacturing facility on the tract.*] The Board of County Commissioners has determined that the value of the tract is $11,400 an acre, for a total value of $193,800. The purchaser of the tract intends to pay the County the full value of the tract at closing. The Board of Commissioners believes this project will stimulate and stabilize the local economy and result in the creation of a substantial number of new, permanent jobs in the County.

The XYZ County Board of Commissioners will hold a public hearing on the County's proposed conveyance of this tract of land at 7:30 P.M. on Monday, March 10, 200x, in the Commissioners' Room in the XYZ County Office Building in the City of ABC. The Commissioners invite all interested persons to attend and present their views.

---

* The name of the purchaser of the land is included in the notice because in most instances the local government will want to identify the purchaser and thereby allow for a more informative public hearing. That sentence is set in brackets, however, because the statute does not require that the notice include this information, and there may be instances in which the information is not yet public.

Resolution Authorizing Sale of Real Property for Economic Development

WHEREAS, North Carolina General Statute 158-7.1 authorizes a county to undertake an economic development project by conveying property to a company in order to cause the company to locate or expand its operations within that county; and

WHEREAS, XYZ County is the owner and developer of the Eastside Industrial Park, Parcel 6 of which is a 17-acre tract; and

WHEREAS, XYZ County and Michigan Industries, Inc., have engaged in private negotiations for the conveyance of Parcel 6, to the end that Michigan Industries, Inc., may construct a surgical instrument manufacturing facility on the tract, and have reached tentative agreement on the terms for conveyance; and

WHEREAS, the Board of Commissioners of XYZ County has held a public hearing to consider whether to approve conveyance of the tract to Michigan Industries, Inc.;

THEREFORE, THE BOARD OF COMMISSIONERS OF XYZ COUNTY RESOLVES THAT:

1. The chairman of the Board of Commissioners is authorized to execute the necessary documents to convey to Michigan Industries, Inc., the real property more particularly described below:

[Description]*

2. The conveyance of the property to Michigan Industries, Inc., will stimulate the local economy, promote business, and result in the creation of a substantial number of jobs in XYZ County that pay at or above the median average hourly wage in the County. The median average hourly wage in XYZ County, as determined by the North Carolina Employment Security Commission, is $X.XX per hour. The probable average hourly wage at the facility to be constructed by Michigan Industries, Inc., is $X.XX, which is above the current median hourly wage in the County. This determination of the probable average hourly wage at the facility is based upon materials provided to the County by Michigan Industries, Inc. [upon testimony from officials of Michigan Industries, Inc., at the public hearing and materials provided at that time to the County by Michigan Industries, Inc.].

3. The fair market value of the property, subject to the covenants and conditions associated with the Eastside Industrial Park, is $193,500. This determination of fair market value is based upon an appraisal of the property by London Appraisal Company, a copy of which is on file in the office of the XYZ County Economic Development Department, XYZ County Office Building. [This determination of fair market value is based upon the sales prices of comparable tracts of land in XYZ County, as reported to the Board of Commissioners.]

4. As consideration for the conveyance of the property, Michigan Industries, Inc., has agreed to construct on the property a surgical instrument manufacturing facility at a cost of at least $13,500,000. A copy of the contract is attached to this resolution. This facility will generate property tax revenues over the next 10 years in an amount at least sufficient to return to the County the fair market value of the property.

Adopted June 23, 200x.

---

* The description should be adequate to identify the property. If a surveyed description exists, it should be used, but other forms of description will adequately identify the property.

Notice of Public Hearing Pursuant to G.S. 160A-457

NOTICE OF PUBLIC HEARING

The City of ABC proposes to convey land located on Killingsworth Road for a community development project pursuant to North Carolina General Statute 160A-457. The ABC City Council intends, subject to public comment at the public hearing for which notice is hereby given, to consider approval of the conveyance of a fee simple interest in a 5-acre tract of land that the city acquired on February 19, 1999. This tract fronts on Killingsworth Road, approximately 200 yards south of its intersection with Prescott Street. It is bounded by Killingsworth Road on the west, property owned by Fremont Manufacturing Company on the north and east, and property owned by Sandy Ceramics on the south. A map of the tract and its environs is available at the Office of the City Planning and Development Department, Third Floor, ABC City Hall. The conveyance will be made to Harvey Scott, Inc., which has committed to construct a broom manufacturing facility on the tract. Harvey Scott, Inc., will pay $30,000 for the site, which is the appraised value of the property.

The ABC City Council will hold a public hearing on the City's proposed conveyance of this tract of land at 7:30 P.M. on Monday, March 10, 200x, in the Council Chambers, ABC City Hall. The Council invites all interested persons to attend and present their views.

Resolution Approving Conveyance of Property Pursuant to G.S. 160A-457

WHEREAS, North Carolina General Statute 160A-457 authorizes a city to convey by private sale real property located in a community development project area; and

WHEREAS, the ABC City Council has designated the Killingsworth Road district as a community development project area and has adopted a community development plan for the area; and

WHEREAS, the City of ABC owns a 5-acre tract on Killingsworth Road that is zoned for industrial use; and

WHEREAS, the City of ABC and Harvey Scott, Inc., have engaged in private negotiations for the conveyance of the 5-acre tract, to the end that Harvey Scott, Inc., may construct a broom manufacturing facility on the tract, and have reached tentative agreement on the terms for conveyance; and

WHEREAS, the ABC City Council has held a public hearing to consider whether to approve conveyance of the tract to Harvey Scott, Inc.;

THEREFORE, THE ABC CITY COUNCIL RESOLVES THAT:

1. The City is authorized to convey to Harvey Scott, Inc., the 5-acre property more particularly described below:

[Description]*

2. The appraised value of the property, as determined by an appraisal made by London Appraisal Company and on file with the city clerk, is $30,000, and Harvey Scott, Inc., has agreed to pay this price to the City upon closing.

3. The Mayor of ABC is authorized to execute all documents necessary to convey the property.

Adopted May 15, 200x.

---

* The description should be adequate to identify the property. If a surveyed description exists, it should be used, but other forms of description will adequately identify the property.

Resolution Approving Conveyance of Property Pursuant to G.S. 160A-279

WHEREAS, the City of ABC owns property in the ABC Gateway Industrial Park, which has been developed by the City; and

WHEREAS, North Carolina General Statute 160A-279 authorizes a city to convey real property by private sale to a nonprofit corporation if the city is authorized by law to appropriate money to the corporation; and

WHEREAS, North Carolina General Statute 160A-20.1 authorizes a city to contract with and appropriate money to any private entity to carry out any purpose that the city is authorized to carry out, and the city is authorized by North Carolina General Statute 158-7.1 to engage in economic development; and

WHEREAS, the City of ABC has negotiated with the ABC Economic Development Corporation [hereafter, Corporation] to convey a 15-acre tract in the ABC Gateway Industrial Park to Corporation in order that Corporation may construct a shell building on the property and then market and arrange for the sale of the building; and

WHEREAS, the construction and availability of the shell building will enhance the economic development of the City of ABC and provide jobs for its citizens;

THEREFORE, THE ABC CITY COUNCIL RESOLVES THAT:

1. The mayor of ABC is authorized to execute all documents necessary to convey fee simple title to a 15-acre tract of land in the ABC Gateway Industrial Park, more particularly described as follows:

[Description]*

2. The consideration for the conveyance is the following set of conditions and restrictions, which shall be agreed to by contract (a copy of which is attached) by the ABC Economic Development Corporation:

a. Corporation will construct on the property a shell building of at least 100,000 square feet, adaptable for either industrial or distribution purposes.

b. Corporation will market the land and building, in cooperation with the City, to potential businesses. In marketing the building and negotiating with potential buyers, Corporation will comply with the economic development goals and policies of the City.

c. Before the land and building may be sold by Corporation, the sale must be approved by the ABC City Council and the following conditions must be met:

First, the conveyance must stimulate the local economy, promote business, and result in the creation of a substantial number of jobs in the City that pay at or above the median average wage in XYZ County.

Second, the consideration for the conveyance must at least equal the fair market value of the property, as affected by whatever covenants, conditions, and restrictions the property is subject to; in determining the amount of consideration received, the City may take into account prospective property tax revenues, sales tax revenues, and other taxes and other revenues generated because of improvements made to the property over the 10 years following the conveyance.

Third, the purchaser of the property must be contractually bound to construct within 5 years any additional improvements on the property that will be the basis for the taxes and other revenues received by the city as consideration for the conveyance.

---

* The description should be adequate to identify the property. If a surveyed description exists, it should be used, but other forms of description will adequately identify the property.

Fourth, the ABC City Council must have held a public hearing on the proposed conveyance pursuant to the terms of North Carolina General Statute 158-7.1.

3. The city clerk shall publish a notice summarizing the contents of this resolution, and the property may be sold at any time after 10 days after publication of the notice.

Adopted October 12, 200x.

Notes

1. N.C. Gen. Stat. § 143-318.11(a)(4) (1999). Hereinafter the General Statutes are referred to as G.S.
2. 1993 N.C. Sess. Laws ch. 570 (1994 Reg. Sess.).
3. Letter to John L. Holshouser, Jr. (Feb. 13, 1995) (letter #171, Advisory Opinions, Department of Justice, www.jus.state.nc.us/lrframe.htm).
4. *Id.*
5. G.S. 143-318.11(a)(5) (1999).
6. Holshouser letter, *supra* note 3.
7. G.S. 143-318.11(a)(4) (1999).
8. SL 1997-290.
9. 342 N.C. 708, 467 S.E.2d 615 (1996).
10. *Id.* at 732, 467 S.E.2d at 630.
11. *Id.*
12. Pages 46–47.
13. Pages 50–51.
14. The public records exception for trade secrets is found in G.S.132-1.2 (1995).
15. G.S. 158-7.1(b)(6) (1994).
16. G.S. 153A-275 (1991) (counties) and 160A-312 (1994) (cities).
17. Page 63.
18. 342 N.C. 708, 467 S.E.2d 615 (1996).
19. *Id.* at 724, 467 S.E.2d at 625.
20. *Id.* at 731, 467 S.E.2d at 629.
21. G.S. 159-28(a) (1994). *See also* David M. Lawrence, *Local Government Finance in North Carolina*, 2d ed. (Chapel Hill, N.C.: The University of North Carolina at Chapel Hill, Institute of Government, 1990), pp. 195–96.
22. The usual procedures for disposing of property held by counties and cities are found in Chapter 160A, Article 12, of the General Statutes.
23. Lawing v. Jaynes, 285 N.C. 418, 206 S.E.2d 162 (1974). In *Sandlin v. Weaver*, 240 N.C. 703, 83 S.E.2d 806 (1954), the court quoted a passage from AMERICAN JURISPRUDENCE that included a statement that an option conveys no interest in property. The court seemed to rely on the passage as a whole in support of its interpretation of a will, but it did not specifically discuss whether an option is an interest in land. At the time, though, the prevailing national view was that options did not convey interests. *See* 3 AMERICAN LAW OF PROPERTY §11.17 (1952) (an option "transfers no title or right *in rem*").

24. George Lefcoe, *Obtaining Land and Rights for Development,* in *Thompson on Real Property,* ed. David A. Thomas (1994) §85.02(a) (an "option is an interest in land").

25. *See* G.S. 40A-2(7) (1984), which defines *property* for eminent domain actions as "any right, title, or interest in land, including leases and options to buy or sell"; and G.S. 160A-400.8(3), which allows an historic preservation commission to acquire "the fee or any lesser included interest, including options to purchase, to [historic] properties."

26. The determination of the interest's value and the calculation of consideration are discussed in the next part of this chapter.

27. G.S. 105-129.4 (1998 Cum. Supp.). This system of tax credits is discussed in Chapter 5, beginning on page 166.

28. G.S. 159C-7(1)a. (1998 Cum. Supp.). Industrial revenue bond financing is described in Chapter 2, beginning on page 48.

29. G.S. 158-7.1(d2) (1994).

30. 342 N.C. 708, 467 S.E.2d 615 (1996). At least one of the projects upheld by the court in *Maready* involved the donation of land to a company.

31. Page 63.

32. G.S. 105-487 & 105-502 (1998 Cum. Supp.).

33. G.S. 160A-211 (1994) authorizes cities to levy privilege license taxes.

34. G.S. 105-116.1 (1997) provides for sharing a portion of the state's electric utility franchise tax with cities.

35. G.S. 105-187.44 (1998 Cum. Supp.) provides for sharing the piped natural gas tax with cities.

36. G.S. 159-13(b)(14) (1994).

37. Actually the Employment Security Commission determines the "average weekly insured wage" for each county. G.S. 96-8(22) (1998 Cum. Supp.). Presumably this is the figure meant in G.S. 159-7.1(d2).

38. *See* 24 C.F.R. § 570.209 (1998); N.C. Division of Community Assistance, *Guidelines for the Community Development Block Grant Program,* 1 (found on the Internet at www.commerce.nc.us/finance/99gl.pdt) ("Program priorities are placed on permanent, full-time jobs, at least 60 percent of which are made available to persons with prior low and moderate family income status.").

39. N.C. CONST. art. I, § 32, is the basis of the constitutional prohibition. This section reads: "No person or set of persons is entitled to exclusive or separate emoluments or privileges from the community but in consideration of public services." The case applying this Privileges and Emoluments Clause to the disposition of public property is *Redevelopment Commission v. Security National Bank,* 252 N.C. 595, 114 S.E.2d 688 (1960).

40. 225 N.C. 691, 36 S.E.2d 281 (1945).

41. Other states accept this general principle. *E.g.,* Ulrich v. Board of Comm'rs, 676 P.2d 127 (Kan. 1984) (county may transfer hospital to nonprofit corporation that will provide hospital facilities; continued operation of hospital constitutes sufficient consideration).

42. G.S. 160A-267 actually states that the resolution "may, but need not, specify a minimum price" for the property. When a local government is conveying real property to a nonprofit organization, the consideration is almost certainly going to have been determined by the time the governing body adopts its resolution or order; therefore, it makes much more sense for the board's action to include the actual consideration agreed to.

4

FINANCING AND ORGANIZING

ECONOMIC DEVELOPMENT ACTIVITIES

• • •

4

FINANCING AND ORGANIZING

ECONOMIC DEVELOPMENT ACTIVITIES

• • •

Financing Current Operations

A North Carolina local government may finance current economic development operations, including incentives, with any non-earmarked revenue in that government's general fund. It may finance incentives involving the local government's enterprises (such as water or sewer line extensions) from the appropriate enterprise fund (or from the general fund). At one time the North Carolina Constitution[1] and, later, state statutes,[2] required that counties and cities receive voter approval before using property tax revenues to finance economic development. In 1983, however, the legislature amended the statutes to list economic development and industrial development among the purposes for which counties and cities may levy property taxes without voter approval, subject only to the overall rate limitation of $1.50 per $100 of valuation.[3] This action removed the only remaining limitation upon the revenues that counties and cities may use for economic development projects and activities.[4]

The Local Government Budget and Fiscal Control Act[5] governs the moneys expended by a county or city for economic development. All economic development moneys expended must be included in the local government's annual budget ordinance (or a capital project ordinance), and all such moneys must be run through the local government's books of account. These requirements extend not only to moneys raised by the local government from its own resources but also to moneys it receives for economic development from the state and federal governments (such as community development block grant funds and moneys from the state Industrial Development Fund) and from private sources.

Borrowing for Capital Projects

Some economic development capital projects are sufficiently large that the county or city will wish to fund them from borrowed moneys rather than from current revenues. The kinds of economic development projects for which a local government might wish to borrow fall into two broad categories:

infrastructure projects and projects that develop sites that are or will be owned or used by private businesses. The first category, which will be called *infrastructure development projects*, is illustrated by projects such as water and sewer line extensions to serve a manufacturing plant; other water or sewer facilities, such as pretreatment plants or water towers, that serve specific private facilities; roads constructed to give access to a manufacturing facility; downtown street and sidewalk improvements; parking facilities that serve a downtown office building; and stormwater drainage improvements undertaken as part of site improvements on private property. The second category, which will be called *business site development projects*, includes such projects as acquisition and development of land for an industrial park, acquisition of industrial or commercial sites, and construction of shell buildings. This section reviews, for both categories of projects, the state statutory framework for borrowing, the practical availability of various forms of borrowing, and federal tax limitations on borrowing.

State Law and Practice

North Carolina law permits all counties and cities to borrow money in four ways, according to the kind of security that the borrowing government gives to its lenders. Three of those ways—general obligation bonds, revenue bonds, and installment financing agreements—permit borrowing for economic development projects.[6] In addition, the thirteen counties that are within the Global TransPark Development Zone may borrow from the Zone. (The authority for those loans is sketched later in this section.) The North Carolina General Statutes (hereinafter abbreviated as G.S.) offer broad authority to borrow money for the two categories of economic development project, but as a practical matter a local government might have difficulty finding lenders for business site development projects unless the government issues general obligation bonds or a member county borrows from the Global TransPark Development Zone.

General Obligation Bonds

General obligation bonds are secured by a local government's power to levy taxes—its full faith and credit. If a local government does not meet its debt service obligations, the lender can seek a judicial order requiring the local government to levy property taxes to repay the debt. General obligation bonds offer a lender the strongest security of any local government debt, and for that reason they usually are the least expensive way for a local government to borrow.[7]

In North Carolina a county or city usually may not issue general obligation bonds unless the bond issue has been approved by the county's or the city's voters. The principal exception to the requirement of voter approval is for so-called two-thirds bonds. Under this exception a local government calculates the amount, if any, by which it reduced its outstanding general obligation debt during a fiscal year. During the next fiscal year, that local government is entitled to issue, without voter approval, general obligation bonds in an amount up to two-thirds of the reduction so calculated. That is, if in Fiscal Year One a local government reduced its general obligation debt by $1.8 million dollars by retiring that much in principal, in Fiscal Year Two that government may issue $1.2 million dollars in new general obligation bonds without voter approval.[8] Finally, any general obligation bond issue must be approved by the Local Government Commission, an agency in the Department of State Treasurer.

G.S. 159-48 lists the purposes for which counties and cities may issue general obligation bonds. With respect to infrastructure development projects, the statute lists the following purposes:

- Providing *water systems*, "including without limitation facilities for the supply, storage, treatment, and distribution of water."[9] Under this authority, a county or city may issue general obligation bonds to pay for such projects as extending water lines to a private facility, constructing new supply or treatment facilities necessary to serve a private facility, or constructing special storage facilities, such as a water tower.

- Providing *sanitary sewer systems*, "including without limitation community sewerage facilities for the collection, treatment, and disposal of sewage or septic tank systems and other on-site collection and disposal facilities or systems."[10] Under this authority, a county or city may issue general obligation bonds to pay for such projects as extending sewer lines to a private facility, adding treatment capacity to serve a private facility, or constructing an on-site system to serve a private facility.

- Providing *parking facilities*, "including on- and off-street parking."[11] Under this authority, a county or city may issue general obligation bonds to construct a parking garage in support of new private facilities.

- Providing *storm sewers and flood control facilities*, including without limitation levees, dikes, diversionary channels, drains, catch basins, and other facilities for storm water drainage."[12] Under this authority, a county or city might be able to issue general obligation bonds to finance the storm water drainage portion of site improvements at an industrial or commercial site.

- Providing *streets and sidewalks* (cities only).[13] Under this authority, a city may issue general obligation bonds to construct an access road to a new private facility or to improve downtown sidewalks in order to attract business to the downtown.

In addition to listing these purposes that fall into the infrastructure development project category, G.S. 159-48 also specifically permits counties and cities to issue general obligation bonds for the following business site development purposes: "providing industrial parks, land suitable for industrial or commercial purposes, [and] shell buildings."[14] This listing is very specific and is based on the projects included in G.S. 158-7.1(b).

G.S. 159-48 does not include in its specific list of authorized bond purposes those infrastructure or business site development projects that a local government might wish to undertake pursuant to G.S. 158-7.1(a). For example, it was suggested in Chapter 2 that Subsection (a) authorizes a county to finance construction of a road as an incentive and authorizes both counties and cities to finance, as an incentive, extension of railroad lines to a facility.[15] Neither county roads nor local government railroad construction is listed among the specific purposes for which G.S. 159-48 permits borrowing, however, leaving it unclear whether a county or city could issue general obligation bonds for this last sort of project. G.S. 159-48(b)(22) contains a catch-all provision that allows local governments to issue general obligation bonds for any purpose for which they are authorized by statewide laws to raise or appropriate money. Bond counsel, however, might not be sufficiently comfortable with the statutory authority of counties to construct roads or of cities or counties to construct railroad lines to rely on the catch-all as authority for borrowing for those purposes.

If a local government is able to secure voter approval of general obligation bonds for any of the sorts of economic development projects—in both categories—listed above, the local government should find a market for the bonds. If a local government attempts, however, to issue general obligation bonds under its two-thirds authority without voter approval, it may run into constitutional difficulties under the loan of credit provision of the state constitution.

The most important restriction in the state constitution's restrictions on loans and gifts of credit (see pages 16–25) is the requirement of voter approval of any loan or gift of credit. Because general obligation bonds are secured by the borrowing government's full faith and credit, the bonds trigger the restrictions. But if the bonds have been approved by the voters and if they are issued pursuant to clear statutory authority, general obligation bonds meet the restrictions and may be issued even if they do amount to a loan or gift of credit. Two-thirds bonds, however, are issued without voter approval and therefore do not meet the restrictions. The situations that constitute a loan or gift of credit to a private entity are detailed in Chapter 1. Clearly some of the projects authorized by G.S. 159-48 and 158-7.1 meet the relevant criteria. Therefore, if a local government attempts to issue general obligation bonds without voter approval, the intended use of bond proceeds may violate the constitution's restrictions on loans or gifts of credit. A local government must consult with bond counsel with regard to particular economic development projects it may want to finance with nonvoted general obligation debt.

Revenue Bonds

Revenue bonds are secured by the revenues generated by the bond-financed project or by the governmental enterprise of which the bond-financed project is a part. For example, water revenue bonds are secured by water system revenues, airport revenue bonds by airport revenues, and parking revenue bonds by parking system revenues. If a local government does not meet its revenue bond debt service obligations, the lender can seek a judicial order requiring the local government to increase rates in the appropriate enterprise in order to repay the debt. Obviously if a project does not generate revenues or is not part of a revenue-producing governmental enterprise, that project cannot be financed by revenue bonds. Lenders generally consider revenue bonds to be riskier than general obligation bonds, and therefore they charge a higher rate of interest for revenue bonds and require the borrowing government to agree to a range of covenants that attempt to protect the revenue-raising capacity of the bond-financed project or of the governmental enterprise of which it is a part. Revenue bonds issued by a North Carolina local government do not require voter approval, but they must be approved by the Local Government Commission.[16]

G.S. 159-81(3) lists the purposes for which counties and cities may issue revenue bonds. With respect to infrastructure development projects, the statute lists the following purposes:

- Providing *water systems or facilities*, "including all plants, works, instrumentalities and properties used or useful in obtaining, conserving, treating, and distributing water for domestic or industrial use . . . or any other public or private use."[17] Under this authority, a county or city may issue revenue bonds to pay for such projects as extending water lines to a private facility, constructing new supply or treatment facilities necessary to serve a private facility, or constructing special storage facilities, such as a water tower.
- Providing *sewage disposal systems or facilities,* "including all plants, works, instrumentalities, and properties used or useful in the collection, treatment, purification, or disposal of sewage."[18] Under this authority, a county or city may issue revenue bonds to pay for such projects as extending sewer lines to a private facility, adding treatment capacity to serve a private facility, or constructing a pretreatment plant that serves a private facility. The revenue bond statute does not include any specific reference to financing septic tank and other on-site systems (as does the general obligation bond statute); it is not clear what effect this omission might have on the scope of projects for which sewer revenue bonds might legally be used.

- Providing *public parking lots, areas, garages* and other vehicular parking structures and facilities.[19] Under this authority, a county or city probably may issue revenue bonds to construct a parking garage in support of new private facilities, although it is unclear what restrictions, if any, the word *public* places on the kinds of parking facilities that can be financed with parking revenue bonds.
- Providing *structural and natural stormwater and drainage systems* of all types.[20] Under this authority, a county or city might be able to issue revenue bonds to finance the stormwater drainage portion of site improvements at an industrial or commercial site.

In addition to this listing of purposes that fall into the infrastructure development category, G.S. 159-81(3) also specifically permits counties and cities to issue revenue bonds for the following business site development purposes: "economic development projects, including the acquisition and development of industrial parks, the acquisition and resale of land suitable for industrial or commercial purposes, and the construction and lease or sale of shell buildings."[21] This is a more expansive authorization than that in the general obligation bond statute in that the specific projects are included here as examples rather than as an exclusive listing. Therefore the revenue bond statute grants stronger authority to finance economic development projects undertaken under G.S. 158-7.1(a)—that is, projects that are not specifically listed in Subsection (b) of that statute.

This apparently expansive authority to issue revenue bonds for economic development projects of both categories seriously overstates the practical availability of this form of financing. In order to find a market for revenue bonds, it is not enough that a local government be able to demonstrate that the bond-financed project, or the governmental enterprise of which it is a part, generates revenues or earns enough money to pay debt service. Prospective bondholders will demand that the borrowing government *promise* that the project or enterprise generate a sufficient profit each year so that the revenues available to pay debt service on the bonds will be at least 120 to 140 percent of the amount of each year's debt service.[22] Moreover prospective bondholders also will demand that *independent* estimates of the earnings of the project or enterprise demonstrate that the revenues available for debt service will actually be at least 150 percent of each year's debt service. These demands of the bond market significantly affect the practical availability of revenue bond financing for economic development projects.

With respect to the infrastructure development category of projects, many public water and sewer systems generate revenues adequate to support and find a market for water or sewer revenue bonds. Parking facilities are considerably more problematic, however, because of the inherent instability of the market for parking. Suppose a city issued revenue bonds to construct a parking deck that primarily served a new downtown office building. If the principal company housed in the building merged with another company and moved its operations elsewhere, that private business decision would have an obvious effect on the market for parking in the city garage. As a result, many cities are unable to find lenders for parking revenue bonds.

Stormwater facilities are even more problematic. The statutes that authorize construction and maintenance of stormwater systems as a revenue-producing enterprise specify that stormwater system fees and charges "may not exceed the [local government's] cost of providing a stormwater and drainage system."[23] The quoted language may make it legally impossible for a local government's stormwater enterprise to earn the level of revenues that prospective bondholders demand before they will purchase revenue bonds.

With respect to the business site development category of projects, these projects present two difficulties for revenue bond financing. First, in some instances the local government intends that there be no revenues arising from the project. If a local government acquires land or constructs a shell building and intends to give the land or building to a company, there are literally no revenues to support revenue bonds. (A local government cannot characterize the property taxes it intends to count as consideration for the conveyance as enterprise revenues supporting the bond issue.) Second, even if the local government intends to recoup its investment by selling the land or the building for real monetary consideration, there is no guarantee it will find a buyer, certainly not on a schedule that fits its debt service obligations. Therefore as a practical matter there is no market for revenue bonds for this category of projects.

In summary, revenue bond financing is practicably available only for water and sewer projects and perhaps for parking projects.

Installment Financing Agreements

Installment financing agreements are secured by the project they finance. That is, if a county finances a new jail with an installment financing agreement, the loan is secured by a deed of trust on the jail; if a city finances renovations to city hall, the loan is secured by a deed of trust on city hall. If a local government does not meet its debt service obligations under an installment financing agreement, the lender can foreclose on the asset under the deed of trust.

Because of provisions in the Internal Revenue Code, local governments use two different mechanisms to borrow through installment financing agreements. Banks are allowed to make smaller loans—up to roughly $10 million—and retain the loans in their loan portfolios. Therefore, for these smaller loans, a local government can go directly to a bank and borrow the money. These are fairly simple transactions, and the interest rates are not much higher than those for comparably sized general obligation bonds. Indeed, if the loan amount is less than $2 or $3 million, installment financing agreements often have lower transaction costs than general obligation bonds and thus the overall cost might be comparable. Banks, however, may not make and retain loans above $10 million. These larger loans must be structured as certificates of deposit, which are sold to investors through the public bond market. Certificates of deposit are highly complex financings, the most complex form of borrowing that a North Carolina local government is authorized to undertake.[24]

Installment financing agreements are not subject to voter approval, but in some instances they require approval from the Local Government Commission. If an installment financing agreement is to finance any sort of *construction* or *repair*, the borrowing government must obtain Local Government Commission approval. But if the agreement is to finance the *purchase* of an asset only, even the purchase of land or a building, the borrowing government must obtain Local Government Commission approval only if both of two conditions are met. First, the government's total payment obligation under the agreement must exceed either $500,000 or one-tenth of 1 percent of the government's property tax base, whichever is smaller. Second, the agreement must extend for five years or longer. If either of the conditions is not met, the borrowing government need not seek the commission's approval.

G.S. 160A-20 is the statute that permits counties and cities to use installment financing agreements. The statute is broad: It permits installment financing of "the purchase of real or personal property" and of "the construction or repair of fixtures or improvements on real property." Therefore a county or city may use this form of financing for any capital project for which some other statute permits the local government to acquire property or construct improvements on property. Legally, then, a county or city may use an installment financing agreement to finance the full range of capital projects in both categories of economic development projects. In reality, however, installment financing agreements are not broadly available for economic development projects. Two reasons underlie the practical limitations on use of installment financings for economic development.

First, as was noted earlier, installment financing agreements are secured by a deed of trust on the asset that has been financed. Although the lender relies more on the government's general credit than on the deed of trust (see the following discussion), any lender wants the property to remain subject to the deed of trust as long as the loan remains outstanding. But with some economic development projects, those in the second category of business site development projects, the borrowing government plans to convey the property to a private company long before the loan is repaid. The obvious examples of such projects are shell buildings, industrial or commercial sites, or parcels in an industrial park. If the property is used as an incentive, the local government does not recover its costs in the property upon sale and therefore is likely still to be liable on the loan even though it no longer owns the property. The company is not likely to be willing to take title to the property subject to the government's deed of trust, and so using an installment financing agreement to finance the government's acquisition or construction costs is probably impracticable.

Second, and more fundamentally, the lender does not want to rely on the asset as the real security for the loan.

> The market does not judge the attractiveness of [installment financings] on the basis of the value of the pledged asset for private use. Rather, the market in effect rates such loans on its perception of the value of the asset to the borrowing government, on the government's willingness or unwillingness to lose the asset. If the asset is perceived as essential to the continued operation of the local government, the loan will be a stronger credit than if the asset is perceived as one that the government could lose without much harm to basic operations. The underlying assumption is that a borrowing government will be unwilling to lose an essential asset through foreclosure.[25]

If a particular kind of asset is perceived by lenders as scoring low in *essentiality*, a local government may not be able to find lenders willing to finance such an asset through an installment financing agreement. Water and sewer lines and facilities score high in essentiality and therefore are relatively easy to finance through installment financing agreements. Because of federal environmental mandates, stormwater systems also might be considered relatively high in essentiality. Parking facilities do not score as well, however, and industrial parks, industrial sites, and shell buildings score even lower. If the economy turns down and a local government finds itself with a shell building it cannot sell or lease, lenders perceive the government as more likely to walk away from the shell building than most other governmental activities. For that reason, many lenders are unwilling to make loans through installment financing agreements for business site development projects, the second category of economic development projects.

Global TransPark Development Zone Loans

There is one exception to the gloomy prediction just made about whether a local government can find a lender for an installment financing of an economic development project. The Global TransPark Development Zone, the thirteen-county special district surrounding the Global TransPark cargo airport, has levied a temporary registration tax on all motor vehicles resident within the zone, and the enabling legislation under which it did so requires that 85 percent of the proceeds from this tax be placed in a special trust account.[26] (In addition, the General Assembly has made at least one special appropriation to the Zone, which also has been placed in the trust account.) The Zone's loan policies permit loans from the trust account to the thirteen counties for economic development projects in both categories defined earlier,[27] and the Zone makes both secured and unsecured loans. Its loans may be unsecured if they are for less than $200,000 or if they are for a project undertaken pursuant to G.S. 158-7.1 and for which the county has followed the procedural requirements of that statute. Otherwise the Zone requires that the borrowing county provide security. The most appropriate vehicle by which a county might do so is an installment financing agreement.

If a county borrows money from the Global TransPark Development Zone through an installment financing agreement, the agreement is subject to Local Government Commission approval as described above. If the Zone makes an unsecured loan to a county, the loan is subject to the commission's approval only if two conditions are met. First, the repayment period must extend for five years or more. Second, the amount of the loan plus interest must exceed the lesser of $500,000 or one-tenth of 1 percent of the county's tax base. The approval requirement does not, however, depend on whether the county will use the proceeds for construction or for purchase, and in that way the unsecured loan differs from an installment financing agreement.

Federal Tax Treatment of Debt Issued for Economic Development Projects

In general the Internal Revenue Code (the Code) excludes from federal taxation the interest on state and local government bonds.[28] (These bonds are usually referred to collectively as *municipal bonds*. They also include installment financing agreements, including certificates of participation.) Not all bonds issued by state and local governments, however, are tax-exempt under federal law.[29] Federal tax policy attempts to restrict the use of tax-exempt bonds by state and local governments to those projects that build or buy assets that are used by the government itself or by the public generally, so-called traditional governmental projects. If the proceeds of a municipal bond issue are used to finance the activities of private persons or entities, the Code directs that, in many cases, the interest paid on that bond issue be included in taxable income. Plainly one usual effect of the kinds of economic development financing projects under discussion in this chapter is to benefit a private company in its business.

Private Activity Bonds

Under federal law, if a private company participates in the ownership or operation of a bond-financed project or otherwise benefits from the project, the bond issue may become a *private activity* bond issue.[30] Although the Code makes some exceptions (discussed below), in general the interest paid on a private activity bond issue is not exempt from federal income tax.[31] The Code's definition of a private activity bond issue and the implementing tax regulations are dense and complex, and the following discussion makes no attempt to convey the details of either. Rather it seeks to summarize briefly some rules on private activity bonds so that local officials can recognize when they might be facing a taxable debt issue. Officials should consult with their bond counsel about the details of any particular project to determine whether the bonds will be tax-exempt or taxable.

The Code establishes two basic tests under which a bond issue might be classified as a private activity bond. The test more likely to be implicated in economic development projects looks to two elements: the use of the bond proceeds and the sources of money and security for repayment of the debt.[32] If more than ten percent of the bond-financed project is used in the trade or business of a private person or entity (the *private business use* test), and if more than ten percent of the debt service on the bond issue is secured by, or derived from payments made with respect to, bond-financed property used by a private business (the *private security or payment* test), the bond issue is a private activity bond. (Both tests must be satisfied for the bond issue to become a private activity bond. If one but not the other is satisfied, the bond issue is a governmental bond and the interest is tax-exempt. It should be noted, finally, that satisfying—or "passing"—these two tests has a negative outcome: The bonds lose their tax exemption.)

Beginning with the private business use test, the range of projects that satisfies the test under these rules is best suggested by a series of examples, based on examples in the tax regulations promulgated by the U.S. Treasury.[33]

- A local government borrows money and constructs an industrial building. The building is sold or leased to a manufacturing company. The bond issue satisfies the private business use test because a private company is using the bond-financed project. This is true whether the building is given to the company or sold or leased at a market rate.[34]
- A local government borrows money and constructs a sewage pretreatment plant on land adjoining a manufacturing plant. Although the sewage pretreatment plant theoretically will be available to treat sewage from any source, as a practical matter the manufacturing plant will be the only customer. The bond issue satisfies the private business use test

because the manufacturing plant derives a special economic benefit from the bond-financed project.[35] This outcome should be contrasted with a project for which a local government uses borrowed money to construct a water tower near a manufacturing plant primarily to allow sprinklers to be installed at the plant, but the water tower will also serve other customers. Because of the water tower's more general availability, the bond issue does not satisfy the private business use test.

- A local government borrows money and constructs a parking deck adjacent to a downtown office building. Although the deck is open to the public generally, the city gives employees of the building's tenants priority for long-term leases of parking spaces.[36] Because of that priority, the bond issue satisfies the private business use test if at least ten percent of the spaces are leased to those employees. If no priority is offered, the parking deck is considered to serve the general public and the bond issue does not satisfy the private business use test. (A comparable deck in a remote location and adjoining a private industrial or commercial facility, even if "open" to the public generally, might be treated like the sewage pretreatment plant noted above. It probably satisfies the private business use test.)
- A local government borrows money and constructs a road into a manufacturing plant. Although the plant is the only facility currently located along the road, because it is open to the general public, it does not satisfy the private business use test.[37] The same result probably would follow if a local government borrowed money to extend utility lines to a private facility because others could tap into the lines over time.

If a bond issue satisfies the private business use test, the private security or payment test is applied. (Recall that a bond issue must satisfy both tests to become a private activity bond.) The value of any property that is security for the debt and that is used by a private entity is combined with the present value of any lease, sale, or other payments from private users of bond-financed property that are available to pay debt service. This total is compared with the present value of debt service requirements on the bonds. If the privately used property and private payments total more than ten percent of the debt service requirements, the private security and payment test is satisfied.[38]

Four points about this test are important in the economic development context. First, generally applicable tax payments (such as property tax payments) are not counted in determining the private user's contribution to debt service.[39] Second, unlike taxes, generally applicable user charges are counted in determining the private user's contributions. Only that portion of the charges attributable to debt service, however, is counted. The portion used for general operating and maintenance costs is not counted. Third, if the borrowing is done through an installment financing agreement, so that it is secured by the financed asset, private use of that asset probably will cause the bond issue to satisfy the private security and payment test. Finally, if a local government gives a bond-financed facility to the private user, who pays nothing for the facility (that is, the facility is used as an incentive), there is no private payment. In such a case, as long as the facility does not continue as security for the debt, the bonds are not private activity bonds but rather governmental bonds and are tax-exempt. Let's apply the private security and payment test to the examples set out above.

- A local government borrows money through general obligation bonds and constructs an industrial building and then conveys the building to a private company. If the company pays for the building and if the present value of the company's total payments exceeds ten percent of the present value of total debt service on the bonds, the private payment test is satisfied. If, however, the local government gives the building to the company, the private security and payment test is not satisfied and the bonds remain tax-exempt.[40]
- A local government borrows money and constructs a sewage pretreatment plant on land adjoining a manufacturing plant. The company's payments for sewage treatment qualify as private payments. If the present value of that portion of the payments made during the term of the bond issue and attributable to debt service is more than ten percent of total debt service, the private security and payment test is satisfied.
- A local government borrows money and constructs a parking deck adjacent to a downtown office building, giving the building's tenants priority in use of the deck. If expected payments from tenants exceed ten percent of debt service, the private security and payment test is satisfied.

Qualified Private Activity Bonds

The Internal Revenue Code exempts from taxable income interest on several categories of private activity bonds collectively known as *qualified* private activity bonds.[41] One category of qualified private activity bonds is "small-issue" industrial revenue bonds of the sort used in North Carolina's industrial revenue bond program. This program is described in Chapter 2 (see pages 48–50).[42] A second category consists of so-called *exempt facilities*, which include facilities that are part of a public water system and facilities that are part of a public sewage system.[43] Even when these bonds benefit a private company, their interest remains tax exempt because they finance exempt facilities. To qualify as exempt facilities, however, water or sewer facilities must serve the general public. Water or sewer lines serve the general public, as does a sewage treatment facility and a water tower (as long as there are other possible users of the treatment facility or water tower). The tax regulations state, however, that a sewage *pretreatment* facility does not serve the general public but only the company whose sewage is being treated before entering the public system. Therefore a private activity bond issue used to finance such a facility is not a *qualified* private activity bond and the interest on it is not exempt from federal income tax.[44]

Table 3 summarizes the likely tax treatment of bonds issued to finance economic development projects of the sort authorized by G.S. 158-7.1 and described in this section. Readers should remember, however, that the tax status of any issue is likely to be complex and dependent on the details of the issue. Therefore readers should rely upon the advice of bond counsel.

Organizing Economic Development Activities

North Carolina local governments use a variety of organizations to manage their economic development activities. This section reviews three basic organizational structures: the city or county line department; the economic development commission established pursuant to G.S. Chapter 158, Article 2; and the nonprofit corporation established pursuant to G.S. Chapter 55A. The discussion reviews *legal* characteristics that might differ among the organizational structures. Nonlegal issues, of course, might cause a local government to select one structure over another. It also is possible for a local government to use more than one of these structures in its economic development operation. A county might, for example, have a county economic development department and also be served by (and contribute money to) a private economic development corporation.

The discussion that follows reviews the status of each of the following six legal characteristics for each of the organizational structures.

Organizational powers. Does this organizational form have legal authority to (1) own real property and convey real property to private companies, (2) borrow money, (3) construct shell buildings, or (4) develop and own an industrial park?

Financial and tax issues. Is this organizational form subject to the Local Government Budget and Fiscal Control Act? Is this organizational form exempt from federal or state income tax? Is property held by this organizational form exempt from property tax? May individuals or businesses deduct from their taxable income contributions made to this organizational form?

Procedural issues. Is this organizational form subject to the public records or open meetings laws? Must this organizational form comply with G.S. 158-7.1(c) (public hearing before making appropriation or expenditure for economic development), 158-7.1(d) (public hearing before conveying real property for economic development), or 158-7.1(d2) (procedural requirements before using real property as an incentive)?

Table 3
Tax Treatment of Bonds That Finance Economic Development Projects

Project	Status	Tax-Exempt?
Water tower	Governmental	Yes
Sewage line extension	Governmental	Yes
Sewage pretreatment plant	Private activity	No
Parking garage, no priority to nearby tenants	Governmental	Yes
Parking garage, priority to nearby tenants	Private activity	No
Public road providing access to plant	Governmental	Yes
Stormwater improvements on industrial site	Private activity	No
Industrial park	Private activity	No
Industrial site, sold to company	Private activity	No
Industrial site, given to company	Governmental	Yes
Shell building	Private activity*	No
Railroad spur to plant; line operated by RR with no revenues to government	Governmental**	Yes

* It is possible to structure this project as a small-issue industrial development bond, which is a qualified private activity bond. Therefore the interest would not be taxable. (See note 42).

** If the railroad spur was financed with an installment financing agreement, so that the spur was security for the debt, it would satisfy the private activity bond tests and the financing would be taxable.

Policy coordination issues. How closely may a city council or board of county commissioners control this organizational form? How closely may a city or county manager control or coordinate the activities of this organizational form? What kind of financial control does a county or city have over this organizational form?

Employee benefits. Are the employees of this organizational form public employees with the benefits and burdens associated with that status?

Private sector involvement. In what ways does this organizational form permit or require involvement by the private sector in economic development activities?

The City or County Line Department

A local government can manage its economic development activities through a line department of the government, either as a separate economic development department or as part of another department, such as a department of planning and development. Counties and cities enjoy broad authority to create, combine, and abolish departments and assign responsibilities to departments,[45] and they can use that authority for economic development activities.

Organizational Powers

A county or city engaging in economic development through a department enjoys all of the powers to undertake economic development activities set out in this book. The government may acquire and convey real property, borrow money, build and convey shell buildings, and own and develop industrial parks. It may offer incentives to private companies. It also is subject to constitutional and statutory limitations on those powers, although those limitations are not many. The government may not, however, guarantee loans made to and other obligations of private companies; it may not offer real property as an incentive unless it will receive the value of the property in taxes and other revenues within ten years; and there are certain projects for which it may not borrow money in certain ways.

Financial and Tax Issues

A county or city is subject to the Local Government Budget and Fiscal Control Act. All moneys received by the county or city must be run through the local government's books of account, and all of the county's or city's expenditures must be authorized in either the annual budget ordinance or a separate capital project or grant project ordinance.

Counties and cities enjoy broad tax advantages. Their income is not subject to federal or state income tax.[46] Their property is not subject to property tax by themselves or another government.[47] Individuals or businesses making gifts to them may deduct the payments as charitable contributions.[48]

Procedural Issues

Counties and cities must comply with all the procedural requirements described in Chapter 3 of this book, both the open meetings and public records laws and the procedural requirements of G.S. 158-7.1.

Policy Coordination Issues

If economic development is located in a county or city department, the governing board has as much control over it as over any other department and the county or city manager has as much managerial control as over other departments. As a result, it is probably easier to coordinate economic development activities with other activities of the government when economic development is provided through a department than when it is organized in some other way.

Employee Benefits

The employees of a county or city line department are public employees. They are members of the Local Government Employees Retirement System (or any local alternative to that system). Federal tax law permits certain fringe benefit programs to be offered only to governmental employees. The federal constitution establishes special protections for public employees vis-à-vis their employers, especially in the area of free speech.

Private Sector Involvement

If a local government manages economic development through a department, it has no automatic mechanism for involving the local business community in economic development efforts. (If the business community is not involved in and supportive of economic development, governmental efforts might be unavailing. Companies thinking of locating in a community always want to talk with existing businesses; if those businesses are negative about new companies or about the local government, the prospective company will probably go elsewhere.) The government can, though, create mechanisms for private sector involvement. For example, North Carolina law gives counties and cities broad authority to create advisory boards and commissions for any of their activities.[49] A county or city with an economic development department can establish an economic development advisory commission and seek the commission's involvement in a variety of economic development activities. Less structurally, a department can present an annual economic development update to community business leaders to keep them informed about the local economy and the government's economic development programs and plans. And a comprehensive economic development program includes regular meetings between economic development officials and the owners or managers of existing businesses so that the officials can learn about and discuss the plans, problems, and frustrations of the businesses.

Statutory Economic Development Commission

G.S. 158-8 authorizes the governing body of any county or city to create an economic development commission. Such a commission may have from three to nine members, with the number, their terms, and their compensation (if any) established by the governing body. The remainder of Article 2 of Chapter 158 sets out the powers of such a commission. G.S. 158-13 indicates the general idea of how such a commission is to work: It is to receive the county's or city's economic development program from the appropriate planning agency; formulate projects to implement the program; undertake general economic development activities such as surveys, advertisement, and business assistance; and encourage the development of private development corporations.

Organizational Powers

The General Statutes do not give economic development commissions the authority to undertake the kinds of economic development projects listed in G.S. 158-7.1. Economic development commissions have no authority to acquire an industrial or commercial site, to acquire land for and develop an industrial park, or to construct and sell a shell building.[50] They have no authority to borrow money. Thus while a local government can charge a commission with general economic development activities—such as economic development planning, business advertisement, business assistance, and coordinating business location and expansion activities—the county or city itself must acquire, develop, or improve land, and only the county or the city itself may borrow money.

Financial and Tax Issues

An economic development commission is part of a county or city government and therefore subject to the Local Government Budget and Fiscal Control Act. All moneys received by a commission must be run through the county's or city's books of account, and all of the commission's expenditures must be authorized in either the county's or the city's annual budget ordinance or in a separate capital project or grant project ordinance adopted by the county commissioners or city council.

As a part of county or city government, an economic development commission enjoys the same broad tax advantages of county or city government. Its income is not subject to federal or state income tax.[51] Any real or personal property owned by an economic development commission for administrative purposes is exempt from property tax.[52] Individuals or businesses making gifts to a commission may deduct the payments as charitable contributions.[53]

Procedural Issues

Economic development commissions, as part of local government, are subject to both the open meetings and the public records law. Because such commissions have no statutory authority to offer economic development incentives, however, the procedural requirements of G.S. 158-7.1 are irrelevant to them.

Policy Coordination Issues

One reason to set up a separate commission for economic development is to achieve some degree of independence for economic development activities from the county or city governing board and county or city manager. The extent of independence can differ from one community to another.

There is always budgeting dependence. An economic development commission is part of the county or city for the purposes of budgeting and fiscal control. The governing body has as much control over appropriations to an economic development commission as it does over those to an economic development line department.

The county's or the city's ability to control and coordinate with the employees of a commission is more difficult (if even desired). G.S. 158-10 authorizes economic development commissions, within the limits of their appropriations, to hire and set the pay of their own employees. Thus the county or city manager does not appoint or supervise these employees. It is, of course, possible for the county or city governing body not to appropriate any money to an economic development commission for personnel. Such a step would in effect force the commission to use county or city employees to carry out its work. In most cases, though, economic development commissions appoint their own employees.

Finally, a governing body can control (or not) the independence of an economic development commission through its power to appoint members of the commission. If the governing body dislikes the direction taken by a commission, it can appoint new members as terms expire. Indeed a governing body can go further: It can restructure the commission by adding members or changing term lengths, and as a last resort it can abolish a commission.

Employee Benefits

The employees of an economic development commission are public employees. They are members of the Local Government Employees Retirement System (or any local alternative to that system). Federal tax law permits certain fringe benefit programs to be offered only to governmental employees. The federal constitution establishes special protections for public employees vis-à-vis their employers, especially in the area of free speech.

Private Sector Involvement

Local governments use operating and advisory commissions to involve citizens in government operations and policy making, and one likely purpose of the economic development commission statute is to provide local business people, through their membership on the commission, a formal role in economic development. Because commission members provide direction to the commission's employees, a commission probably gives its members a potentially stronger role in economic development policy than is true of a board established simply to advise a city or county line department.

Nonprofit Corporations

A nonprofit corporation engaged in economic development may take a wide variety of forms. A traditional example is the local chamber of commerce; local governments contracted with chambers for economic development activities during much of the twentieth century.[54] In recent decades, local governments have been contracting with organizations established specifically to undertake economic development: economic development corporations, committees of 100, and similar organizations. Local governments also have been contracting with and contributing to nonprofit organizations with specialized economic development goals: to encourage development of a specific community within the county or city, to operate a business incubator, to encourage a specific kind of business, such as tourism.

Nonprofit corporations engaged in economic development may or may not be independent of the county or city. On their face, nonprofit corporations are private entities; they are set up under a state statute (G.S. Chapter 55A) that is intended to authorize private corporations rather than government agencies. Sometimes, however, a local government is actively involved in the creation or operation of a nonprofit corporation. The government seeks freedom from some of the constraints that apply to governments but not to the private sector; but the government doesn't want the nonprofit corporation to operate fully free of governmental control. Thus the local government retains some formal control over the nonprofit: appointing or approving some or all members of the board of directors, approving the corporation's annual budget, placing public employees on the board of directors. In addition, a government may provide assistance to the corporation through appropriations, loaned employees, or office space. At some point the government's formal controls over and other relationships to the nonprofit become so significant that the courts treat the corporation as if it were a governmental agency and not a private organization. Two North Carolina court decisions, both involving hospitals, illustrate this point.

In *Coats v. Sampson County Memorial Hospital, Inc.*,[55] the plaintiff sued the hospital in a county other than the one in which the hospital was located. A venue statute required that local government agencies be sued in the county in which they were located, and the hospital argued that the statute applied to it. Although the hospital was organized as a private nonprofit corporation, the county commissioners appointed its board of directors, and it occupied a county-owned hospital. Without much discussion, the state supreme court held that the hospital was a county agency and that the local government venue statute applied.

In *News & Observer Publishing Company v. Wake County Hospital System, Inc.*,[56] the newspaper sought records held by the hospital system, which was organized as a nonprofit corporation. The newspaper was proceeding pursuant to the state public records law, and the hospital claimed that, because it was organized as a nonprofit corporation, the records statute did not apply. The court agreed with the newspaper. It noted that the county commissioners approved appointments to the hospital corporation's board of directors, the commissioners approved the corporation's annual budget, the county was entitled to audit the corporation's books, the corporation operated the county's hospital under a one-dollar-a-year lease, the hospital's revenues were pledged to payment of county hospital bonds, and the corporation could not change its articles of incorporation without county approval. In total, these connections gave the county sufficient control over the corporation that the latter was characterized as a county agency.

Organizational Powers

The private sector operates under a different presumption with respect to organizational powers than does the public sector. A local government in North Carolina may undertake only those activities that it has statutory authority to undertake; a private organization can undertake any activity permitted by law, unless its charter imposes additional limitations.[57] For that reason, absent some charter-based prohibition, a nonprofit corporation may undertake any sort of economic development activity, including some (such as loan guarantees) prohibited to counties and cities. Similarly a nonprofit corporation may borrow money for any purpose and through any form for which it can find lenders. The restrictions on its power to borrow are practical (i.e., its ability to repay), not legal.

If a nonprofit corporation is too closely tied to a local government, however, it may find that its power to borrow or otherwise use its credit is subsumed within that of the local government. For example, assume that a county board of commissioners appoints all of the members of the corporation's board of directors and must approve the corporation's annual budget. Although neither of the two cases discussed earlier involved borrowing, a court might extend its rationale to the question of whether such a corporation may borrow on its own. It would not be surprising if a court were to hold that the corporation is actually a county agency and therefore any borrowing must be done on its behalf by the county government; it can no more borrow itself than can the county board of health.

Financial and Tax Issues

Budgeting and accounting. As private organizations, nonprofit corporations engaged in economic development are not subject to the Local Government Budget and Fiscal Control Act. They are not included in the annual budget ordinance of the county or city, and typically their funds do not run through the books of account of the county or city. As a matter of practice, this is true even for those corporations subject to considerable formal control by a county or city. A county or city may find, though, that it must include the finances of such a controlled corporation in the county's or city's annual financial statements. The accounting profession's rule-making entity, the Governmental Accounting Standards Board, is not restricted by state law in determining whether an apparently private organization is sufficiently related to a county or city so that the organization's financial results must be reflected in the government's audited financial statements.

Federal income tax. Just because an organization is established pursuant to North Carolina's nonprofit corporation statute does not mean that the corporation's income is exempt from federal income tax. That is a matter of federal tax law, and Section 501(c) of the Internal Revenue Code specifies the kinds of nonprofit organizations that are exempt from federal tax. It appears that nonprofit corporations engaged in the kinds of economic development activities discussed in this book are exempt organizations under Section 501—that is, their income is not subject to federal income tax. What is not clear is which paragraph of Section 501(c) supports their exemption. The importance of the source of the exemption is not in whether the exempt organization has to pay tax on its exempt activities—it does not—but on whether private donors to the organization may treat their gifts as *charitable* contributions and therefore deduct them from their otherwise taxable income.

Section 501(c) includes three paragraphs that might be the source of exemption for a nonprofit corporation engaged in economic development. The first of these is Section 501(c)(3), which extends an exemption to organizations organized and operated exclusively for religious, charitable, scientific, testing for public safety, literacy, or educational purposes. If economic development organizations fit within this category, they do so as charitable organizations.[58]

Clearly an economic development organization that focuses its work in an economically depressed area is engaged in charitable work and is entitled to exemption under Section 502(c)(3). The Internal Revenue Service (IRS) has characterized the work of such an organization as charitable because it is engaged in relieving poverty, reducing community tensions that arise from widespread unemployment, and combating the community's physical and personal deterioration.[59]

The IRS, however, has also extended Section 501(c)(3) status to economic development organizations that do not focus solely on deteriorating areas but operate communitywide.[60] The IRS recognizes as a charitable activity actions that lessen the burdens of government, and this probably is the basis for extending Section 501(c)(3) status to communitywide economic development organizations. If an organization assumes responsibility for an activity that otherwise would be the province of government, and thereby lessens the government's need to engage in the activity, the IRS accepts that the organization is engaged in a charitable activity.[61] The determination of whether a specific organization is so engaged is fact-based, and apparently the IRS will consider such issues as whether the government exercises some control over the organization's operations, whether the government provides funding to the organization, whether the organization meets expenses that the government would have to otherwise, and whether the government itself may undertake the organization's activities.[62] The more "yes" answers, the better.[63]

The second paragraph is Section 501(c)(4), which extends an exemption to civic leagues and other organizations organized and operated exclusively for the promotion of social welfare. The tax regulations characterize organizations qualifying for exemption under this paragraph as "promoting in some way the common good and general welfare of the people of the community" and as bringing about "civic betterments and social improvements." The published revenue rulings grant exemption under this paragraph to organizations that are engaged in activities comparable to those of the clearly charitable organizations discussed in the preceding paragraph—that is, organizations involved in economic development in economically distressed areas.[64] But the IRS has issued determination letters that grant exemption under Section 501(c)(4) to communitywide economic development corporations.

The third paragraph is Section 501(c)(6), which extends an exemption to business leagues, chambers of commerce, boards of trade, and other groups with common business interests. The Internal Revenue Service has identified the common business interest of a chamber of commerce as the general economic welfare of a community,[65] a purpose shared by other nonprofit corporations engaged in economic development. The IRS has granted the exemption to a chamber of commerce that was developing an industrial park, to another organization that was

constructing and marketing a shell building, and to a community group organized to attract and arrange national conventions.[66]

Thus Section 501(c) includes three potential bases for exempting from federal
income tax a nonprofit corporation engaged in economic development. Of the
three, only Section 501(c)(3) status as a charitable organization carries the additional benefit that donations to the organization can be deducted as charitable
contributions;[67] it also carries the associated burden of limitations on the
organization's ability to lobby.[68] Because of the charitable deduction possibility,
an organization might wish to seek exemption under paragraph (c)(3) in the first
instance.

State income tax. Under G.S. 105-130.11(a), if a nonprofit organization is
exempt from federal income tax, it is exempt also from state income tax.

Deductibility of contributions. As was discussed earlier in the section on
federal income taxes, if a nonprofit corporation engaged in economic development is determined to be exempt from taxation pursuant to Section 501(c)(3) of
the Internal Revenue Code, the Code allows taxpayers to deduct contributions
to the corporation as charitable contributions. Contributions to such an organization are deductible also for state income tax purposes.[69] If the organization is
determined to be exempt pursuant to Section 501(c)(4) or 501(c)(6), however, the
only basis for deducting contributions would be to determine that they were
ordinary and necessary business expenses of the entity making the contribution. To be deductible, the contributions must bear a direct relationship to the
donor's business and be made with a reasonable expectation of a financial return that is commensurate with the contribution.[70]

Property taxes. There is no exemption or classification of property for taxes
that applies to nonprofit economic development organizations. Therefore their
property is fully subject to local property taxes.

Procedural Issues

If a nonprofit corporation is independent of local government, and its only
connection is a contract to engage in economic development on behalf of one or
more local governments, it is not subject to the open meetings law or the public records law. It is a private organization, and those statutes do not apply to
private organizations. If a nonprofit corporation is closely connected to local
government, however, as was the hospital corporation involved in the earlier
discussion of *News & Observer Publishing Company v. Wake County Hospital
System, Inc.*,[71] then the corporation is considered an agency of local government
and is subject to the open meetings and public records statutes.

The situation with respect to the procedural requirements of G.S. 158-7.1 is
somewhat more complex. The statute applies to counties and cities only; it makes

no reference to nonprofit corporations engaged in economic development. For that reason, a nonprofit need not hold any of the hearings required by the statute. But a nonprofit might find nonetheless that the hearing requirements affect its operations, if it has received money or property from a county or city.

Assume two kinds of transactions between a county or city on the one hand and a nonprofit corporation on the other. First, the county or city gives a parcel of property to the nonprofit and asks the nonprofit to market the parcel to an industrial company. Second, the county or city appropriates money to the nonprofit and asks the nonprofit to buy a parcel of property and then market the parcel to an industrial company. The concluding section in Chapter 3 of this book suggests that in the first situation the county or city should hold the property conveyance hearing required by G.S. 158-7.1(d) once the nonprofit corporation is ready to convey the property to a company. That is, the local government may not obviate the need for the hearing by conveying the property to a nonprofit organization, but the burden of the hearing probably remains with the county or city rather than being transferred to the corporation along with the property. Similarly a local government ought not to be able to avoid the public discussion of economic development expenditures required by G.S. 158-7.1(c) by appropriating money to a nonprofit and having the nonprofit make the specific expenditures. G.S. 158-7.2 requires a county or city that appropriates money to another entity for economic development to approve all expenditures made by the other entity before those expenditures are made. (This requirement is discussed further in the next section.) Putting this requirement together with the hearing requirement of G.S. 158-7.1(c) suggests the following procedure when money is appropriated to a nonprofit for discrete economic development projects: The local government need not hold a hearing at the time that it makes the appropriation to the corporation but rather when the corporation is about to make one or a series of expenditures for an economic development project using the money appropriated from the county or city. The county or city should then hold the public hearing, following the general outline of G.S. 158-7.1(c) and following the hearing approve the expenditure pursuant to G.S. 158-7.2.

Policy Coordination Issues

A county or city normally has less ability to control the operations of a nonprofit corporation engaged in economic development than the operations of the other two organizational structures, even when the nonprofit's board of directors is appointed by a local government governing body and when the governing body must approve the nonprofit's budget each year. In the latter case, the relationship between the local government and the nonprofit is quite close to the relationship between a local government and an economic development commission established pursuant to G.S. Chapter 158, but it is not exactly the same. The economic development commission is part of the local government's budget ordinance, subject to the continuing fiscal control of the county or city finance department. The nonprofit corporation receives an appropriation from the local government, but the money is thereafter administered by the corporation itself.

If the nonprofit is truly independent, its relationship to the local government is no different from that of any other contracting entity. The only vehicle that a local government has for influencing the operations of such a nonprofit is its appropriation to the nonprofit and any express contract that accompanies the appropriation.

Approval of expenditures. As was noted in the preceding section, G.S. 158-7.2 provides:

> In the event funds appropriated for the purposes of [G.S. 158-7.1] are turned over to any agency or organization other than the county or city for expenditure, no such expenditure shall be made until the county or city has approved the same.

This is a perplexing statute if read literally. So read, it seems to require that a county or city that has appropriated money to a nongovernmental economic development agency approve each expenditure that the agency proposes to make using public funds. If the agency wishes to purchase $125 of office supplies, the county or city must first give its okay. Such a reading seems so cumbersome that the statute cries out for some other understanding of its meaning.

The statute is probably based on the procedures followed by the city of Raleigh in the late 1950s, which were given specific approval by the state supreme court. In *Dennis v. Raleigh*,[72] the issue was whether the city could appropriate funds for economic development to the local chamber of commerce. Some years earlier the supreme court had invalidated an appropriation made by the city of Burlington to its local chamber of commerce. Burlington's appropriations had been unspecific, and the chamber had mingled the city money with its other revenues. The court was concerned that public money might be spent on nonpublic activities.[73] In apparent response to this judicial concern, Raleigh had made its appropriation to the chamber more specific; it was to be used for "advertising the advantages of the city . . . in an effort to secure the location of new industry within the city." In addition, the city retained the power to approve specific advertisements before any money was expended.[74] The court upheld the Raleigh appropriation.

This history gives some support to the literal reading of the statute, but it also suggests an alternative reading. If the nongovernmental entity proposes a specific economic development program, the county or city appropriating the money can give approval to the specific programmatic design. The nongovernmental entity may then make expenditures within the approved program without further approvals from the government. Programmatic approval could be used for such matters as developing an economic development plan, undertaking a program to visit and support existing businesses, undertaking a program of general business recruitment, or operating a microloan pool for small businesses. On the other hand, if the nongovernmental entity proposes to offer an incentive to a specific company or to engage in any of the projects listed in G.S. 158-7.1(b) and to use county or city money to do so, the statute probably requires a discrete approval by the county or city of such a significant use of its funds. As was noted in the preceding section, that approval might best be given after a public hearing that follows the procedures of G.S. 158-7.1(c).

Annual accounting. In addition to requiring that the county or city approve expenditures by any nongovernmental agency receiving economic development funds, G.S. 158-7.2 also requires that the agency account for its expenditures to the county or city at the end of each fiscal year. The agency should provide to the county or city a listing of the uses it has made of the county's or city's money to ensure that those uses were consistent with the appropriation made to the agency and with the expenditure approvals made by the county or city.

Employee Benefits

The employees of a nonprofit corporation are not public employees. Therefore the various pension and benefit programs that are available to public employees are not available to these employees. Furthermore the constitutional protections available to public employees because their employer is a governmental entity also are unavailable to employees of private organizations.

Private Sector Involvement

The nonprofit corporation offers the strongest possibilities for involvement of the private business sector in economic development activities. If the corporation is closely controlled by a county or city, the governing body of the county or city usually appoints some or all of the members of the corporation's board of directors; it's likely that local business people will be among those selected. If the corporation is structurally independent of local government, it is probable that it was established by and is controlled by the local business community.

Table 4
Summary of Legal Characteristics of Economic Development Organizations

Characteristic	Line Department	Economic Development Commission	Dependent Nonprofit	Inde-pendent Nonprofit
Organizational Powers				
Own property	Yes	No	Yes	Yes
Develop industrial park	Yes	No	Yes	Yes
Construct shell building	Yes	No	Yes	Yes
Borrow money	Yes	No	Yes	Yes
Guarantee private loans	No	No	Probably no	Yes
Finance and Taxation				
Subject to Budget/Fiscal Control Act	Yes	Yes	No	No
Income tax status	Exempt	Exempt	Exempt	Exempt
Contributions deductible	Yes	Yes	If 501(c)(3)	If 501(c)(3)
Property tax status	Exempt	Exempt	Taxable	Taxable
Procedural Issues				
Subject to Open Meetings/ Public Records laws	Yes	Yes	Yes	No
Follow 158-7.1 procedures	Yes	NA	No	No
Policy Coordination/Control				
Policy coordination	High	Fair	Fair	Low
Financial control	Appropriation	Appropriation	Contract	Contract
Employee Benefits	Public	Public	Private	Private
Private Sector Involvement	Low	Good	Good	High

Table 4 summarizes the distinctions between the different possible organizational structures.

Notes

1. Before 1973, the state constitution required local governments to secure voter approval before levying local taxes for "non-necessary expenses" of local government. N.C. Const. art. VII, § 7 (repealed 1973). Whether a local government expense was necessary or not was a judicial question, and thus the state supreme court decided what local government activities could be funded by property taxes without voter approval. In *Ketchie v. Hedrick*, 186 N.C. 392, 119 S.E. 767 (1923), the court held that economic development was not a necessary expense, thereby requiring voter approval for the levy of local taxes for that purpose. In 1973, Section 2(5) of Article V of the state constitution came into effect and shifted from the supreme court to the General Assembly the deci-

sion as to which local government activities could be funded by property taxes without voter approval.

2. The statutes through which the General Assembly regulates whether voter approval is necessary to levy property taxes are N.C. Gen. Stat. 153A-149 for counties and 160A-209 for cities. From 1973 until 1983, both of these statutes required voter approval before property taxes could be levied for economic or industrial development. Hereinafter the General Statutes will be abbreviated as G.S.

3. 1983 N.C. Sess. Laws ch. 511.

4. There is still some statutory residue from the time when local governments could not levy property taxes for economic development without voter approval. Chapter 158, Article 3 (Tax Election for Industrial Development Purposes), authorizes twenty-one counties to call a referendum on whether to levy property taxes, up to a rate of five cents, for industrial development; if a referendum is successful, the county commissioners may establish an industrial development commission. There no longer is a need for such statutory authority.

5. Chapter 159, Article 3, of the General Statutes.

6. The fourth form of borrowing is through special obligation bonds, but these are only available for solid waste projects. G.S. 159I-30 (1997). *See also,* David M. Lawrence, *Financing Capital Projects in North Carolina,* 2d ed. (Chapel Hill, N.C.: Institute of Government, The University of North Carolina at Chapel Hill, 1994), especially pp. 16–19.

7. Lawrence, *supra* note 6, at 5-9, discusses the nature of general obligation debt in greater detail.

8. *Id.* at 73–80 explains two-thirds bonds.

9. G.S. 159-48(b)(21) (1994).

10. G.S. 159-48(b)(17) (1994).

11. G.S. 159-48(b)(12) (1994).

12. G.S. 159-48(b)(19) (1994).

13. G.S. 159-48(d)(5) (1994).

14. G.S. 159-48(b)(24) (1994).

15. Pages 62–63.

16. Lawrence, *supra* note 6, at 9–16, discusses the nature of revenue bonds in greater detail.

17. G.S. 159-81(3)a. (1994).

18. G.S. 159-81(3)b. (1994).

19. G.S. 159-81(3)f. (1994).

20. G.S. 159-81(3)o. (1994).

21. G.S. 159-81(3)m. (1994).

22. Lawrence, *supra* note 6, at 12.

23. G.S. 153A-277(a1) (1991) for counties and 160A-314(a1) (1994) for cities.

24. Lawrence, *supra* note 6, at 19–22, 24–28, and 56–67, discusses installment financing agreements and certificates of deposit in more detail.

25. *Id.* at 20.

26. G.S. 158-42 (1998 Cum. Supp.).

27. Global Transpark Development Zone, Loan Policy and Procedure, § 6.1, adopted Feb. 9, 1995 (copy in author's files).

28. I.R.C. § 103 (West 1999). North Carolina law also excludes from *state* taxation the interest paid on bonds of the state, of state agencies, and of North Carolina local governments. G.S. 105-130.5(b)(1a)a. (1997) (corporate income tax) and 105-134.6(b)(1)b. (1997) (individual income tax).

29. North Carolina's exemption for interest on municipal bonds does not differentiate between exempt and nonexempt purposes; if the bonds have been issued pursuant to state law by the state, a state agency, or a North Carolina local government, the interest paid on the bonds is exempt from state income tax. *Id.*

30. I.R.C. § 141 (West 1999).

31. I.R.C. § 103 (West 1999).

32. The other private activity bond test is used when bond proceeds are loaned to private persons or entities.

33. Treas. Reg. § 1.141-3(f) (1997).

34. *Id.,* examples 1 and 2.

35. *Id.,* example 7.

36. *Id.,* example 9.

37. *Id.,* example 11.

38. Treas. Reg. § 1.141-4(b)(2) (1997).

39. Treas. Reg. § 1.141-4(e)(1) (1997).

40. Under North Carolina law, the local government receives its consideration for the building in the form of property tax payments or other tax revenues. (See Chapter 3 at pages 105–10.) Because the property tax payments or other taxes are generally applicable revenues, however, they are not counted for purposes of the private payment test under the Code.

41. The categories of qualified private activity bonds are set out in I.R.C. § 141(e) (West 1999).

42. If a local government borrowed money and constructed a shell building, which it sold to a private company, the government's borrowing might qualify as a small-issue industrial revenue bond. The primary difficulty to reaching that end is that tax regulations require that the owner or operator of the building be identified before the money is borrowed. Temp. Treas. Regs. § 5f.103-2(f)(2), found at 4 U.S. Tax Rep. 15,261 (1999). If the shell building was being built on speculation, there is no buyer to identify. The tax laws also limit the portion of proceeds from small-issue industrial revenue bonds that can expended on land to 25 percent of the total proceeds. I.R.C. § 147(c)(1)(A) (West 1999). Therefore bonds used to purchase industrial or commercial sites could not qualify as small-issue industrial development bonds, and bonds used to acquire and develop land for an industrial park probably could not qualify.

43. I.R.C. §§ 142(a)(4) (facilities for the furnishing of water) and 142(a)(5) (sewage facilities) (West 1999).

44. Treas. Reg. § 1-142(a)(5)-1(a) (1994).

45. G.S. 153A-76 (1991) (counties) and 160A-146 (1994) (cities).

46. Generally gross income for federal tax purposes does not include income earned by a state or local government. *See* Rev. Rul. 87-2, 1987-1 C.B. 18; G.S. 105-130.3 and 105-130.2(5c) (1997) (state income tax only on federal taxable income adjusted and apportioned).

47. G.S. 105-278.1(b) (1997).

48. I.R.C. § 170(c)(1) (West 1999). Contributions to state and local government also are deductible for state income tax purposes. G.S. 105-130.9(b) (1997) (corporate income tax) & 105-134.6(a) (1997) (individual income tax, in that there is no adjustment to federal taxable income because of charitable contributions).

49. *Id.*

50. G.S. 158-11 (1994) permits an economic development commission to purchase and own real property but only for the purpose of providing its own office space.

51. Generally gross income for federal tax purposes does not include income earned by a state or local government. *See* Rev. Rul. 87-2, 1987-1 C.B. 18; G.S. 105-130.3 and 105-130.2(5c) (1997) (state income tax only on federal taxable income adjusted and apportioned).

52. G.S. 105-278.1(c)(1) (1997).

53. I.R.C. § 170(c)(1) (West 1999). Contributions to state and local government also are deductible for state income tax purposes. G.S. 105-130.9(b) (1997) (corporate income tax) & 105-134.6(a) (1997) (individual income tax, in that there is no adjustment to federal taxable income because of charitable contributions).

54. The economic development expenditure at issue in the 1923 case that held economic development was not a necessary expense of local government, *see supra* note 1, was a contribution to the local chamber of commerce. Ketchie v. Hedrick, 186 N.C. 392, 119 S.E. 767 (1923).

55. 264 N.C. 332, 141 S.E.2d 490 (1965).

56. 55 N.C. App. 1, 284 S.E.2d 542 (1981).

57. G.S. 55A-3-01(a) (1993) ("Every corporation incorporated under this Chapter has the purpose of engaging in any lawful activity unless a more limited purpose is set forth in its articles of incorporation."). In order to become an exempt organization under the Internal Revenue Code, however, a nonprofit corporation's charter must limit it to activities that will qualify the corporation for that status. See the discussion in the next section on the status of nonprofit economic development corporations under the federal income tax code.

58. A specialized economic development organization that engaged solely in providing training to persons seeking employment would probably qualify under Section 501(c)(3) as an educational organization.

59. Rev. Rul. 76-419, 1976-2 C.B. 146 (organization that purchases blighted land in economically depressed community, converts the land to industrial park, and encourages industrial enterprises to locate in the park in order to provide employment opportunities for low-income residents of the area qualifies as charitable organization); Rev. Rul. 74-587, 1974-2 C.B. 162 (organization that provides financial assistance to businesses in economically depressed areas by making loans or acquiring equity qualifies as charitable organization).

60. In Tech. Adv. Mem. 98-11-001 (Aug. 11, 1997), the IRS referred to a community-wide economic development organization and noted that it was a Section 501(c)(3) organization. The organization operated a business incubator, did workforce training, and engaged in business recruitment and retention.

61. Treas. Reg. § 1.501(c)(3)-1(d)(2) (1990).

62. Theodore J. Hopkins, Jr., *Lessening the Burdens of Government Can Provide Exemption,* 5 J. TAX'N OF EXEMPT ORGANS 260 (May-June 1994).

63. If a nonprofit corporation is closely controlled by a local government, the Internal Revenue Service may consider it part of the government and exempt for that reason. In Priv. Ltr. Rul. 98-53-016 (Sept. 29, 1998), the IRS considered a nonprofit corporation established by a city. The corporation received title to a vacant downtown shopping center and held the property during its environmental rehabilitation. The property was to be developed for public use, including a new city hall. The city appointed the directors and officers of the corporation, all of whom were city staff; and the city funded the corporation's operations. The city established the corporation in order to keep the city out of the chain of title for the property until the environmental problems were cleaned up and also to avoid state bidding laws on the environmental cleanup. The IRS's letter

held that the corporation was an integral part of the city and was to be treated as such for tax purposes.

64. Rev. Rul. 67-294, 1967-2 C.B. 193 (organization that makes loans to businesses to induce them to locate in an economically depressed area in order to alleviate unemployment in the area qualifies for exemption as a social welfare organization); Rev. Rul. 64-187, 1964-1 C.B. (Part 1) 187 (organization that makes loans to businesses to induce them to locate in redevelopment area qualifies for exemption as a social welfare organization).

65. Rev. Rul. 73-411, 1973-2 C.B. 180.

66. Rev. Rul. 70-81, 1970-1 C.B. 131 (chamber developing industrial park); Rev. Rul. 81-138, 1981-1 C.B. 358 (shell building); and Rev. Rul. 76-207, 1976-1 C.B. 158 (convention bureau).

67. I.R.C. § 170(c)(2) (West 1999).

68. "[N]o substantial part of the activities of [a 501(c)(3) organization may be] carrying on propaganda, or otherwise attempting, to influence legislation." I.R.C. § 501(c)(3) (West 1999).

69. State income tax law essentially follows federal law on charitable contributions (with some differences for corporate taxpayers not relevant to this discussion). G.S. 105-130.9(a) (1997) (corporate income tax) and 105-134.6(a) (1997) (individual income tax, in that there is no adjustment to federal taxable income because of charitable contributions).

70. Treas. Reg. § 1.162-15 (1965). In *Commissioner of Internal Revenue v. The Hub*, 68 F.2d 349 (4th Cir. 1934), the court indicated that a retail merchant could deduct, as ordinary business expenses, subscriptions it made to a nonprofit corporation that was established to attract new industrial development to the community. The new jobs created by the efforts of such a corporation would help build the business of the taxpayer.

71. 55 N.C. App. 1, 284 S.E.2d 542 (1981).

72. 253 N.C. 400, 116 S.E.2d 923 (1960).

73. Horner v. Chamber of Commerce of City of Burlington, 235 N.C. 77, 68 S.E.2d 660 (1952). The court argued that the city had made "an absolute gift" of city moneys to the chamber "without specifying how they were to be spent, and without reserving the right to direct or control their use." *Id.* at 81, 68 S.E.2d at 663.

74. *Dennis*, 253 N.C. at 401, 116 S.E.2d at 924. The case has the smell of a test case, inasmuch as Raleigh only appropriated $500 for these purposes.

5

STATE GOVERNMENT INCENTIVES

• • •

5

STATE GOVERNMENT INCENTIVES

• • •

THE STATE OF NORTH CAROLINA takes a leading role in economic development, especially in the process of attracting new business location and existing business expansion. The state Department of Commerce has long been recognized nationally as a leading practitioner in this field, and the department's representatives work closely with local economic development officials in dealing with business location and expansion. The state offers a number of incentives for economic development that complement those offered by local governments, and this chapter briefly summarizes these state incentives.

Tax Credits

During the 1990s, the state established a system of tax credits that has become the core of the state's economic development incentive system. When a new or expanded private facility is announced and the amount of state incentives revealed, tax credits make up most of that amount. The credit system reflects the state's economic development priorities. The state is seeking to channel economic development into counties that have not shared in its prosperity.[1] Therefore companies that locate or expand in the state's poorer counties receive larger credits. Indeed, in the very poorest counties the credits are significantly larger. In addition the state is encouraging creation of higher-quality jobs for its citizens,[2] and therefore credits are available only to companies that provide jobs at or above current wage levels. As incentives, credits carry two significant advantages. First, like local government incentives staged over time, tax credits are not received by the company until after it has made its new investments, created its new jobs, or trained its employees. Even then most of the credits are staged over several years, and during that period the company must keep in service the property and retain the jobs for which credits have been given. Second, tax credits do not cost the state anything in appropriated funds; rather, they represent revenues that are never received.

165

The William S. Lee Quality Jobs and Business Expansion Act (commonly called the Bill Lee Act), enacted in 1996, established a comprehensive set of tax credits;[3] subsequent amendments to the original legislation have expanded the kind and availability of credits. Although a few of the tax credits have been tailored for specific projects,[4] for the most part the credits are general in nature and available to any company that meets the criteria set forth in the North Carolina General Statutes (to be abbreviated from here on as G.S.).

Tax Credits for New and Expanding Businesses

G.S. Chapter 105, Article 3A, establishes a system of tax credits for new and expanding businesses. In general a company may choose to use the credit against the corporate franchise tax, the company's state income tax, or the state's gross premium tax. These credits are currently scheduled to expire on January 1, 2006, but the General Assembly has extended them in the past and may well do so again.

Eligibility

Article 3A makes its credits available only to companies engaged in the following kinds of businesses: companies engaged in manufacturing, warehousing or wholesale trade, data processing, or air carrier services; telecommunications or financial services companies that establish call centers in Enterprise Tier 1 or 2 areas; companies that establish electronic mail order houses that create at least 250 new jobs and are located in Enterprise Tier 1 or 2 areas; and companies that establish a central administrative office with at least 40 new jobs. (Enterprise tiers are explained in the next section.)

In addition to limiting the kinds of businesses or facilities for which a credit is available, the statute establishes a wage threshold that the company must meet in order to qualify for credits. The threshold is somewhat complicated, but the basic policy is that (except in the poorest counties or communities) a company must pay at least 110 percent of the statewide average weekly wage or 110 percent of the county average weekly wage, whichever is less.[5] Thus to qualify for credits, a company must provide jobs of somewhat better quality than the current state or county average. (In the state's poorest counties—those in Enterprise Tier 1—the wage threshold is 100 percent of that county's average weekly wage. It is also 100 percent within development zones, explained below.)

Finally, the statute conditions eligibility for credits upon the company providing health insurance for its employees and upon the company's not being in significant violation of environmental laws or occupational safety and health laws.

The Enterprise Tier System

Article 3A establishes five *enterprise tiers* and directs how the state's secretary of commerce is annually to assign North Carolina's one hundred counties among the five tiers.[6] The amount of or eligibility for some of the credits established by Article 3A differs among the tiers, with the largest credits available to companies conducting business in the state's poorest counties. In assigning the counties among the tiers, the commerce secretary establishes three statewide rankings:

(1) a ranking of counties by average rate of unemployment, from the lowest to the highest, over the preceding three years;

(2) a ranking of counties by average per capita income, from the highest to the lower, over the preceding three years; and

(3) a ranking of counties by percentage growth in population (apparently in the most recent year).

The secretary assigns each county an *enterprise factor*, which is the total of the county's rank in each of the three rankings. For example, if a county ranks 95th in the unemployment rate ranking, 92d in the per capita income ranking, and 75th in the percentage growth ranking, its enterprise factor is 262. Another county might rank 7th in unemployment, 4th in per capita income, and 12th in growth, and its enterprise factor is 23. The counties are assigned among enterprise tiers according to their enterprise factors, as follows:

Enterprise Tier 1	10 highest-scoring counties[7]
Enterprise Tier 2	15 next highest-scoring counties
Enterprise Tier 3	25 next highest-scoring counties[8]
Enterprise Tier 4	25 next highest-scoring counties
Enterprise Tier 5	remaining counties

Development Zones

G.S. 105-129.3A establishes the criteria for *development zones* and charges the Department of Commerce with designating such zones. The statute allows development zones to be designated in (or partly in) cities with a population of at least 5,000. A zone, which comprises one or more contiguous census tracts or census block groups, must have a population of at least 1,000, and at least 20 percent of its residents must be below the poverty level. Once designated, an area remains a zone for twenty-four months; it then needs to be redesignated, assuming it still meets the statutory criteria.

Zones are proposed by local governments or by citizens; if an area meets the statutory criteria, the department must designate the area as a development zone. As of the winter of 2000, the department had designated development zones in fifty-six different cities and towns. For certain of the tax credits for new and expanding businesses, development zones are treated as if they were in Enterprise Tier 1 counties, thereby giving companies located in the zones larger credits than they would qualify for otherwise.

The Credits

Article 3A establishes six tax credits for new and expanding businesses. These tax credits are briefly summarized in this section.[9]

Credit for Creating Jobs

A company with at least five employees qualifies for a credit for each additional full-time job it creates.[10] The amount of the credit depends on the enterprise tier in which the job is created, as follows:

Enterprise Tier 1	$12,500 per job
Enterprise Tier 2	$ 4,000 per job
Enterprise Tier 3	$ 3,000 per job
Enterprise Tier 4	$ 1,000 per job
Enterprise Tier 5	$ 500 per job

In addition, if the company is located in a development zone, it is entitled to an additional credit of $4,000 per job. Thus if a company located in Enterprise Tier 2 created six new jobs in Year 1, it is entitled to a credit of $24,000; if it is also in a development zone, the credit increases to $48,000.

The company must take the credit in four equal installments, beginning in the year after the job is created, and during those four years the company must maintain at least as many jobs as it had before it created the job for which the credit is given.

Credit for Investing in Machinery and Equipment

A company that purchases or leases machinery or equipment and places it in service in North Carolina may be entitled to a credit.[11] Leased property is included if it is capitalized on the company's books. The credit is 7 percent of the *eligible investment amount* over the *applicable threshold*, which differs among the five enterprise tiers. Usually the eligible investment amount is the cost of the investment, but it might be less if the company has taken other machinery or equipment out of service. The thresholds in the five tiers are as follows:

Enterprise Tier 1	$ 0
Enterprise Tier 2	$ 100,000
Enterprise Tier 3	$ 200,000
Enterprise Tier 4	$ 500,000
Enterprise Tier 5	$1,000,000

Thus if a company in tier 3 invested $650,000 in machinery and equipment, it is entitled to a credit of 7 percent of $450,000, or $31,500. The same investment in tier 1 is 7 percent of the full $650,000, or $45,500. In tier 5 there is no credit at all because the investment is below the applicable threshold. A company located in a development zone is treated as if it were in Enterprise Tier 1. A company takes this credit in seven annual installments, beginning in the year after the investment is made, and the equipment or machinery must continue in service to qualify for each installment.

Credit for Technology Commercialization

Instead of taking the credit for investing in machinery and equipment, a few taxpayers may be eligible to take the technology commercialization credit.[12] The credit is triggered by purchasing or leasing, and placing into service, machinery or equipment for use in production based on technology that has been developed by and licensed from a research university. The machinery and equipment must be placed into service in a county located in enterprise tiers 1, 2, or 3. The credit is 20 percent of the eligible investment amount if the secretary of commerce certifies that the taxpayer will invest at least $150 million in such machinery and equipment within five years. The credit is 15 percent of the eligible investment amount if the secretary certifies that the taxpayer will invest at least $100 million within five years. (If the investment is less than $100 million, the taxpayer is limited to the more general credit for investing in machinery and equipment.) Unlike the other credits, a company may divide this credit against the various taxes against which credits may be taken. The credit is taken in the year in which the machinery and equipment is placed into service.

Credit for Research and Development

If a company qualifies for the federal tax credit for increasing research activities, it is entitled to a state tax credit as well.[13] The amount of the state credit is a percentage of the state's apportioned share of the company's expenditures for research and does not vary among enterprise tiers. The company takes the credit in the year that the expenditures are made.

Credit for Worker Training

A company that provides training for five or more employees may be entitled to a credit for the wages it paid the workers during their training.[14] The workers must be in jobs that are nonexempt under the Fair Labor Standards Act; in addition, each worker must be in either a job for which the job creation tax credit is available or a job that involves the operation of machinery or equipment for which the investment tax credit is available. In both Enterprise Tier 1 and development zones the maximum credit is $1,000 per employee; elsewhere it is $500. The company takes the credit in the year in which the training is given.

Credit for Investing in Central Administrative Offices

A company that establishes a central administrative office and creates at least forty new jobs at that location is entitled to a credit.[15] The amount of the credit is 7 percent of the capital cost (or a lesser amount if the company has taken other central administrative offices in North Carolina out of service), and the company takes it in seven annual installments beginning in the year after the investment is made. The amount of the credit does not depend on the enterprise tier in which the investment was made.

Usage

In May 1999 the Department of Commerce issued a report on the use of the tax credits for new and expanding businesses for the 1997 tax year.[16] (Data from later years were not yet available, and data from 1997 were incomplete.[17]) Based on the 1997 tax returns that were available for analysis, the credits claimed for that year cost the state about $10.8 million in foregone tax revenue. The largest dollar amount of credits, about 55 percent, was claimed for research and development; about 38 percent, for investments in machinery and equipment; almost all the rest, for job creation.[18] Well over 95 percent of the dollar amount of credits was claimed by companies already located in North Carolina.[19] Finally, although the largest dollar amount of credits was claimed in enterprise tiers 4 and 5, the credits do appear to have encouraged companies to invest and create jobs in tiers 1 and 2; counties in the latter tiers witnessed an increase in business investment of almost 600 percent after enactment of the Bill Lee Act.[20]

Tax Credits for Development Zone Projects

The Bill Lee Act was amended by the 1999 General Assembly to create a new credit for contributions, in cash or property, to a development zone agency for the support of an improvement project the agency is undertaking in a development zone.[21] (*Development zone* has the same meaning for this credit as it does for the various credits for new and expanding businesses, described above.) The statute defines *development zone agencies* to include community-based development organizations, community action agencies, community development corporations, community development financial institutions, community housing development organizations, and local housing authorities. To qualify for the credit, the agency's project must be for community development purposes, as defined in G.S. 160A-456, -457, or -457.2. The credit is for 25 percent of the taxpayer's contribution to the development zone agency. The statute establishes a $4 million annual limit on the amount of credits that can be awarded statewide pursuant to its terms.

Tax Credits for Business Purchases

Article 3B of G.S. Chapter 105 establishes a credit for purchasing or leasing business personal property; leased property is included if it is capitalized on the company's books. A business may take this credit against the corporate franchise tax or the state income tax. A taxpayer may not, however, take this credit for the same property that was the basis for the investment tax credit described in a previous section (beginning on page 168). Unlike the credits described above, this credit does not depend on the nature or location of the business; it is available to all businesses, and the amount is the same in all counties. The credit is 4.5 percent of the cost of purchase or lease, with a maximum credit of $4,500. The company takes the credit over five years, beginning with the year the property is acquired, and the property must remain in service in each future year if that year's installment is to be used.

Credits for Recycling Facilities

Article 3C of G.S. Chapter 105 establishes credits for very large investments in manufacturing plants that are located in Enterprise Tier 1 counties and that use significant amounts of recycled materials. At least three-fourths of the products of such a plant must be made of at least 50 percent recycled materials. G.S. 105-129.25 defines two categories of recycling facilities: a *major* recycling facility represents a capital investment of at least $300 million within four years and creates at least 250 new jobs; a *large* recycling facility represents a capital investment of at least $150 million within two years and creates at least 155 new jobs. The credit is for investments in equipment and machinery and is 50 percent of cost for major facilities and 20 percent of cost for large facilities. A company may take the credit against both the corporate franchise tax and the state income tax.[22]

As was previously noted, these credits for recycling facilities were enacted to attract two specific projects; it is unlikely that they will find further use.

Tax Credits for Qualified Business Investments

G.S. Chapter 105, Article 4, Division V, establishes tax credits that may be taken by individuals (but not corporations) who invest in selected smaller companies. The purpose of the credit is to encourage investment of venture capital in North Carolina companies. An individual who purchases equity securities or subordinated debt directly from a *qualified business venture* or a *qualified grantee business* is entitled to an income tax credit of 25 percent of the amount invested, up to $50,000.[23] Statewide the annual amount of such credits may not exceed $6 million; if an amount greater than that is claimed, the secretary of revenue reduces each individual's credit pro rata. In 1997, for example, the amount of such credits claimed was about $9.2 million; therefore, each claimed credit was reduced by about 35 percent. The current credits are scheduled to expire at the end of 2002, but they have been extended before and may be again.

A qualified business venture is a new company or an existing company with annual gross revenues of $5 million or less. The company may be engaged in manufacturing, processing, warehousing, wholesaling, research and development, or a service-related business (but not in professional services, construction, retail, investments, cosmetics, entertainment, sports, or real estate). A qualified grantee business is a business that during the preceding three years has received a grant from one of seven entities that invest in technology companies.[24] Qualified business ventures and qualified grantee businesses must be registered as such with the secretary of state.[25] As of winter 2000, about 150 qualified business ventures and qualified grantee businesses had registered.

Other Tax System Incentives

Corporate Income Tax Rates and Apportionment

In addition to beginning the system of tax credits described above, the William S. Lee Quality Jobs and Business Expansion Act reduced state income tax rates over several years. When the act was enacted, the state's corporate income tax was levied at a rate of 7.75 percent. The act reduced the rate over several years, so that for tax years beginning after 1999 the rate is 6.9 percent.[26]

When a company operates in more than one state, each state is entitled to tax a portion of the corporation's income, but the portion taxed must bear a reasonable relationship to the amount of business the corporation does in the state. Traditionally most states have used a three-factor formula to apportion a corporation's income. The three factors are the percentages of the corporation's property located in the state, payroll paid in the state, and sales made in the state. The formula averages the three percentages. For example, if a company has 20 percent of its property in a state, pays 18 percent of its payroll in that state, and makes 7 percent of its sales in that state, the average is 15 percent. That state would tax the corporation on 15 percent of its apportioned income.

North Carolina, however, has modified the traditional formula by counting the sales factor twice—that is, the average is now calculated by adding the property factor, the payroll factor, and two sales factors and then dividing by four.[27] The effect of the change is to lower the apportionment average if a corporation makes a significant percentage of its sales outside of North Carolina. To return to the example, adding the 7 percent sales factor twice and dividing by 4 results in an average of 13 percent, as opposed to 15 percent under the three-factor formula.[28]

Sales Tax Incentives

The General Assembly encourages business investment by reducing or eliminating sales and use tax on certain kinds of purchases. The most important of these is found in G.S. 105-164.4A, which sets the tax rate on manufacturing machinery and equipment at 1 percent and places an $80 cap on the amount of tax on any single acquisition. In addition, if a company acquires machinery and equipment and locates it in a county that has been designated as an Enterprise Tier 1 or 2 county,[29] and if the company is eligible for the tax credits for new and expanding businesses enacted in G.S. Chapter 105, Article 3A, it is entitled to a refund for those sales taxes it has paid on the machinery and equipment.[30]

Infrastructure Incentives

The state offers a number of programs that pay for infrastructure serving new private facilities, usually facilities that qualify for tax credits as new and expanding businesses under the Bill Lee Act. Most of these programs transfer money to local governments to pay for infrastructure, but one program pays directly for road improvements.

Department of Transportation Site Access Fund

Since 1957 one of the line items in the state appropriations act has funded the site access program of the North Carolina Department of Transportation. (There is no other statutory basis for the program.) The money is available for constructing roads to new industrial facilities, and departmental policies provide that the number of employees at the facility and the amount of truck traffic to and from the facility will be primary justifications for assistance. (The money is available also for constructing public school drives and driveways at public medical facilities and public airports and for paving entrance aprons at volunteer fire departments and rescue squads located outside cities.)

The General Assembly appropriates $2 million annually to this program. Over time about two-thirds of the funds appropriated to the program have been used for industrial projects.

Department of Transportation Rail Industrial Access Program

Since 1994 the state Department of Transportation, through its Rail Division, has operated the Rail Industrial Access Program.[31] The program pays a portion of the cost of constructing or refurbishing spur tracks to new or expanded industrial facilities. The funded portion is between 35 percent and 50 percent of eligible project costs, with the percentage funded determined by the project's score in an economic benefit point system that credits jobs created, amount of capital investment, number of rail carloads to be generated, and whether the project is in a distressed county or will preserve a shortline railroad. The remaining portion of the cost is the responsibility of local government, private sources, or both. The program will pay for site preparation, track construction, switches, and grade crossings and signals. (It will not pay for engineering, utility relocation, right-of-way relocation, or rail docks.)

The program accepts applications from local governments, private community development agencies, railroads, and industries, although industry is the usual applicant. If a local government is not the applicant, the appropriate county or city governing board must nonetheless indicate support for the project. After an application is approved, the applicant constructs the project; the program reimburses its share once the first rail car has operated over the new or refurbished tracks.

From its beginning in 1994 through March 1999, the program had approved forty projects, totaling roughly $3.5 million. In most years the program has funded between $550,000 and $850,000 in projects. Over its first six years the program has assisted industrial projects representing $712 million in new private investment and the creation of more than 4,700 new jobs.

Industrial Development Fund: Infrastructure

The Department of Commerce administers the Industrial Development Fund, established by G.S. 143B-437.01 and funded each year (in varying amounts) by the General Assembly. The General Assembly established the fund in 1987 and added the fund's Utility Account in 1996. The department uses moneys in the fund to make grants or loans to local governments to be used by the local government as an incentive to those companies that are eligible for tax credits for new and expanding businesses under the William S. Lee Quality Jobs and Business Expansion Act. This section discusses those grants and loans used for infrastructure; loans used to purchase or improve private facilities are discussed in the next section of this chapter.

The fund does not assist local governments or companies statewide. Rather only the fifty or so most economically distressed counties—those in enterprise tiers 1, 2, and 3—and the cities within those counties are eligible to apply for the money. Except for grants from the fund's Utility Account, the amount that can be allocated to a particular project depends on the project cost and the number of jobs to be created by the business location or expansion. The fund will provide up to $5,000 per job, with a maximum of either $500,000 or the cost of the project, whichever is less.[32] There are no funding limits for grants from the Utility Account; these grants are available only to local governments in tier 1 and 2 counties and finance only the extension or expansion of utility lines to a project.

Fund moneys may be used to provide utility infrastructure to existing buildings that are being renovated or modified and to newly constructed buildings. With existing buildings, fund moneys can be used to finance off-site facilities and facilities located on company property; with new buildings, the moneys may be used only for extension or expansion of utility lines. When the money is used to extend publicly owned utility lines to the project or to pay for other utility facilities that serve the public as well as the company, the money is a grant and need not be repaid to the fund unless the promised jobs target is not met. If the money is used to provide infrastructure that serves only the company, however, such as a water storage tank located on company property, the money is a loan. The company is responsible for repaying the local government applicant, and the local government then returns the money to the state. With two exceptions, grants from the fund require a 25 percent matching contribution by the local government. The first exception is for any project in an Enterprise Tier 1 county; the second is for projects financed from the fund's Utility Account. Grants are made on a reimbursement basis.

Since the fund's inception in 1987 through March 1999, the General Assembly has appropriated a total of $25.3 million to the fund. In recent years the appropriation has been around $2 million annually. The legislature has appropriated another $5.5 million to the Utility Account since it was established in 1996.

Clean Water Bond Proceeds

In 1998 North Carolina voters authorized the state to issue $800 million in bonds to assist local governments with water and wastewater projects. The bond legislation directed that $20 million of the proceeds be used for economic development projects.[33] The Department of Commerce administers this portion of the Clean Water program, using policies similar to those governing the Industrial Development Fund. They are as follows:

- The moneys are divided into two accounts, one tracking the basic Industrial Development Fund policies and the other tracking the Utility Account policies.
- Moneys in the first account are available to any local government in a county in enterprise tiers 1, 2, or 3. Moneys in the utility account are available only to local governments in tiers 1 and 2.
- No match is required from local governments in tier 1 counties, but a 25 percent match is required from other local governments.

The legislation directs that the Clean Water program moneys be distributed subject to a few other policies that differ slightly from those governing the Industrial Development Fund, as follows:

- The state only makes grants of clean water moneys for these purposes; no money is loaned.
- The companies whose facilities will be served by the financed projects must be engaged in manufacturing, warehousing, or wholesale trade. This is a narrower list than that applicable to the Industrial Development Fund.
- Any project that is funded must further the state's clean water objectives, such as by reducing reliance on wells or septic tanks or extending service to additional users.
- A project may include improvements on a company's property if the improvements further the state's clean water objectives.

Community Development Block Grants

The Department of Commerce, through its Division of Community Assistance, operates the small cities Community Development Block Grant (CDBG) program. A portion of the CDBG money coming from the federal government—about

Table 5
CDBG Grants for Each Job Created

Enterprise Tier	Business Eligible for Lee Act Tax Credits	Business Not Eligible for Tax Credits
1	$15,000	$10,000
2	12,000	8,000
3	12,000	8,000
4	9,000	4,000
5	8,000	3,000

$8.7 million in 1999–2000—is earmarked for economic development projects. Under federal and state guidelines, CDBG economic development moneys may be used to help finance public facilities needed to serve targeted businesses and populations. (The moneys are used also to make loans to businesses serving community development areas. These loans are made in conjunction with bank loans, and the bank services both loans.) The guidelines require that the recipient local government match each three program dollars with one local dollar, except that no match is required from governments in Enterprise Tier 1 counties.

The CDBG program is intended to benefit persons of low or moderate income, and therefore the state guidelines emphasize creation of "permanent, full-time jobs, at least 60 percent of which are made available to persons with prior low and moderate family income status." No more than $1 million annually may be granted to any single local government (no more than $750,000 to a local government in enterprise tiers 4 or 5), and the guidelines establish the maximum amount that can be awarded for each job that is being created. The maximums for each enterprise tier appear in Table 5. The per-job maximums go up another $4,000 for projects in state development zones and $3,000 for each WorkFirst participant who is hired by the benefiting company.

Paying Company Costs

Community College Industrial Training Program

Beginning in 1958 the state appropriations act has included a line item in the budget of the community college system for industrial training. (There is no other statutory basis for the program.) The amount appropriated has varied from year to year; in 1997–98 it was $6 million. The program trains workers for any new or expanding business that has created at least twelve new jobs. The program pays the instructors' wages and travel costs (even if an instructor is a company employee), for classroom materials, and for the use of the training facility.

This program has been a mainstay of the state's economic development program for forty years and has been widely emulated around the country.[34] In the past several years, the program has provided training for about 18,500 people annually.[35]

Industrial Development Fund: Company Costs

The preceding part (see pages 175 and 176) described the Industrial Development Fund and the grants and loans made from it to local governments for construction of utility lines and facilities. The fund also makes loans to companies, through local governments, for the renovation or improvement of existing buildings and for purchasing and installing manufacturing equipment in such buildings. (The fund does not finance any part of a company's cost of new buildings.) These loans must be matched by a bank loan to the company, and the bank administers both its and the state's loan. The fund's program for these company costs is available only to companies that are eligible for the tax credits for new and expanding businesses and that locate in counties in enterprise tiers 1, 2, or 3. The same per job and per project limitations apply to projects funded by these loans as to utility infrastructure projects. The company repays the loan to the local government, and the local government returns the money to the fund.

The Industrial Recruitment Competitive Fund

The Industrial Recruitment Competitive Fund was first established in 1993 in that year's appropriations act. The original appropriation to the fund was $5 million, but later General Assemblies have appropriated smaller amounts. (The most recent appropriation, in 1999–2000, was $2 million.) Through April 1999, $14.6 million had been disbursed through the fund to more than eighty projects, with another $800,000 announced but not yet disbursed.

Acting through the Department of Commerce, the state makes grants from the fund (through local governments) to pay for equipment purchase and installation, building renovation for expanding businesses, utility lines for existing buildings, or utility lines for new or proposed manufacturing or industrial buildings. The state's policies suggest that each grant is usually in the order of $1,000 per job, but many grants are in fact smaller than that. Whatever the amount, the local governments affected by the project must match the state's grant. The state makes the grants on a reimbursement basis in four increments. Each increment is awarded as each 25 percent of the promised jobs is created. The state uses the fund to try to close deals with new or expanding companies—that is, to add one final incentive that might cause the company to come to North Carolina.

Industrial Revenue Bonds

Although industrial revenue bonds are issued by county agencies, the process is significantly controlled by the Department of Commerce. For that reason, the Industrial Revenue Bond program is often included in lists of state incentives. Because of the county involvement, however, the program was included among county incentives in this book. It is described in Chapter 2 (beginning at page 48).

Notes

1. The first goal of the state's economic development plan is to "build a high-growth economy in all parts of the state shared by all people."
2. The second goal is to "achieve high wages and high incomes for North Carolina's workforce."
3. William S. Lee was a retired chief executive officer of Duke Power Company who led a blue-ribbon study that proposed the first comprehensive set of tax credits. Mr. Lee died unexpectedly while the General Assembly was considering the proposal, and the final legislation was named in his memory.
4. For example, the credits for recycling facilities, found in Chapter 105, Article 3C, appear to have been designed for two projects: a large steel mill using recycled steel and a paper products plant using recycled paper.
5. N.C. Gen. Stat. § 105-129.4(b) (1998 Cum. Supp.). The applicable average weekly wage might actually be lower than the county's average weekly wage if the county suffers from significant unemployment. (Hereinafter the General Statutes are abbreviated as G.S.)
6. G.S. 105-129.3 (1998 Cum. Supp.).
7. Once a county has been designated as an Enterprise Tier 1 county, it must stay in that tier for at least two years. *Id.* For that reason, tier 1 usually includes more than ten counties. The tier included fourteen counties in 1997, fifteen in 1998, and thirteen in 1999. Beginning in 2000, any county with fewer than 10,000 residents and more than 16 percent of its population below the federal poverty level is legislatively designated a tier 1 county. Furthermore, also beginning in 2000, any county with fewer than 50,000 residents and more than 18 percent of its population below the federal poverty level is legislatively placed one tier below the designation it would have otherwise. *Id.* (as enacted by SL 1999-360).
8. Beginning in 2000, a county with fewer than 25,000 residents can be designated no higher than tier 3. *Id.*
9. A company may not use credits to reduce its taxes by more than 50 percent. Unused credits may be carried forward for five years, except that if a company makes a very large investment, $150 million or more within two years, it qualifies for a much longer carryforward period for its credits—twenty years. G.S. 105-129.5(b) (1998 Cum. Supp.).
10. G.S. 105-129.8 (1998 Cum. Supp.).
11. G.S. 105-129.9 (1998 Cum. Supp.).
12. G.S. 105-129.9A (as enacted by SL 1999-305).
13. G.S. 105-129.10 (1998 Cum. Supp.).
14. G.S. 105-129.11 (1998 Cum. Supp.).
15. G.S. 105-129.12 (1998 Cum. Supp.).

16. N.C. Dep't of Commerce, William S. Lee Quality Jobs & Bus. Expansion Act: Progress Rep. (May 1999).

17. The Department of Revenue identified 772 1997 tax returns as eligible for Bill Lee Act tax credits; the report was able to analyze 592 returns. *Id.* at 9.

18. *Id.*

19. *Id.* at 3.

20. *Id.* at 8.

21. G.S. 105-129.13 (as enacted by SL 1999-360).

22. G.S. 105-129.28 (1998 Cum. Supp.) creates an additional credit for major recycling facilities for costs the facility incurs for transportation and transloading because it is not accessible to seagoing barges or ships.

23. G.S. 105-163.011 (1998 Cum. Supp.). A person may invest as an individual or as part of a partnership or comparable entity. The investor may not, however, participate in the business for compensation. G.S. 105-163.014 (1998 Cum. Supp.).

24. The seven entities are the North Carolina Technological Development Authority; the North Carolina Technological Development Authority, Inc.; North Carolina First Flight, Inc.; North Carolina Biotechnology Center; Microelectronics Center of North Carolina; the Kenan Institute for Engineering, Technology, and Science; and the Federal Small Business Innovation Research Program.

25. G.S. 105-163.013 (1998 Cum. Supp.).

26. G.S. 105-130.3 (1997).

27. G.S. 105-130.4(i) through 105.130.4(l) (1977).

28. The state's tax system includes a variety of other provisions intended to attract business development. These include the property tax exemptions and classifications listed in Chapter 1 at notes 53–58, as well as some of the exemptions allowed to the state's sales and use tax. For example, G.S. 105-164.13 (1998 Cum. Supp.) exempts from sales tax a variety of transactions important to the state's agricultural industries.

29. The enterprise tier system is explained, *supra,* in the text accompanying notes 6 through 8.

30. G.S. 105-164.14(h) (enacted by SL 1999-360).

31. The program is explained in an excellent Web site, www.bytrain.org/industry.htm. In addition, the department's administrative regulations governing the program are found at 19A NCAC 6B.0400 through 6B.0417 (1998).

32. These numbers have increased over time. When the fund was first established in 1987, the amounts were $1,200 per job and $250,000 per project; the amounts per job and per project have been increased several times.

33. SL 1998-132, § 5.1(e). These economic development grants are to "pay the cost of clean water projects in connection with the location of industry to, and expansion of industry in, the State."

34. The community college system also offers small business centers at each of the colleges. These centers focus on small businesses and offer training to business owners, counseling, a resource library, and referrals to other sources of assistance. Some of the centers operate business incubators.

The University of North Carolina operates the Small Business and Technology Development Center, with twelve regional offices. These offices offer general business counseling to new and small businesses on a one-on-one basis.

35. N.C. Community College Sys., Annual Statistical Rep., Table 3, Student Enrollment by Program Area, 1987–88 through 1997–98 (1998).

INDEX

• • •